Cross Currents
in the International Women's Movement,
1848-1948

Cross Currents
in the International Women's Movement, 1848-1948

Patricia Ward D'Itri

Bowling Green State University Popular Press
Bowling Green, OH 43403

Library of Congress Cataloging-in-Publication Data

D'Itri, Patricia Ward.
    Cross currents in the international women's movement, 1848-1948 /
Patricia Ward D'Itri.
        p.   cm.
    Includes bibliographical references and index.
    ISBN 0-87972-781-0 (clothbound). -- ISBN 0-87972-782-9 (pbk.)
    1. Feminism--International cooperation--History. 2. Women's
rights--International cooperation--History. 3. Women--Societies and
clubs--History.   I. Title.
HQ1154.D55   1999
305.42'09--dc21   98-40947
                                                                         CIP

Cover design by Dumm Art

To my spouse:

Frank M. D'Itri

CONTENTS

ACKNOWLEDGMENTS

The final version of this book and related citations provide a very limited and incomplete listing of individuals, organizations, libraries and other sources consulted. My obligations are numerous, and I begin with an apology to those who were left out. Such oversights were inadvertent and unintentional. The great generosity and cooperation of many persons made this a very rewarding project. First of all, at Michigan State University I am indebted to the Department of American Thought and Language and the College of Arts and Letters for sabbatical leaves to conduct research.

The staff of the library at Michigan State University have been most helpful to obtain materials through interlibrary loan. Other libraries where staff provided very cordial assistance were the Schlesinger Library at Radcliffe, Boston, Massachusetts; the Sophia Smith Collection, Women's History Archives at Smith College, Northampton, Massachusetts; the Women's Collection of the Special Collections Department of the Library of Northwestern University, Evanston, Illinois; and the Archives of the Chicago Historical Society, Chicago, Illinois.

In England my debt begins with Douglas Dougham and his marvelous staff at the Fawcett Library, London Guildhall University. I also was cordially received and provided access to files at the library of the London School of Economics, The Salvation Army, the City of London Archives, and the British Museum. In Manchester I am indebted to David Tyler and the staff of the Manchester Central Library. In Geneva, Switzerland, I wish to thank the staff of the WYWCA, the IFWA, and the WILPF, particularly Edith Ballantyne, who has been unfailingly helpful. In the Netherlands I wish to thank Anne Marie Kloosterman.

Many people facilitated my research in Asia as well. First, I wish to thank the faculty and staff at Tokyo University of Agriculture for providing housing and numerous services during my sabbaticals there. In addition, I am indebted to Professor Fumi Takano who introduced me to a number of remarkable women at Tsuda College, including former president Taki Fujita. Besides dispelling any illusions I retained about Japanese Madame Butterflies, Takano sensei introduced me to the Japanese Association of University Women and the International Federation of University Women. Fugita sensei, in turn, acquainted me with the current and past efforts of the Pan Pacific and Southeast Asian Women's Association and arranged my introduction to Diet member and suffragist, Fusae Ichikawa. I owe another special debt to Yoko Nuita who graciously opened to me the library facilities at the National Women's Education Centre and the Fusen Kaikan (the Fusae Ichikawa Memorial Association) in Tokyo. Also at the National Women's Education Centre I was aided by Director Mizue Maeda and librarian Hiroko Hashimoto as well as other staff members: Chieko Seta, Sumiko Yoshida, and senior researcher Chikako Uemura.

At the Fusen Kaikan, staff members Kimiko Kubo and Mitsuko Yamaguchi put me in contact with Ichikawa associate and women's suffrage researcher, Katsuko Kodama, and scholar Haruyo Lieteau. For personal recollections of Fusae Ichikawa I am also obliged to two of her former secretaries, Kimiko Kubo and Keiko Kihara of the Japanese League of Women Voters, as well as Bernice Guthmann of Evanston, Illinois. I also wish to thank Professor Akiko Kumagai of Tokyo University of Agriculture for arranging my introduction to Shidzue Kato.

I was also assisted by Masako Sato, editor of the history of the first 100 years of the JWCTU as well as Eiko Nagano, Kikue Takahashi, and Aiko Carter, to mention only a few supportive members of that organization. Others were Etsuko Kaji, editor of *80 Years of the Japanese YWCA,* and officers Tomoko Yunomae and Uoki Asa. Numerous members of the Japanese WCTU, YWCA, and WILPF also provided information about Tsume Gauntlett; and I am particularly indebted to her grandson, David Gauntlett, biographer, T. Kiyohara; Yoshiko Moriya, director of the Japanese branch of WILPF, and Tazuko and James B. Harris.

Much time and assistance were generously donated to assist me in translations of documents and between individuals. I would especially like to thank Dr. Kikuji Saito, Masuko Muraoka, and Masako Yamazaki as well as Hisako Inaba for their generous efforts as well as Jun Ui for translation of some of Fusae Ichikawa's papers. In Korea, Youn Hee Lee, Professor of Sociology at Inchon University, was also very helpful. I would also like to thank Madonna Marsden for the care she used in editing this volume.

At home I thank my patient spouse, Frank, my daughter, Julie, for her WCTU connection, and my other children and their spouses: Michael and Suzanne, Angel and Mike, and Trish for assistance with computer questions at all hours of the day and night.

ABBREVIATIONS

AA	Alcoholics Anonymous
AWSA	American Woman Suffrage Association
CNS	Central National Society for Women's Suffrage
DAR	Daughters of the American Revolution
ERA	Equal Rights Amendment
ECOSOC	Economic and Social Council (United Nations)
FBPWC	Federation of Business and Professional Women's Clubs
FDR	Franklin Delano Roosevelt
IAW	International Alliance of Women for Suffrage and Equal Citizenship
ICW	International Council of Women
IFBPWC	International Federation of Business and Professional Women's Clubs
IFUW	International Federation of University Women
ILO	International Labour Organization
ILPF	International League for Peace and Freedom
IWFL	Irish Women's Franchise League
IWSA	International Woman Suffrage Alliance
LN	League of Nations
LNA	Ladies' National Association for the Repeal of the Contagious Diseases Acts
LWV	League of Women Voters
MADD	Mothers Against Drunk Drivers
NAPSS	National Association for the Promotion of Social Science
NCL	National Consumer's League
NOW	National Organization of Women
NWEC	National Women's Education Centre (Japan)
NWP	National Woman's Party
NGO	Nongovernmental Organization
NWSA	National Woman Suffrage Association
NAWSA	National American Woman Suffrage Association
NUWSS	National Union of Women's Suffrage Societies
PPWA	Pan Pacific Women's Association
PPSAWA	Pan Pacific and South East Asian Women's Association
SCAP	Supreme Command Allied Pacific

UN	United Nations
UNO	United Nations Organization
USA	United States of America
WCTU	Women's Christian Temperance Union
WFMS	Women's Foreign Missionary Society
WIL	Women's International League
WILPF	Women's International League for Peace and Freedom
WLF	Women's Liberal Federation
WYWCA	World Young Women's Christian Association
WWCTU	World Women's Christian Temperance Union
WTUL	Women's Trade Union League
WWP	World Woman's Party
YWCA	Young Women's Christian Association

PART I

GOALS AND LIMITATIONS,
THEORETICAL FRAMEWORK

The so-called Second Wave Women's Movement has not only generated great interest in current women's roles, education, and potential but also in the foremothers upon whose shoulders the current leaders symbolically stand. From the early expressions of discontent with women's circumstances and identity as constrained by the separate spheres doctrine, theorists have disagreed on what should constitute women's appropriate role in society. In the late eighteenth and nineteenth centuries, spokespersons like Mary Wollstonecraft, John Stuart Mill, and Elizabeth Cady Stanton built on the views of predecessors like Mary Astell and William Thompson as they applied the Doctrine of Natural Rights and tried to expand women's role in society. Between 1848 and 1948, the women's rights movement evolved in a crazy quilt pattern of interactions among individuals and organizations that became international networks.

Legions of talented women devoted their lives to women's rights. Many of the leaders have been described elsewhere in personal accounts, biographies, and descriptions of organizations and movements. Although most of these accounts have focused on the story of a leader or an organization in a particular nation, women's call for equal rights and opportunities strengthened as it extended across national boundaries and cultures. American and British leaders joined with those from other nations in affiliations that gradually belted the world, and many of their accomplishments resulted from international cooperation. In the exchanges, women learned from one another, and their political skills improved. They shared concerns, exchanged organizing techniques, and set priorities to achieve women's rights on a global basis. These efforts led to declarations of equality in the United Nations Charter and formed the basis of the current women's rights struggle. In this study, the focus is on cross-cultural interactions among groups and between individuals. Often women not only participated in organizations and movements in their own countries, but they supported one another on an ongoing international basis that was really quite extraordinary in eras of slow communication and travel.

Little formal, scholarly attention was paid to this earlier history until Women's Studies became a major part of the Second Wave

Women's Movement in the early 1970s. Since then, feminist scholars have sought to reconstruct the history of women's accomplishments, many of which had been seriously diminished or deleted altogether from historical accounts. As the study of women became identified as a profession, a remarkable array of scholarship examined the contemporary women's movement and sought to discover its foundations in earlier women's history.

Sources of information are fairly abundant. As international organizations developed agendas and activities to create awareness and lobby for women's rights, their achievements were described in various minutes and annual reports. Individuals like Elizabeth Cady Stanton and Susan B. Anthony were conscious of how readily women's accomplishments faded out of historical accounts. Determined not to let that happen, they began the six-volume *History of Woman Suffrage,* which their successors completed. Leaders also exchanged letters and wrote journals and memoirs that provide extensive and often highly subjective accounts. In later years, especially during the slump in women's rights activities between the two world wars, historian Mary Ritter Beard was exceptional as she recognized the importance of collecting women's history.

As modern feminists researched these materials, they have attempted to analyze and explain their findings within a theoretical construct, identifying western women leaders as Socialist, Radical, Welfare, and Liberal or Bourgeois women's rights or equal rights feminists. The preponderance of this volume has to do with the latter group. However, recent attempts to retrofit equal rights feminists into a modern theoretical construct does them some disservice. Unlike the Socialist Feminists, who wanted to revamp society as a whole, the so-called equal rights feminists wanted a more equal share in patriarchal societies. While they were often short on feminist theory, they were very tuned to immediate social concerns such as alcohol abuse. They largely assimilated their doctrines and their goals from the patriarchy and redefined women's roles as their organizations expanded. The broader, more varied interpretations feminism has now are an outgrowth of these earlier battles for education, employment, and political rights.

The Seneca Falls convention in 1848 is a benchmark for this study. Elizabeth Cady Stanton crystalized many issues when she adopted the model of the Declaration of Independence for the Women's Declaration of Sentiments. Although the British women's movement was already underway, the small American convention was a defining moment. It generated a series of conventions and reinforced the movement in the United States as well as abroad.

In England, for example, John Stuart Mill and Harriet Taylor Mill were subsequently encouraged to publish their justification of women's equal rights. In his theoretical construct, Mill concluded that a society's progress could be determined by the standing of its women. Mill's theories and prestige lent support to what Ray Strachey termed "the Cause." Yet, many women leaders were pragmatists who threaded their way through the minefields of public opinion however they could. In Stanton's case, expediency more often overrode theory as she claimed various rights for women, often with highly controversial results. Over the next fifty years, her objectives remained the same, but Stanton often anchored her women's rights theory and claim to suffrage in current doctrines. One was that women's purity entitled them to the vote in order to improve society. In the backlash against ex-slaves and immigrants, she argued that white middle-class women would help maintain white male supremacy if they were given the vote. Stanton's most radical step was to directly challenge contemporary Biblical teachings. To counter the argument that God created Eve as Adam's helpmeet and subordinate, Stanton reconstructed religious texts and published her version as *The Woman's Bible*.

This study considers several feminists in three major aspects. Initially, women leaders had to develop their own feminist consciousness. Often, women were opposed just for asserting their right to speak in public. Second, male resistance had to be overcome as women's determination reflected a self-imposed moral obligation to oppose social injustices such as slavery. Their individual and collective voices went virtually unheard when they began to object to their own unfair treatment. Finally, a primary task was to overcome the well-entrenched custom of separate spheres for men and women. As women banded together in local and regional groups, they began to take public stands and attract more attention (often in the form of ridicule) as they identified cultural and legal inequities.

Some of the most complex women's issues related to sex and domesticity. In England, social tabus inhibited speaking out against the sexual double standard until laws were passed that would permit any woman to be casually categorized as a prostitute. Josephine Butler's early campaign to halt this degradation represents another significant but inadequately developed theme, although organization against the Contagious Diseases Acts brought attention to this issue in various parts of the world. Women then addressed the double standard under the dainty rubric of "social purity." Even some conservative women gradually began to campaign for an equal standard between men and women— chastity before marriage and fidelity afterwards. However, women were essentially defensive as they spoke out and banded together to protect their reputations and persons from being defiled.

Women stepped out of the domestic sphere to oppose violations of their ethics, such as slavery or their morals, such as prostitution. But since alcohol abuse most immediately jeopardized their home lives, it was often the first cause to raise their consciousness. Once they began to support one another in temperance work, they soon accepted responsibility for making changes in other areas as well. Self-improvement also quickly became a major goal, notably through better education and opportunities for employment. In addition, radicals like Elizabeth Cady Stanton promoted domestic equality in property rights and divorce. Woman suffrage was seen as only one of the tools needed for advancement. When women were educated to both recognize their own subordination and desire its overthrow, they reasoned that informed men would want to give them equal rights in employment, politics and law. As leaders struggled to improve their lives and those of other women less able to participate, the activists encountered deeper and more intense resistance as the battle for equality with men continued from one generation to the next.

Nineteenth-century women who had no access to positions in government or many other kinds of employment, channeled their talents into women's organizations and built power bases within female networks that gradually spanned the globe. Often with a racist and ethnocentric perspective, western women leaders sought not only to impose their ideas as colonial powers, but also to cooperate in improving the status of women overall. The scope of the second part of this volume has been narrowed to a few movements and cross-cultural interchanges as women bridged the substantial barriers of language, nationality, culture, and arduous travel to associate with others in common efforts to address "the woman question." Not included are the legions of women who were active in their own countries, but were not as prominent in the international movement. Many women struggled in heroic isolation, castigated locally and denied the support and consolation of their international sisters. In some cases they were not allowed to leave their countries or even their homes.

However, the creation of a network to support national efforts and to lobby for recognition in international bodies was a significant achievement. As organizations were formed to work for women's rights in the last half of the nineteenth and the first half of the twentieth centuries, their affiliations extended from local to national to international. Women gained strength and support from one another as they recognized their common suppression, despite its diverse cultural manifestations. As international organizations and individuals furthered women's cooperative efforts, the peace movement emerged as a common goal.

Much of this account demonstrates the long, piecemeal struggle of individuals and organizations to band together to achieve various women's rights. Wars, however, also exerted enormous cross-cultural influences. Often women's rights underwent dramatic and sudden repression under militaristic regimes. When democratic ideas were imposed after both world wars, women attained suffrage in more countries. Whatever the circumstances of their final success, these victories also culminated long campaigns by women on their own behalf. This was true in Japan where woman suffrage was awarded under American occupation, but the climate for acceptance had been prepared earlier by the Japanese suffragists.

The final phase of this study illustrates how women's input into the development of the League of Nations Charter set a precedent for the equal rights charter and system of input from nongovernmental organizations (NGOs) at the United Nations. The battle for equal rights took the time, talent, and energies of many capable women over not just decades but centuries. This account of only a few individuals and organizations that worked for women's rights after 1848 ends with the adoption by the United Nations of the Universal Declaration of Human Rights on December 10, 1948. This Declaration stipulated equality of all persons and opposition to all forms of discrimination. With the establishment of a Commission on the Status of Women in 1946, women's organizations had gained standing to collect information, air grievances, and lobby for redress. Liberal, Socialist, and nonaffiliated women of myriad political interests could express their views and lobby for change through official committees as consultants in NGOs. Cross-cultural cooperation and dissension could be expressed and widely publicized.

This achievement formed the basis for contemporary international efforts. As information was collected on the status of women around the world, intense publicity was generated by the International Decade for Women with its three major conferences in Mexico City, Copenhagen, and Nairobi between 1975 and 1985. Women also lobbied for rights in the international forum of the 1995 Conference in Beijing, and such conferences continue to be scheduled. These meetings raise new hopes and renew old conflicts over both priorities and leadership between women in underdeveloped and developed nations.

Despite official acknowledgment through consultantships such as NGOs, women's organizations have not always benefitted. As the post World War II era opened more occupations to women, they were less likely to expend their talents in older women's organizations. In the United States, new ones like the National Organization of Women (NOW) emerged in the Second Wave Women's Movement. The largest of the new women's organizations, NOW has recently lobbied more publicly than the older women's groups whose memberships vary in numbers and activity around the world. Despite major victories, their ranks are still divided, especially between western and developing nations. This is one reason the goal of equality remains elusive. However, improvements in transportation and communication as well as recognition in international political forums now facilitate the struggle. Consequently, cross-cultural exchanges of information and tactics more readily integrate national and international efforts in the ongoing struggle for women's rights.

1

THE EARLY PHASE

Arnold Whittick notes that, "There were, of course, some differences in European countries, but the remarkable circumstance is the general similarity in the legal and moral subjection of women throughout Europe during the nineteenth century, and the gradual but slow movement towards improvement."[1] Whittick argues that the industrial revolution contributed to the degradation of women because it forced them out of their homes to work for low pay in Europe and America. This was true in Asia as well. But factory work also opened new opportunities, especially for young, single women. However, the separation of home and work crystallized the concept of a separate domestic sphere for women as the middle class emerged.

This chapter describes some of the earlier efforts to call attention to the plight of women and steps toward the beginnings of local equal rights organizations. Before the 1848 Seneca Falls Convention was publicized, individual equal rights efforts attracted little attention in the United States during the first half of the nineteenth century. Earlier manifestos had decried women's lack of education or its trivialization, but between 1820 and 1880 opportunities were extended either through co-educational or women's colleges. Even though education became the right of more women, they were still denied access to paid employment and government service. Consequently, they sought alternatives such as teaching and proselytizing in missionary schools abroad. These cross-cultural interchanges became a basis on which to build an international movement.

Before the mid-nineteenth century, women's calls for a larger role in society were individual and isolated, usually expressed in publications that generated some interest but few results. Mary Astell (1668-1731), the best known English feminist before Mary Wollstonecraft, was a member of the Anglican Church and had no sympathy for religious dissenters. In anonymous publications between 1694 and 1705, Astell expressed her conviction that female inferiority resulted from educational rather than natural deficiencies.[2] Mary Wollstonecraft (1759-1797) took the same approach in *A Vindication of the Rights of Women* (1792). She argued that women's limitations were due to social conditioning and a lack of education. Because their capacity to reason was equal to men's, Wollstonecraft reproached women for letting themselves be turned into useless ornaments.

Susan B. Anthony (left) and Elizabeth Cady Stanton (right), pioneers in the American and international woman suffrage movement. Picture from Ida Husted Harper, *The Life and Work of Susan B. Anthony*, Volume II, Indianapolis, The Hollenbeck Press, 1898.

French feminist Olympe de Gouges published a pamphlet on women's rights in 1794. Yet well into the beginning of the nineteenth century, women continued to lose out as working men's political power increased. For example, the Napoleonic Code of 1804 "made the husband as much the dictator of the home as Napoleon was of France."[3] Anne-Louise-Germaine de Staël, better known as Madame de Staël (1766-1817), raised one of the few opposing voices as women lost control over family property and encountered more stringent rules of marriage and divorce. Like Wollstonecraft, de Staël rejected Jean Jacques Rousseau's contention that women should be educated to please men. She saw the relationship between "the equality of woman in the family and in marriage" and "the cultivation of her mind in terms of her own value and her capacity to endure the hardships of life."[4]

Irish women took a step backward when the Act of Union abolished the Irish parliament in 1800. Thereafter, they were represented in England, and the struggle for Irish nationalism complicated interactions between the Irish and English women's suffrage movements.[5] In England two articles in the *Westminster Review* (one written by a member of Parliament) advocated woman suffrage in 1831 and 1832.[6] However, when the 1832 Reform Act introduced the word "male," women were formally denied suffrage legally as well as by custom, while more men received the parliamentary franchise. The first draft of the 1837 People's Charter contained a provision for women's suffrage, but it was dropped on the grounds of lack of expediency.

Also in the 1830s, British middle-class women of letters like Harriet Martineau and Harriet Taylor began to revise their views on women's proper place in society, although they were not yet ready to support women's suffrage publicly. Initially, they accepted Jeremy Bentham's doctrine of utilitarianism and based their argument for women's rights on natural equality. The right to vote would follow in the struggle for the greatest happiness of the greatest number.[7]

During the Anti-Corn Law agitation in 1848, Richard Cobden supported a motion in the House of Commons to give all householders, women and men, the vote. Benjamin Disraeli seemed to favor the motion before he was elected to government office, but not afterwards.[8] The next year Anne Knight's pamphlet in favor of woman suffrage received little attention.[9] In 1850, Lord Brougham proposed a ruling which specified "that in English law the word 'man' shall always include 'woman' unless the contrary is stated."[10] That ruling did not apply when male suffrage was extended in 1868 and 1884. But men's progress was gradual, too. Although masculinity was increasingly seen as the basis for suffrage, even by 1911 only sixty percent of British males and even fewer Irish men were eligible to vote.[11]

New domestic legislation did improve some of women's circumstances in Great Britain. In 1836 civil marriages outside the state church or dissenting chapel were legalized. And in 1839 a Custody of Infants Act established the mother's rights to her children provided that she had not been proved guilty of adultery.[12] In 1854 Barbara Leigh-Smith (later Bodichon) published *A Brief Summary, in Plain Language, of the Most Important Laws of England Concerning Women, Together with a Few Observations Thereon.* Then petitions called for a Married Women's Property Bill. It failed in Parliament in 1857, but a less comprehensive Matrimonial Causes Act allowed divorced women to return to the same legal standing as single women.[13] This bill was subsequently amended numerous times. In 1878 the legal separation of wives and their custody of children were permitted.[14] Matters having to do with the property of husband and wife were placed on a more equitable basis in 1882.

As legal advances improved their circumstances, women also traveled between countries in efforts to achieve cross-cultural understanding. British observers who went to America in the 1820s and 1830s were disappointed that American women did not profit from their much-touted democratic principles. After a two-year visit, author Harriet Martineau described the limitations on American women in her six-volume study, *Society in America*. Maria Weston Chapman introduced Martineau's account:

She was seeking for the cause, in order to find the cure, in such openings of various careers suited to women's capacities and education as should furnish them with a truer stimulus than the hours of pernicious excitement which varied the dullness of their lives. She had fathomed the cause: American women were then educated, and had been for half a century, beyond the sphere of action permitted them; and some of them were strenuously labouring for the temperance cause as a safeguard from the dangers of such a life, others were yielding to its temptations.[15]

Like Harriet Martineau, Frances Wright contrasted single women's freedom with the restrictions on their married sisters in America. Wright gained much publicity as she pioneered public speaking for women, especially in opposition to slavery. After that, other women who spoke out might be derogatorily called "Fannie Wrightists."

Two southern sisters from slave holding families, Sarah and Angelina Grimke, attracted much attention when they spoke for abolition. Women who were denied admission to men's abolitionist societies met in their homes and then formed female antislavery societies. In 1837 after a National Female Anti-Slavery Convention, Angelina Grimke wrote to Theodore Weld that "we are placed very unexpectedly in a very trying situation, in the forefront of an entirely new contest—a contest for the *rights of woman* as a moral, intelligent and responsible being"[16] From then on American women generally addressed "the woman question" in the singular whereas the British were more apt to mind their singulars and plurals to speak of women's rights. Many Quakers and Congregationalists as well as affiliates of other evangelical Protestant sects challenged the social biases against women speaking in public to oppose slavery openly.

Quaker women were early leaders in what subsequently became two movements—antislavery and women's rights. Some of them had leadership experience because they were allowed to preach as well as manage their own church-related affairs. Especially in coastal communities that depended on fisheries for a livelihood, the women tended to business while the men were at sea.[17] One such Quaker was Lucretia Mott (1793-1880) of Nantucket. In the Enlightenment tradition, like the Grimkes and Wollstonecraft, Mott argued that women were entitled to the same rights as men because of their moral and rational natures.

Mott was a minister and a delegate to the World's Anti-Slavery Convention in London in 1840. Her rebuff there may not have been a reaction solely to her gender. English Quakers were antagonistic to the Hicksite dissenters that Mott represented.[18] Elias Hicks (1748-1830) had organized the Hicksite or Liberal Quakers when he broke with the Society of Friends. They relied on the Bible for guidance, whereas Hicks insisted that the "Inner Light" alone was sufficient. Whether or not that division added to the men's reluctance to accept the American women delegates, publicity surrounding this convention drew the attention of Europeans and Americans. While the women delegates were sidelined as observers, Mott socialized with Elizabeth Cady Stanton (1815-1902), who was honeymooning with her delegate husband, Henry Stanton.

Mott later challenged Stanton's famous recollection that the American women's rights movement began with the refusal to seat the women delegates at this antislavery convention. Mott wrote to Stanton in 1855 that the conversation about a possible women's rights convention had taken place in Boston in 1841, not in London in 1840.[19] Stanton also suggested that her consciousness might have been raised somewhat later. She wrote to Susan B. Anthony (1830-1906) on April 2, 1851: "I have been re-reading the report of the London convention of 1840. How thoroughly humiliating it was to us! How I could have sat there quietly and listened to all that was said and done I do not now understand."[20] Perhaps the seeds of discontent with women's lot required longer to germinate than Stanton later recalled, but the antislavery convention in London in 1840 certainly promoted the struggle for women's rights. Between then and the Women's Rights Convention held at Seneca Falls, New York, on July 19, 1848, other women also spoke out. Transcendentalist Margaret Fuller published her essay, "The Great Lawsuit. Man versus Men. Woman versus Women," in 1843.[21] That same year in Great Britain Mrs. Hugo Reed's *A Plea for Women* called for absolute political and educational equality between the sexes.[22]

Before the Civil War in the United States, an early sign of progress came in efforts to overturn the old laws of coverture adopted from the British. According to William Blackstone's *Commentaries on the Laws of England* (1765-1769), married women (*femme covert*) were not entitled to hold property, collect wages, or retain custody of their children in the event of divorce. Discord would be prevented, at least in theory, if only one head of the household were permitted—the man. In 1836 Ernestine Rose began a campaign in New York State to legalize married

women's right to hold property. In 1846 the state constitutional convention raised this issue, and in March 1848, legislators passed a Married
Women's Property Law. It reinforced the women's resolve at the convention in Seneca Falls.[23, 24]

In the same year as that first American Women's Rights Convention, the French colonies abolished slavery.[25] However, the French
Assembly also passed a law that barred women from participating in the
political clubs and associations that had sprung up since the February
Revolution. Although Fourierist, Victor Considerant, proposed a constitutional amendment to give political rights to women. It was quickly
rejected.[26] Subsequently, Hubertine Auclert started the French women's
suffrage movement.[27]

So the issue of women's rights was being raised in other places
around the time when Elizabeth Cady Stanton and Lucretia Mott held
their convention at Seneca Falls. After the Women's Declaration of Sentiments with its call for woman suffrage was adopted there, the pioneers
subsequently disagreed on how to proceed. In later years, Elizabeth
Cady Stanton contended that women were morally superior and should
have the right to vote because they would improve men. This assumption
and Stanton's dominant personality antagonized many potential supporters. Also, as the decades passed, this position became less politically
expedient. In later years, Stanton tried to appeal to nativist and racist
white male voters on the basis that educated white women could reinforce their numbers.

Half a century earlier, Stanton's call for the first women's rights
convention struck the right note. Other women's rights conferences soon
followed, and more women leaders were recruited. According to Ross
Evans Paulson, Susan B. Anthony first participated in the second meeting held in Rochester, New York on August 2, 1848.[28] However, Alice
Stone Blackwell claimed a later debut for this hardy champion of
women's rights. Another convention was held in Salem, Ohio, in 1850 as
well as one billed as the first national convention called by Sarah H.
Earle at Worcester, Massachusetts.[29] It brought Lucy Stone (1818-1893)
to national and international attention. Blackwell's biography of her
mother recalls that a *New York Weekly Tribune* report of Lucy Stone's
speech at the Worcester convention converted Anthony to the woman
suffrage cause.[30] Biographer Ida Husted Harper says Anthony still was
not quite won over although her father, mother, and sister Mary attended
the Seneca Falls convention. Her cousin, Sarah Anthony Burtis, had
acted as secretary.[31] Suffrage perhaps did not seem so important to
Anthony initially because Quaker men did not vote either. They thought
it was wrong to support a government that believed in war.[32] According
to Alice Stone Blackwell, Anthony made her women's rights debut at the
third national convention held at Syracuse, New York, in 1852.[33]

Anthony had already met Elizabeth Cady Stanton in Seneca Falls in 1850 on her way home to Rochester from an antislavery convention in Syracuse.

Anthony's consciousness was also substantially raised through the temperance movement. In 1852 the Sons of Temperance invited the Daughters of Temperance to a mass meeting at Albany, but the women delegates were not allowed to speak. Some of them left the hall and, on the advice of Lydia Mott (Lucretia's sister) held their own meeting at the Presbyterian church. Although some of the ladies objected that a letter from Stanton was too radical to read, Anthony read it along with other letters that had been intended for the Sons' meeting.[34] Afterwards, Anthony called for a Woman's State Temperance Convention. When it was held in Rochester, New York, on April 20, 1852, Elizabeth Cady Stanton was elected president. That June the women accepted an invitation from the Men's State Temperance Society to send delegates to their meeting. Once again the women were denied the right to speak, so they held their own meeting and drew away much of the crowd.

Anthony's employment as a school teacher also raised her consciousness. When she attended a teachers' convention in Elmira, New York, three-fourths of the participants were women. Yet none spoke, were appointed to committees, or voted on any question. Anthony resolved then to attend the next teachers' convention and demand equal privileges for women with men. Between temperance and the teachers, she was well prepared for her first Woman's Rights Convention.[35]

Stanton and Anthony worked together to persuade the New York state legislature to extend women's property rights.[36] In addresses in 1854 and 1860, Stanton played on antislavery sentiments and drew parallels between the circumstances of slaves and married women. She declared in 1854 that "The wife who inherits no property holds about the same legal position that does the slave on the Southern plantation. She can own nothing, sell nothing. She has no right even to the wages she earns; her person, her time, her services are the property of another."[37] In 1860 Stanton was more explicit. "The negro has no name. He is Cuffy Douglas or Cuffy Brooks, just whose Cuffy he may chance to be. The woman has no name. She is Mrs. Richard Roe or Mrs. John Doe, just whose Mrs. she may chance to be."[38] The 1860 Married Women's Property Act spelled out a woman's right to possess and dispose of property, to sue and be sued, to be the joint guardian of her children, to inherit one-third of her husband's property, and to manage the remainder during the minority of the youngest child.[39]

As these new laws improved their legal circumstances, women also pressed for better education. In the American colonies, the early settlers had emphasized the importance of being able to read the Bible and so had encouraged the education of a wider population, not just the elites.

As women were gradually included, they perceived education as the foundation for political and civil rights. In the nineteenth century higher education was also offered. In Ohio, Oberlin College first admitted women on a co-educational basis in 1833. Consequently, two early feminists, Lucy Stone and Antoinette Brown Blackwell, were college graduates. In 1837, Mary Lyon founded the female seminary, Mount Holyoke, in South Hadley, Massachusetts. It became a college in 1893.[40]

Especially while many men fought in the Civil War, a need for students prompted the admission of women to colleges and universities in the Midwest. The Morrill Land Act of 1862 endowed colleges with a gift of public lands to teach agriculture and mechanical arts. Women were not excluded, so coeducation was gradually extended. In the East with its tradition of prestigious, all male universities, separate women's colleges developed such as Vassar (1865), Wellesley and Smith (1875), and Bryn Mawr (1884). Coordinate colleges such as Radcliffe (1879) at Harvard and Barnard (1889) at Columbia gave women an alternative and kept them out of the more prestigious men's colleges.[41]

England followed a similar pattern. When Queen's College was founded in 1848, girls twelve years of age and older were admitted. Then Bedford College for women was established in 1849. Barbara Leigh Smith, a pioneer British suffragist, was one of the first students.[42] North London Collegiate School came into existence in 1850. In 1869, Emily Davies started a women's college at Hitchin. In 1874 it was moved to Cambridge and became Girton College. In 1871 Newnham College was founded at Cambridge, and in 1879 Lady Margaret Hall and Somerville College were established at Oxford. Westfield College, Hampstead (a women's college) later became part of London University. It was established in 1882, as was the Girls' Public Day School Trust, which gave girls a secondary education.[43] Royal Holloway College was founded in 1886. Universities in the Commonwealth opened to women in the same era. The University College of Otago at Dunedin, New Zealand, admitted women very soon after its founding in 1869 and graduated the first woman in the Commonwealth in 1877. The University of Sydney, Australia, opened its degrees to women in 1881.[44]

In Ireland, women's opportunities for education also improved. The Intermediate Education Act of 1878 and the Royal University Act of 1879 allowed girls to compete with boys on equal terms. In 1904 Trinity College, Dublin, opened to women; and in 1909 so did the National University, Dublin, and Queens University, Belfast. As women took advantage of new educational opportunities, they began to demand that more occupations be opened to them, and in 1898 they were given the right to hold some local political offices. With this wedge the women argued that their experience in local politics demonstrated their ability to handle national responsibility as well.[45]

Although more of the second generation women's rights leaders were college graduates, many were still denied opportunities for suitable employment and sought challenges abroad. As missionaries they took their educations and faith in progress and women's rights to the far corners of the world, to "redeem the heathen," as Page Smith expressed it.[46] The broad expanse of the British empire not only imposed the male-dominated colonial system, but also afforded the opportunity to initiate a worldwide women's movement. The missionaries assumed their own racial and cultural superiority and often opposed the extension of women's rights. In many instances their goal was primarily to shift the male-dominant hierarchy onto a Christian basis. However, where indigenous customs like foot binding and polygamy conflicted with English values, the missionaries worked for change. Whatever their intentions, as they educated the local people in the English language and culture, they constructed a mutual basis for communication.

India was an example. Ross Paulson argued that "What held together the various aspects of women's rights, women's suffrage, temperance and prohibition was Gandhi's vision of India's future." However, legions of missionaries were followed by other women's rights workers with their own visions. They reinforced indigenous women. One of these, independence leader Sarojini Naidu, argued that had there been no Mrs. Besant [a reference to English Theosophist Annie Besant] there would have been no Gandhi."[47] Indians gradually shifted from their traditional, hierarchical caste law to the English system of at least theoretical equality before the law. At the same time, through pioneering educational ventures, the number of girls and women in the schools and colleges continued to grow. Enrollment trebled between 1921 and 1947 when India gained independence from England.[48]

While missionaries carried their message around the world, American and British women's rights leaders struggled to organize and define their objectives. In the United States conferences were called on an ad hoc basis before the Loyal League was formed after the Civil War. Petitions became another common weapon in the women's rights movement. One was circulated to support passage of the Thirteenth Amendment to emancipate the slaves in 1865. Theodore Tilton advocated that women's rights be linked with abolition by creating an Equal Rights Association. Accordingly, in May 1866, Elizabeth Cady Stanton and Susan B. Anthony, the leaders of the Woman's Rights Convention, formed the American Equal Rights Association. Their old comrade-in-arms, Frederick Douglass, was a vice president.[49]

In that same year, women's suffrage was debated in the Senate in connection with a bill to extend the vote to freed male slaves in the District of Columbia. The women who had supported the Republican war effort expected to be granted suffrage with the freedmen.[50] Instead, the legislators raised charges that were frequently heard later. First, they contended that most women were not interested in the vote and were content with their domestic sphere. Contradictory arguments were that women were both too weak and too threatening to be enfranchised. Other familiar cries were that the family would be jeopardized and the rights of labor threatened.[51]

Women subsequently lost an opportunity to achieve state suffrage and set a precedent for the federal government when the state constitution was revised in New York in 1867. A bid to add "negro" and remove "male" from the voting requirements was also defeated in Kansas. Stanton and Anthony became notorious for their outspoken objections to these slights. When the Equal Right Association held its annual convention in May 1868, Lucy Stone acknowledged the divisions in the organization as she summarized the status of the women's suffrage movement in England and the United States. Stone represented conservatives who favored giving black men the vote without women if that was what they could get at the time. In contrast, Stanton and Anthony opposed the Fourteenth Amendment, which raised another barrier. The word "male" was introduced in the Constitution for the first time. Then "sex" was not included when the Fifteenth Amendment extended voting rights in 1870. The women's moment had passed, and a constitutional amendment to undo the damage would require a long, hard fight.

In the process Stanton and Anthony had alienated friends like a former slave, Frederick Douglass, who supported the Fourteenth Amendment. Then Stanton also managed to embarrass conservative women because she advocated abortion and birth control. She also went against popular opinion because she blamed society rather than individuals for prostitution. All of this was too much for the conservatives. When Stanton proposed a woman suffrage amendment to the federal Constitution at the 1869 New York meeting of the American Equal Rights Association, the moderates refused their support.

Instead, Lucy Stone rallied them to form The American Woman Suffrage Association (AWSA). They campaigned for the ballot on a state-by-state basis with the expectation that other women's rights would follow. This primarily New England organization attracted conservative women like Julia Ward Howe (1819-1910), who did not wish to alter women's primary roles as wives and mothers.[52] Stanton and Anthony subsequently founded The National Woman Suffrage Association (NWSA) to promote a variety of women's rights in addition to suffrage. The division in the women's movement and the popular perception of Stanton and Anthony as radicals lessened the political effectiveness of both suffrage organizations.

In politics, women usually gained the right to participate in municipal and school board elections first. Their moral superiority or at least conservative social instincts were assumed to entitle them to a special voice in matters such as education, morals, and charity. Municipal suffrage was granted in Kansas in 1861. Various parts of Australia soon followed: New South Wales in 1867, the city of Victoria in 1869, and Western Australia in 1871. In Europe and Scandinavia, Sweden extended women municipal suffrage in 1861, England in 1869-71, and Finland in 1872.[53]

A major advance occurred in 1869 when the Wyoming territory gave women their first concrete victory within a larger political unit than municipalities. Diverse stories have been told as to why the Wyoming territory was first to award American women the vote since it had been rescinded in New Jersey in 1807. Suffragists later gave much credit to a little known former New York State milliner, Esther Morris. According to one version, Morris emigrated to Wyoming in 1869, just in time to entertain the candidates for the First Territorial Legislature at a tea party and persuade them to give women the vote.[54]

As recounted by Anna Howard Shaw (1847-1919), a minister, physician, and later president of the NAWSA, Morris helped a neighbor through a difficult birth. Then the grateful husband asked how he might repay the favor. Because he was a member of the legislature, she asked him to introduce a bill that would enfranchise women. The Democratic legislature passed the measure as a joke and expected the Republican governor to be embarrassed at having to veto it. But the governor had heard Susan B. Anthony make a suffrage speech back in Salem, Ohio, one of the first towns in the United States to hold a suffrage convention. That had impressed him, and he signed the bill. The Democrats lacked the votes to override it.[55]

A third version was offered in a history of the American women's suffrage movement published in 1913 by the International Woman Suffrage Alliance. This time Esther Morris led a group of women to the governor's house and intimated that they would stay until he signed, an early example of no-nonsense lobbying. Two years later, the governor vetoed a bill to repeal the law. When Wyoming applied to become a state, the legislators declared that they would remain out of the union a hundred years rather than give up the women's vote. Consequently, on June 27, 1890, they proclaimed that "the first free state was admitted to the Union."[56] Women did not fare as well in Utah, the second territory to accord them suffrage. They had voted for seventeen years before opposition to polygyny complicated the struggle for statehood. In 1887 the federal Edmund Tucker Law declared the women's vote to be illegal.[57]

In the British Commonwealth, women property owners voted for members of the House of Keys, the legislative body of the Isle of Man. Women rate payers received the vote in 1892.[58] But Wyoming placed no qualifications on the women's right to vote, and that state became a beacon of hope. When the Women's Christian Temperance Union of New Zealand waged their campaign two decades later, they obtained information on Wyoming from their American colleagues. In 1893, New Zealand became the first modern nation in the world to let women vote in federal elections. This victory reinforced suffragists' determination elsewhere, but the movement was very divided.

As caricatured and otherwise ridiculed in newspapers, Stanton and Anthony appeared to be too radical for conservative women to support. The NWSA was particularly stigmatized by association with Victoria Woodhull, a self-proclaimed free lover. While she meant that women should choose their mates to improve the species, the press preferred an interpretation of sexual promiscuity. When Woodhull ran for president in 1872, she contended that women already had the right to vote under the Fourteenth Amendment. Susan B. Anthony attempted to follow that line of reasoning and was fined when she attempted to vote in New York State. Lydia Becker (1842-1903) had led a group of British women in a similar attempt in Manchester, England, in 1868, but they also were stopped. In the next decade, Woodhull out-radicaled the radicals and soon split with the NWSA to form her own Equal Rights Party. Then Anthony drafted the first American federal woman suffrage constitutional amendment. It was introduced in 1878, more than a decade after the British made their first attempt.[59] They had already developed a substantial women's rights movement supported by the well-known British economist, John Stuart Mill.

2

HARRIET MILL AND JOHN STUART MILL:
A WORLD INFLUENCE

Before American women adopted their Declaration of Sentiments in 1848, John Stuart Mill (1806-1873) had long supported the English women's rights movement. He evolved a theoretical construct and his prestige lent credibility. Although Mill was sometimes identified as the founder of the women's rights movement in England, he was always careful to point out that the cause had many spokespersons before him. At a speech at Greenwich in 1870, he corrected a previous speaker who had alluded to him as having been the first to advocate the enfranchisement of women. "Several of the most eminent philosophers," he said, "and many of the noblest of women for ages have done this."[1] One who received less recognition than she deserved was his wife, Harriet Taylor Mill.

Mill was a fan of women's rights before he met Taylor, and he later went to great pains to contend that she had no formative influence on him in this matter. Rather, his support for the female franchise dated from his earlier days.[2] When Mill was eighteen, he was arrested for passing out birth control information. This incident could have ruined his budding career at the India House had it not been hushed up.[3] From then on, Mill was more circumspect as he deviated further from his father's views. James Mill asserted in 1820 that political rights could be removed without inconvenience from certain classes of people. Most women could be denied the vote, he argued, because their interests corresponded with those of their fathers or husbands. This declaration provoked a defense of women's right to suffrage by two Irish authors, William Thompson of Cork, and Anna Wheeler, the daughter of an Irish Protestant archbishop.[4] Then Thomas Babbington Macaulay attacked James Mill's views in the March 1829 *Edinburgh Review.*

Without adducing one fact, without taking the trouble to perplex the question by one sophism, he placidly dogmatizes away the interest of one half of the human race. If there be a word of truth in history, women have always been, and still are, over the greatest part of the globe, humble companions, playthings, captives, menials, beasts of burden. Except in a few happy and highly civilized communities, they are strictly in a state of personal slavery.[5]

John Stuart Mill introduced woman suffrage in the British parliament. Reprinted with permission from The Mary Evans Picture Library, London, England.

From Macaulay, Mill incorporated the perception that women's interests were no more identical with their husbands than those of subjects with their kings. Mill's biographer, Michael St. John Packe, said, "The passage about the position of women struck him particularly hard: throughout his life, that question was so much a passion with him that he often made it the final issue, the test on which depended his acceptance or rejection of a philosophic system."[6]

Although Mill's basic position on the woman question was formed before he met Harriet Taylor, she gave the cause new meaning. At the time, Taylor was married to another man. Her private correspondence with Mill reflects their mutual moral and ethical struggle, particularly concerning divorce. Mill later gave Harriet Taylor primary credit for a number of newspaper articles that they coauthored on wife beating and other women's issues. She also is now assumed to have been the primary author of "Enfranchisement of Women."

Taylor set aside writing this small essay while she mourned the death of her first husband, but she resumed after Mill drew her attention to news of women's conventions in Ohio and Massachusetts. In an undated letter written after October 29, 1850, Mill says "you know some time ago there was a convention of Women in Ohio to claim equal rights —(& there is to be another in May) well, there has just been a Convention for the same purpose in Massachusetts—chiefly of women but with a great number of men too. . . ." Based on a long account in the *New York Tribune,* Mill concluded that he and Harriet Taylor had "a good chance of living to see something decisive really accomplished on that of all practical subjects the most important. . . ."[7] The 1851 Worcester convention was the focal point of "Enfranchisement of Women," which was published anonymously in the July 1851, *Westminster Review* three months after Taylor and Mill married. Mill initially let it appear that he had written the essay, and it received much wider distribution and consideration than it would have otherwise.[8] However, he gave most of the credit to Taylor when it was republished in his *Dissertations and Discussions* in 1859.[9] Neither of them felt that it was the best they could write on the subject, but the planned revision was left to Mill to complete after Taylor's death.

Taylor's essay became one of the best-selling tracts of the American women's rights movement. Evelyn Pugh has suggested that "Enfranchisement of Women" appeared at a time when they had "little carefully reasoned and readily available material to turn to for confirmation of their beliefs."[10] The small essay filled the gap because it was relatively straightforward in denouncing such injustices as denying women the right to vote, to hold certain jobs, to receive education, and to compete in the professional world. Mill's presumed authorship and its publication in a well-known British journal enhanced its prestige in the United States. The essay also proved to be very popular in England. Over Mill's protests, a cheap edition was printed and sold by the thousands to the British working classes.[11] In 1864 (thirteen years later), *The English Woman's Review* published a summary and encouraged reading the original.[12]

Mill later also gave his wife credit for incorporating his views on women in works on other subjects. His audience, primarily learned men, was exposed to a positive perspective on women's rights in Mill's treatises on logic, politics and government, and liberty. For example, in the 1840s when Harriet Taylor was writing an essay on the disabilities of women, she encouraged Mill to add a paragraph to his third edition of *Political Economy.* Declaring a need for population control, Mill contended that "There would be no need, however, of legal sanctions, if women were admitted as on all other grounds they have the clearest title to be, to the same rights of citizenship with men."[13]

Ruth Borchard, another Mill biographer, contends that the strong impetus Mill gave socialism and the current British welfare state owe more to Harriet Taylor than to Mill himself. "Mill's *Political Economy* did more than any other single book to bring about socialism in England."[14] This book was read by working men and trade unionists as well as the elites, and Mill's popularity with the working class largely derived from its influence.[15] Mill later acceded to some working men's request to give over his royalties to bring out *Political Economy* in cheap, popular editions.

Mill also acknowledged Taylor's influence on his most famous work, *On Liberty*.[16] Published shortly after her death in 1858, Mill described it as "more literally our joint production than anything else which bears my name. . . ."[17] He made it clear that his assumptions on liberty applied to women as well as men. In fact, Gertrude Himmelfarb contends that "*On Liberty* was the case of women writ large, the liberation of women magnified to the point where it became the liberation of all mankind."[18] This book was translated into nearly all living languages and was read by citizens of all nations. According to Borchard, "It is still one of the great torches of Western civilization."[19] Forbidden by totalitarian regimes, even today *On Liberty* continues to appear in new editions.

Women's rights supporters acknowledged Mill's contribution to their cause. A two-part essay in *The English Woman's Journal* of September and November 1860 summarized some of Mill's statements in volumes more likely to be read by specialists in economics, social welfare, or politics. The essay begins, "There is no name in England which carries with it so much weight, whether it be at Oxford or Cambridge, or in the two Houses of Legislature, as that of John Stuart Mill, the philosopher, logician and political economist."[20] Segments of his writings that were applicable to women's rights were extracted for the readers. For example, from *A System of Logic, Ratiocinative and Inductive, Being a Connected View of the Principles of Evidence, and the Methods of Scientific Investigation*, usually identified as "The Logic," the author quotes Mill:

To add one more example: those who assert, what no one has ever succeeded in proving, that there is in one human individual, one sex, or one race of mankind over another, an inherent and inexplicable superiority in mental faculties, could only substantiate their proposition by subtracting from the differences of intellect, which we in fact see, all that can be traced by known laws either to the ascertained differences of physical organization, or to the differences which have existed in the outward circumstances in which the subjects of the comparison have hitherto been placed.[21]

Despite Mill's convoluted statements, female students were told to be encouraged by what they read. "The whole weight of the book leans to the advantage of the female student; and none, whether men or women, can close these two volumes without holding a more reasonable view of this and all other questions."[22]

In articles in *The English Woman's Journal,* Bessie Raynor Parkes saw similar encouragement for women in Mill's *Principles of Political Economy, with Some of Their Applications to Social Philosophy.* "Mr. Mill distinctly declares his opinion, that the inferior position and help-less submission, is one of the reasons for the misery and poverty of the lower classes." Mill acknowledged that the earnings of whole families might be lower than those of men who worked alone in other trades. Nonetheless, he opposed protective legislation. Mill asserted that "No argument however, can be hence derived for the exclusion of women from the liberty of competing in the labor market." Rather, if the man and woman together earn less than the man alone, Mill argued that "the advantage to the woman of not depending on a master for subsistence is more than an equivalent."[23] Mill further asserted that, "women are as capable as men of appreciating and managing their own concerns, and the only hindrance to their doing so, arises from the injustice of their present social position."[24]

When Mill was elected to the House of Commons in 1865, he attempted to advance the women's cause more directly. On June 7, 1866, he presented a petition signed by 1,499 women to request suffrage.[25] It was intended to counteract the popular belief that women did not want the vote. Then *The English Woman's Review* (formerly *Journal*) summa-rized what was said about it in other publications and explored the prob-able consequences of extending the franchise to female householders.[26] When Mill called for woman suffrage on May 20, 1867, his speech to Parliament was published in full.[27, 28]

The recently elected member moved to amend the Representation of the People Bill (Clause 4) to leave out the word "man" and substitute "people."[29] Mill and his followers received more support on this first hearing than they expected. Millicent Garrett Fawcett, the subsequent leader of the conservative British women's suffrage movement, recalled later that seventy-three members of Parliament voted for the motion, eighty-one counting the tellers.[30] The measure failed against 196 in opposition.[31] While Fawcett cited figures on how many men voted favor-ably, and John Stuart Mill expressed pleasure at the good showing, Henry Labouchere (MP for Northampton) recalled thirty years later that practically all of the MPs had viewed the proposal as a huge joke, "Mill being the only one who voted seriously."[32]

Women suffragists also took the initiative on their own behalf. The Manchester National Society for Women's Suffrage contended that women already had the parliamentary franchise. In 1868, a contingent led by Lydia Becker managed to register women with property qualifica-tion. Most were thrown off the list, but some voted in the election of November 1868.[33] In Chorlton v. Lings the judges ruled that the word "man" does not include "woman" and so invalidated the women's efforts.[34] Ironically, this decision was substantiated on the ground that Mill's motion to include women proved their exclusion.[35]

British women also tried to claim precedent as a basis for their legal right to vote. In *Women's Suffrage: A Short History of A Great Movement*, Millicent Garrett Fawcett contends that British women possessed the necessary legal qualifications to vote as late as 1807. She quotes Mrs. Spencer Stanhope's letter to her son, John. Her husband's party was so certain of success in the forthcoming election that "They determine not to admit the ladies to vote, which is extraordinary and very hard considering how few privileges we poor females have."[36]

Mill's famous speech in Parliament did not turn the tide, but he did win some at least temporary converts. One was John Bright, whose female relatives became major supporters. And Jacob Bright participated in the successful drive to secure women the right to vote in municipal elections under the Municipal Corporations Amendment Act of 1869. The Education Act of 1870 extended the right of women to vote for and sit on school boards.[37] With Mill's support, the women's suffrage committee exerted pressure for these and other gains in London. The original London Suffrage Society founded in 1866 was dissolved in 1867. Then the London National Society for Women's Suffrage was formed with Mill as president. By the time the first meeting was held that July, more than forty other women's suffrage societies were being formed around England.[38] Mill also encouraged the development of the Irish woman suffrage movement. Anna Haslam's husband corresponded with Mill before she founded the Dublin Women's Suffrage Association (the first in that country) in 1876.[39]

After Mill was voted out of Parliament, he and his stepdaughter, Helen Taylor, worked for women's rights through speeches and letters. At the same time, Henry Fawcett continued to represent Mill unofficially in Parliament.[40] This Cambridge professor remained Mill's enthusiastic follower.[41] The two men had become friends before they were both elected to Parliament in 1865.[42] Fawcett married Millicent Garrett, who had read Mill's works when she was sixteen. She benefitted from Mill's support for women public speakers. In 1884, Fawcett recalled that lady speakers had been a novelty in 1868. They were subjected to ridicule even if they appeared on the speaking platform in the company of men like Mill and Henry Fawcett.[43]

Mill now is remembered less for "Enfranchisement of Women" than *The Subjection of Women*. This small book was completed not long after Harriet Taylor Mill died in 1858. However, it was not published until nearly a decade later, almost twenty years after the shorter essay. Mill's book was more theoretical. He focused on the concept of total equality between the sexes, not such basic issues as divorce and employment for married women. Nonetheless, Mill seems very radical even now because he blamed women's subjection primarily on the family.[44] Most of the suf-fragists were not ready to face the fundamental inequities in that institution.

When *The Subjection of Women* was first published in 1868, it was widely praised among Americans like Susan B. Anthony and Lucy Stone. Mill himself had received little attention in the United States from 1851 until he was elected to Parliament.[45] Then his *Considerations on Representative Government* and also his amendment speech that pro-posed woman suffrage were widely quoted. With his renewed popularity, Mill graciously declined many invitations to speak in the United States. He usually sent a letter the suffragists could read at their conventions and publish in local newspapers.[46] These letters of encouragement gave credence to the cause because they were written by the distinguished British theorist. Nonetheless, after *The Subjection of Women* received its initial round of praise, only Elizabeth Cady Stanton spoke out boldly in agreement with Mill's views.[47] In England, *The Subjection of Women* raised a great outcry among men and did not reinforce his standing among women then as it would in later decades.[48] Some critics argued that Mill had damaged his reputation by writing on such a trivial subject. One positive side effect was renewed interest in and enthusiasm for Har-riet Taylor Mill's earlier essay, especially in the United States. American suffragists tried to invoke John Stuart Mill's name while they distanced themselves from some of his views. And some British suffragists, partic-ularly Millicent Garrett Fawcett, saw his idealistic goal of women's complete equality as beyond their reach.

After Mill died in 1873, Fawcett paid tribute to him for giving the women's movement its character of practical good sense and modera-tion.[49] She contended that his famous speech to Parliament motivated women to claim the right to suffrage on the grounds of expediency, on the same basis as men. Fawcett glossed over Mill's staunchly held posi-tion that married women should also be allowed to vote. She favored a compromise that would limit suffrage to women property holders. Widows and single women would be included, but not married women, who were not yet allowed to hold property in their own names. Affronted by this conservative stance, Dr. and Mrs. Richard M. Pankhurst, Mrs. Jacob Bright, and Elizabeth Wolstenholme Elmy withdrew and founded the Women's Franchise League. They followed Mill's lead and promoted the Women's Franchise Bill of 1889. It proposed the vote for women, married or single, who possessed the same qualifications as men.[50]

In addition to his personal support and introduction of the first woman suffrage bill in the British Parliament, Mill contributed to the international women's movement through his exalted reputation as a substantive and respected author. His publications gave the cause stand-ing as Mill asserted that a civilization's advancement could be measured by how far it had progressed toward equal rights for women. Because

Victorian England was the major world power in the nineteenth century and Mill was one of the best-known Englishmen, his influence was enormous. Biographer Ruth Borchard contends that "Mill became indeed a sort of mentor to the world."[51] Moncure D. Conway told of Russian princesses who came out of seclusion to greet him and the American charge d'affaires after they heard that Conway was a personal friend of John Stuart Mill. The four young daughters bowed and said in perfect English that Mill's book with its demand for women's freedom was their Bible. The eldest said she slept with a copy under her pillow. However, the First Wave suffragists were more apt to praise Harriet Taylor Mill's earlier essay and give Mill credit for it. They left *The Subjection of Women* to inspire later feminists. As they organized and began their campaigns, others like Josephine Butler fought to keep women from losing additional rights. One step toward overcoming the double standard was to prevent or rescind government sanction of prostitution.

3

JOSEPHINE BUTLER AND THE CONTAGIOUS DISEASES ACTS

While the woman suffrage campaign began to develop local and national organizations, other women's rights deteriorated. In Great Britain when the Contagious Diseases Acts were passed to regulate prostitution, they created a major fire storm. In ancient Greece, Aristotle recounted the fragmentation of women into two classes. Private women were supposedly cherished wives and mothers while public women were castigated as prostitutes. This system was staunchly institutionalized in Great Britain. For example, the brothels in Winchester belonged to the bishop and were operated under a royal license from 1161 to 1545 AD.[1] In the nineteenth century, the belief continued that Eve was a temptress who misled Adam. It sustained the notion that female prostitutes were depraved beings responsible for leading young men astray. The double standard was also reinforced by the conviction that men had a natural sex drive that required an outlet to protect their health, whereas women did not.

Women who knew nothing about sex were often shocked on their wedding nights. Most of them conformed to the respectable ladies' obligation to suffer in silence. They usually tacitly accepted the double standard out of ignorance or a misguided sense of respectability. An exception was Annie Besant, a contemporary of Butler's. The future president of the Indian National Congress recalled vividly the shock of violation on her wedding night.[2] Her husband, a church pastor named Frank Besant, may well have also been a victim of lack of knowledge and experience. However, the shock could be even greater in first encounters with husbands accustomed to the services of prostitutes. Often the symptoms of venereal disease readily added to the insult.

The largely male medical profession conspired in the silence about sex. When bridegrooms' marriages were imminent, they were often treated with medications that stopped drainage from venereal ailments at least long enough to get them through their honeymoons. Therefore, it was no accident that one of the priorities of the women's movement was to train female physicians. Then they could educate women about the hazards of sexuality and how venereal disease could affect children as well as wives.[3] Prevention and cure were still a long way off.

Like the medical profession, the male dominated political, legal, and religious establishments accepted prostitution as inevitable because

Josephine Butler led the women's movement against regulated prostitution in England. Picture from *Josephine Butler: An Autobiographical Memoir,* edited by George W. and Lucy A. Johnson. Bristol: J. W. Arrowsmith, 1911.

sex was believed to be necessary for men's health. Therefore, they wanted it regulated so male patrons would not contract venereal disease from prostitutes. Male medical, military, and government officials were particularly concerned that venereal disease, especially syphilis, would spread among soldiers and sailors who were away from home for long periods. Men who engaged prostitutes were perceived as victims, both of their own natural instincts and of the depraved creatures who accepted money to meet their needs. Regulatory systems were always flawed, however, because there was no real cure for venereal diseases. Also, although health examinations were favored for the women, this possibility was seldom raised for their male clients.

Although prostitution was a well-entrenched custom, England did not attempt to formalize its regulation under law until the nineteenth century. Before that, local police assumed *de facto* authority. In France, on the other hand, state regulation of vice was initiated in the eighteenth century. Prostitution had been regulated in Japan for centuries, but Paris was the first city in the Western world to try to confine it to certain districts. The *Bureau des Moeurs* (Morals Bureau) claimed to act as a compassionate agency that went to great lengths to prevent girls and women from being officially registered as "public women." However, all men, not just police, could arbitrarily charge them with soliciting. Then the women could be hauled before a magistrate, forced to submit to the indignity of a physical examination, and be registered as prostitutes.

Although the women were licensed and subjected to regular medical inspections, the system did not deter prostitution or limit venereal disease. The number of prostitutes increased from 22,000 in 1815 to 52,000 in 1850.[4] Nonetheless, the French effort motivated calls for similar regulations all over Europe. Two books particularly attracted public attention in England. As a medical resident, William Acton had studied the French system. He contended that women were not registered arbitrarily. In fact, many prostitutes were not registered at all. This undercut the most common argument in favor of the Contagious Diseases Acts— that all prostitutes would be examined regularly. Despite such apparent defects in the system, when Acton published *Prostitution Considered in Its Moral, Social and Sanitary Aspects in London and Other Large Cities, with Proposals for the Mitigation and Prevention of Its Attendant Evils* in 1857, the book generated much attention in England. It was reinforced by numerous studies, including one conducted by William Sanger, *The History of Prostitution: Its Extent, Causes and Effects throughout the World,* published in 1858. This survey conducted in New York City established that the primary reasons women entered prostitution were destitution, seduction, and abandonment, not depravity.[5]

Despite the lack of positive results in Paris, the British medical community strongly endorsed a system of government regulation to reduce venereal disease around Army and Navy posts. The decision to legislate rather than continue *de facto* police control opened the subject to public discussion. In a letter and three articles published in *The Daily News,* Harriet Martineau protested in 1863 that there was no proof that regulation diminished venereal disease.[6] She also attempted to refute the widely accepted belief that sex was necessary to maintain men's health.[7]

Still, the protests were few and generally ignored, perhaps largely because previous legislation titled Contagious Diseases Acts had referred to animals. In 1864, the first of a series of laws permitted the regulation of vice at fourteen military and naval stations.[8] The persuading argument was that large concentrations of military men away from their wives would need to be protected from disease in their inevitable intercourse with local prostitutes. The 1864 Contagious Diseases Act had expired when the 1866 Act extended this authority. By then both opposition and support were growing. Elizabeth Wolstenholme (later Elmy) and Dr. Elizabeth Blackwell were among the women who protested against the 1866 Acts, but their efforts were virtually ignored.

The Acts were verbally extended in 1868, but widespread opposition did not finally crystallize until the last Contagious Diseases Act was passed in 1869. It extended regulation and compulsory examination to women in civilian as well as military communities. Then Josephine Butler (1828-1906) took up what became a sixteen-year campaign between 1869 and 1886 that forced Parliamentary repeal. For the suffragists, the timing could not have been worse, as Butler was well aware. She had signed the original suffrage petition Mill presented to Parliament.[9] He had introduced the first woman suffrage bill in 1867 in the middle of the period when the Contagious Diseases Acts were being passed. Later, Butler would argue that if women had had the vote, these Acts would never have passed in the first place. At the time she felt that she had to follow her conscience, although she realized that publicizing the regulation of the sex industry could have negative consequences for woman suffrage.

Although the leaders of the movements to repeal the Contagious Diseases Acts and to win women's suffrage were very different, both Josephine Butler and Millicent Garrett Fawcett recognized the common origin in the suppression of women by men. The abolitionists sought to protect women's civil rights, while the suffragists wanted to extend their political rights. However, the two women also were very aware that if that most intimate relationship between men and women were placed under public scrutiny, it could reinforce previously suppressed hostility between the sexes. Consequently, after Butler began the fight for abolition, conservative suffragists initially tried to distance themselves from that cause.[10]

Mill was among them, although he did eventually speak out publicly against the Contagious Diseases Acts before they were repealed.[11] Millicent Garrett Fawcett also tried to distance herself from the abolitionists, who were called repealers. In her admiring biography of Butler written in 1927, Fawcett claimed that the two women did not even become acquainted until 1885, one year before the Contagious Diseases Acts were repealed.[12] However, after that, Fawcett campaigned for social purity as well as suffrage.

Despite efforts to maintain some distance between the two causes, Butler's campaign divided the suffrage movement. In 1871 the London National Society for Women's Suffrage split from the National Society for Women's Suffrage on this issue.[13] The two organizations rejoined in 1877 but split again in 1888 over whether other political groups should be allowed to affiliate with the NSWS. Fawcett and Lydia Becker continued to advocate nonpartisanship, but the breakaway Central National Society for Women's Suffrage (CNS) accepted political affiliates.[14] The social purity movement also took a toll on the Irish suffragists.[15] Anna Haslam later said the suffrage campaign was slowed due to efforts to pass the Married Women's Property Acts and to repeal the Contagious Diseases Acts.[16]

Josephine Butler was exceptionally well qualified to lead a movement concerned with such a controversial topic in the latter half of the nineteenth century. Few women could appear in public without risk of having their morals challenged, but Butler was exceptional. She was president of the North of England Council for Promoting the Higher Education of Women between 1867 and 1873, when opposition to the Contagious Diseases Acts became her primary mission. Attractive, fashionably dressed, and soft spoken, she was well educated, highly religious, and married to a supportive scholar/cleric, George Butler. Above reproach morally, they were also well-placed socially. Among their acquaintances were members of the peerage and Parliament. These included Prime Minister and Mrs. William Gladstone.[17]

In England a National Association for the Repeal of the Contagious Diseases Acts was formed in October 1869, and a Ladies National Association developed at about the same time.[18] Recruited by Elizabeth Wolstonholme, Butler became their leader. On December 31, 1869, their manifesto was published in *The Daily News*, one of the infrequent occasions when that newspaper broke its code of silence on the subject.

When she was asked to participate, Butler's first reaction was to get down on her knees and pray for guidance. Next she asked for and received the full support of her husband. Both of them recognized the overwhelming task that lay ahead. Josephine Butler already understood some of the prostitutes' circumstances. Unlike the respectable women who turned their backs, she had offered employment and sanctuary in her own home for women who had just been released from prison or were dying from disease.[19] Butler had also suffered the consequences of breaking the code of silence that underpinned the sexual double standard. After she publicly discussed a novel by Elizabeth Gaskell, Butler had been virtually ostracized while her husband was on the faculty at Oxford.[20] She was convinced that the code of silence gave the Contagious Diseases Acts a permanent endorsement.[21]

Other factors also qualified Butler to lead the fight against the Contagious Diseases Acts. The most important were her bravery and unwavering conviction that these Acts violated not only women's civil rights, but basic human liberty because they were founded on injustice.[22] As the Contagious Diseases Acts put women beyond the law, Butler argued for justice rather than social purity.[23] Her goal was only to abolish the Contagious Diseases Acts, not prostitution itself. Women could sell their bodies without coercion. Butler hoped, however, that both men and women would strive for a higher standard of individual morals that would prohibit them from engaging in such transactions.

As a first principle of her campaign, Butler rejected the notion that women could be separated into private and public spheres.[24] She was convinced that the moral foundation of society was damaged when the government regulated prostitution. Vice and venereal disease increased as consorting with prostitutes became socially accepted. Patrons were given a false sense of security because the government took responsibility for insuring their protection from venereal disease. Men's minds would be difficult to change, especially in the medical community. However, Butler received some support that she did not anticipate.

At ease in the upper echelons of society, Butler initially experienced much trepidation as she called on working men to support abolition. Nonetheless, they had to be convinced because they were in the majority after Disraeli extended the vote in the 1868 Reform Bill.[25] Butler's fears proved to be unfounded, as the laboring class audiences quickly made clear that they understood and supported her. It was their wives and daughters, after all, who would summarily be brought before police magistrates, examined, and branded as prostitutes. The working classes had traditionally been forced to provide sexual services for the elites, and they did not need the matter explained. Millicent Garrett Fawcett later contended that every extension of the suffrage to men helped Butler's cause, but not necessarily her own.[26] By World War I, she feared that women might never get the vote if the remainder of the men were enfranchised without them. Butler began to achieve some victories much sooner because of working-class support.

Well-known women like Harriet Martineau, Florence Nightingale, and Ursula Bright lent their names on placards of support as Butler campaigned before the Colchester election in 1870.[27] A repealer, Colonel Learmouth, won after Sir Henry Storks said that not only prostitutes but also soldiers' wives ought to be examined.[28] His supporters were vicious, but Butler persevered. She was thrown out of hotels wherever she was recognized, and she endured much verbal abuse as well as physical threats. By the end of that struggle she had traveled more than 3,700 miles and addressed ninety-nine public meetings and four conferences.[29] The first repeal bill was introduced that year, but the Contagious Diseases Acts were not abolished for sixteen more.

While working-class men proved to be a bastion of support, some middle-class women also risked their tenuous respectability to join Butler's cause. Married women recognized that they also were sex slaves like the prostitutes, but with less bargaining power. They were private sexual property just as prostitutes were public sexual property. So-called respectable women rejected the argument that prostitutes saved them from shame.[30] Marital rape was not recognized under law, and feminists opposed birth control since men then could force their wives to engage in sex more frequently without the fear of having to support more children.[31] As it was, women were burdened with both child bearing and the unsanitary delivery procedures that frequently caused their untimely deaths. Female physicians like Elizabeth Blackwell supported Butler's cause by challenging the popular notion that sex was necessary to maintain men's health.[32]

As opposition to the Contagious Diseases Acts grew and was publicized in England, the struggle also attracted notice in Europe, the United States, and India.[33] Repeal of the Contagious Diseases Acts and woman suffrage came to a vote in Great Britain in 1873, and both were defeated.[34] The regulationists were winning in Europe, and Josephine Butler became aware of a scheme intended to be applied throughout the world.[35] Consequently, after the 1874 conference at York, the abolitionists agreed to form an international association. On March 18, 1875, the British, Continental, and General Federation for the Abolition of Government Regulation of Prostitution was established in Geneva, Switzerland.[36] Butler was widely traveled and fluent in several languages, so she was well prepared to wage an international campaign. Her ideas were endorsed at the first meeting held at Geneva in 1877.[37] Ironically, that city continued to regulate brothels for the next fifty years. The repealers suffered a particularly humiliating defeat in 1896.[38] Local churches were desecrated as brothel owners celebrated in the name of La Lampe Rouge (The Red Lamp). Regulation was finally only reluctantly abolished in 1927 under a proclamation by the League of Nations.[39]

Fifty years earlier, Butler's ideas attracted international attention as her influential writings were widely translated. The feminist novelist, Camilla Collett, was among her Norwegian supporters.[40] In 1879 she called attention to Josephine Butler's views on the elimination of officially sanctioned prostitution and so spread the antiregulation movement to that country.[41] In France Butler investigated police regulation of prostitution, particularly in Paris where she charmed Inspector Lecour, head of the infamous *Bureau de Moeurs*. He permitted her to visit the women imprisoned at St. Lazare and even sent her copies of his publications. In January 1877, the Butlers were invited to testify before the Paris Municipal Council after newspapers reported numerous arbitrary and cruel actions.[42] Other international cooperation was also underway.

Another repealer, Mr. Aimé Humbert of Neuchatel, Switzerland, went to study the situation in Japan in 1874.[43] Two years later, Henry J. Wilson and the Reverend J. P. Gledstone traveled to New York City where regulation was under consideration.[44] That year, organizers of the Philadelphia Medical Convention faced enough opposition so that the issue was dropped.[45] When the medical community could be restrained, a major source of support was withdrawn from the regulationists. The system was abolished in the Cape Colony, South Africa, in Bombay, India, and in St. Louis, Missouri, USA.[46] Pressure increased to abolish regulation after Butler exposed the traffic in children for sexual purposes between Britain and Belgium in 1880.[47] When the Contagious Diseases Acts were rescinded in 1883, the repealers received messages from well-wishers in Scotland, Ireland, France, Switzerland, and Italy. Butler wrote to her sister, "There was something in the air like the approach of victory."[48] That was reinforced when the Contagious Diseases Acts were actually repealed three years later.

The celebration was brief though, as word soon filtered back from India that prostitution was still regulated there. Butler confirmed this through her emissaries, two American members of the Women's Christian Temperance Union, Kate Bushnell and Elizabeth Andrews. The WCTU had jumped into the campaign for what Americans daintily called "social purity" very early, as they recognized its connection with the abuse of alcohol.[49] Bushnell and Andrews had previously observed prostitution around lumber camps in the American states of Michigan and Wisconsin.

Under colonial authority in India, prostitution had been authorized to provide sexual services for the British military encampments before 1858 under various Cantonment Acts. Clearly, parliamentary repeal in Great Britain did not affect the colonies. In India the same year the Contagious Diseases Acts were repealed, Major-General Chapman issued an Order of Council under instructions from the Commander-in-Chief. Under Special Cantonment Acts, native women would be supplied for British regiments. The Order requested, "To arrange for the effective inspection of prostitutes attached to regimental bazaars, whether in cantonments or on the line of march. . . ." A second part dictated, "To have a sufficient number of women, to take care that they are sufficiently attractive, to provide them with proper houses." Any reasonable expenditure from cantonment funds would be sanctioned to achieve the measure.[50] This so-called Infamous Memorandum aroused public indignation when it was publicized in England in 1888. Then the Indian Contagious Diseases Acts were repealed as well. The Cantonment Acts were amended in 1895.[51] Then all compulsory medical examinations and registrations of women were prohibited.[52] Brothels were also abolished, but various forms of regulation continued.[53]

Nor was vigorous action taken in other parts of the empire. Although the Contagious Diseases Acts were repealed in England in 1886, in Ireland Regulation 40, Defense of the Realm (DORA), was implemented in August 1918.[54] While women were also concerned about the higher incidence of venereal disease in Ireland than in England, they objected to Regulation 40 because any woman could be arrested "on suspicion" and detained until she was proved innocent by a medical examination. She could also be handed over to the police on a verbal charge made by a soldier, just as if Butler's campaign had never been waged.[55] So the fight against regulation continued as abolitionists also challenged the system in Hong Kong, Singapore, Sri Lanka, Gibraltar, Malta, South Africa, and Australia.[56]

In England, suffragists began to see some advantages in the rival cause.[57] Women who first became active in the repeal campaign often later supported woman suffrage. In addition, although the Married Women's Property Act was passed in 1870 and more women were able to receive higher education, the British suffragists, like the Americans, were in a long doldrums and badly needed successes. While the repeal movement spread around the world, it became more central to the women's suffrage movement in Great Britain. As they gradually over-came the code of silence that reinforced the double standard, feminists were able at least to modify the old notion of man as victim and woman as temptress.[58] In the latter part of the nineteenth century, many women became convinced that masculinity is culturally, not biologically, con-structed. They were sure women could never attain equality within a separate sphere or get equitable laws passed as long as they were based primarily on men's self-interest. The heated battle to repeal the Conta-gious Diseases Acts also made clear that the chivalry with which men claimed to protect women was a sham, "that outward sex attraction often masked an inward sex antipathy."[59]

As Josephine Butler broke the code of silence, she and her follow-ers bore the initial brunt of abuse by men who supported regulation of prostitution. This escalated in attacks on the suffragists later, particularly after some women became militant. Male violence was a major reason even the militant suffragists directed their hostility against things such as throwing stones to break windows. Without the guise of gallantry or chivalry, women were forced to face men's brutality directly. Millicent Garrett Fawcett tried to lead the suffragists in a conservative path so as not to crystalize what many of them recognized at least privately as a sex war.[60] Prosuffrage women attributed male violence to social conditioning and at least saw some hope for change. In contrast, the antisuffragists were inclined to see men's brutality as inherent to their natures. The women feared that if the pose of submission were dropped, open sex warfare would result. Because of this fear, many antis worked for educa-tion, property rights, and custody of children, but not for suffrage, the cause they were convinced unleashed the beast in men.[61]

Like the antis, the suffragists were also reluctant to face directly the question of men's potential for brutality against women. They often coded issues related to sex, and Susan Kingsley Kent describes some of the language they used to avoid stating the fundamental concern. When Josephine Butler noted that the language with which men confronted her would be more likely to be heard in a brothel, Fawcett said that the suf-frage campaign could be a way to eliminate "degrading and vulgar" images of women. Other suffragists spoke of the chains forged when a woman permitted herself to be the instrument of man's pleasure (Charlotte Despard), the laws and customs that forced a woman to live with a man who degraded and infected her with disease (Theresa Billington-Greig), and women's desire to "revolt against the ignominious conditions of amatory life as bound by coercive monogamy" (Gasquoine Hartley). Emmeline Pankhurst, leader of the British militant suffragettes, declared that prostitution was a metaphor for the position of all women and perhaps the main reason for militancy.[62]

As Butler led the movement to repeal the Contagious Diseases Acts, she drew attention to the issue of social purity. In one form or another, women's sexual standing became part of the agenda of women's national and international organizations. Josephine Butler's cause was eventually recognized by other leaders of the women's movement as an important if usually hidden basis for the need to achieve political rights. Even so, these women were reluctant to examine the institution of marriage itself too closely. They left for later feminists the task of trying to change fundamental male and female consciousness.[63] Meanwhile, international networks were gradually constructed as women banded together to work more effectively and pressure for improved standing in law and custom.

PART II

INTERNATIONAL WOMEN'S ORGANIZATIONS

While small numbers of largely middle-class women struggled for legal rights and against the deprivation of civil rights, most women were socialized primarily through church and community activities. Social awareness and civic responsibility evolved through accounts sent home by missionaries overseas and work for temperance to lesson male abuse of alcohol at home. Especially when women missionaries were sent abroad, their sisters at home related more personally to world events and recognized the important functions women could perform outside the domestic sphere.

When the temperance movement began in the United States, women were already accustomed to forming their own groups within the churches to support foreign missions. Mary Webb initiated the Boston Female Society for Missionary Purposes in 1800.[1] Sometimes the women's organizations operated on a very modest scale. For example, the Female Cent Society founded in 1802 called on its members to contribute one penny at each meeting to aid women and children in poor countries.[2] Most women could afford this sum, although they usually had little money of their own.

Men organized the American Bible Society in 1816 and sent funds to countries like Thailand to assist the American Board and American Baptist-sponsored missionaries. These efforts were sometimes markedly unsuccessful. They reportedly did not make a single Thai convert from 1831 to 1849 and only forty-five before 1863.[3] The efforts of women missionaries were often not recognized at all because they were wives who accompanied the officially sponsored men. Anne Hazeltine Jackson became the first female Protestant missionary when she was posted to Rangoon, Myanmar, in 1819. She married Adonian Judson and translated his catechism into Thai. The first American woman missionary, Mrs. John T. Jones, arrived in Thailand in 1833. An English woman, Theodisa Ann Barker, reached China in 1836 in the service of The Society for Promoting Female Education in the East.[4] Sophia Blackmore, an Australian, was the first unmarried woman to go to Singapore under the aegis of the American Woman's Foreign Missionary Society (WFMS) of the Methodist Episcopal Church. Her long service was recalled in *A Record of Woman's Work in Malaya, 1887-1927*. Blackmore joined the WCTU when a branch was formed in 1887, and in 1892 Josephine Hebinger came to rescue fallen women.[5]

37

Although foreign missions attracted interest back home, alcohol abuse directly affected women's lives. Women and children stood help-lessly by as their "menfolks" drank up the family's resources at the corner saloon. When women began to organize in opposition, the church was a socially accepted gathering place for them to commiserate with one another. New York State's Daughters of Temperance, a secret society, attracted an increasing membership after the 1847 local option law was repealed. Then some women fought back directly. They went into saloons, broke glasses and bottles, and emptied demijohns and barrels into the street.[6]

Movements to abolish slavery and increase women's rights over-lapped with temperance in the nineteenth century. Men initially founded temperance organizations to oppose the use and abuse of alcohol. When women were not allowed to participate, they soon developed separate organizations. Resentment against alcohol abuse brought out even very conservative women of all ages, classes, and nations. Their effort to protect their homes initially drew them into the public arena where many became politicized and also worked for other causes, including woman suffrage.

After Susan B. Anthony organized the Woman's State Temperance Society in Rochester, New York, in 1852, President Elizabeth Cady Stanton immediately called for reforms for which some members were not ready.[7] One they did favor was implementation of the so-called Maine Law. Maine had been first to initiate statewide prohibition in 1851. A more controversial proposal was to petition the state govern-ment to modify laws that affected marriage and the custody of children, so the drunkard would have no claims on his wife or children. Even Stanton did not use the word "divorce"; she displayed a provincial view-point that contrasted with her later internationalism. She called on women to withdraw from foreign mission societies to concentrate on the problems at home, ". . . let us withdraw our mite from all associations for sending the Gospel to the heathen across the ocean. . . ."[8]

Susan B. Anthony went further as she combined her appeals for new temperance laws and women's rights. She argued that women had not only the right, but the duty to speak out against the liquor traffic. Because women could not vote, she advised them to instruct their male relatives on how to vote. Anthony argued that if men continued to misrepresent her, a woman should "take the right to march to the ballot-box and deposit a vote indicative of her highest ideas of practical temperance."[9]

As the campaigns became more popular, other states followed Maine in mandating prohibition: Kansas in 1880, Iowa in 1882, Maine again in 1884, and Rhode Island in 1886. Then the brewers, liquor dealers, and saloon keepers organized; and the reform movement lost twelve of the next fourteen attempts to enact statewide prohibition between 1887 and 1890.[10] Because temperance and woman suffrage were perceived to be closely connected, sometimes the two causes were defeated together. In the Washington territory, men defeated constitutional amendments for both in the election of October 1, 1889.[11] Americans linked temperance and women's rights from their beginnings to World War I, when two constitutional amendments (the Eighteenth and Nineteenth) prohibited interstate transport of alcohol and permitted women to vote in federal elections.

Temperance groups readily formed international associations. The American Temperance Society, a men's organization, was formed in 1826 and influenced the antispirits movements that began in Belfast, Ireland, and Glasgow, Scotland, in 1829, in North England in 1830, and in the British and Foreign Temperance Society founded in 1831.[12] Their problems were similar. The American Temperance Union had split from the more moderate American Temperance Society by 1837 because the teetotalers favored total abstinence rather than drinking in moderation. The British also split on teetotalism versus abstinence in 1839. Although a World's Temperance Convention was called in London in 1846, such divisions prevented the formation of a world union at that time.[13]

John Stuart Mill waffled on the prohibition question. In *On Liberty* he contends that prohibition would infringe on the liberty of the buyer. However, restrictions could be imposed on the seller because only his pecuniary self-interest and not his liberty was at stake.[14] Whereas the Americans settled on the "one man, one vote concept," the prohibition issue in England represented one phase of the struggle over how to define voting rights. As Mill opted for proportional representation, opposing pressure groups like the prohibitionists could be limited.[15]

As women became more active in social reform, they began to organize groups to support causes like temperance that were often more popular than woman suffrage. These associations frequently expanded from local to national to international. One of them, the Women's Christian Temperance Union, gingerly orchestrated the development of a mass movement, first against alcohol, and then for other social reforms. They also worked with missionaries to establish chapters around the world. With a gospel character but no single church affiliation, the WCTU welcomed women from many religions, although Protestant affiliations were most common. The Catholic acceptance of communion wine inhibited their participation.

Ultimately, Frances Willard (1839-1896) led the WCTU to become the largest women's organization in the world. To protect the home, she challenged women to leave it long enough to work for a great variety of causes. Under her "Do Everything" policy, women by the thousands formed local unions that affiliated with the national. Then autonomous national WCTUs worked together in a world organization that became the pattern for subsequent women's groups such as the International Council of Women.

Whereas the WCTU reached down and out to attract middle-class and working women into a variety of causes, the International Council of Women was the pinnacle of a hierarchy based on National Councils of Women that amalgamated local women's organizations. Willard was also instrumental in its formation in 1888, but Stanton and Anthony originated the idea. They intended the ICW to work primarily for suffrage, but the conservative membership espoused a number of other causes, so the International Woman Suffrage Alliance was formed in 1902. The IWSA initially was devoted exclusively to that one cause. As suffrage was won in some places, it subsequently followed Willard's WCTU and other women's organizations into a "do at least nearly everything" policy. Like Lucy Stone's AWSA, the IWSA was committed to getting the vote first because it would lead to other rights. Despite the division, the ICW and IWSA cooperated on many causes. Both were comprised of leaders of national suffrage organizations.

As women leaders cooperated from one organization to another, eventually all of them established committees that worked for peace. The women differed on whether they supported wars actually in progress. However, the conviction that peace was essential to women's rights led to the foundation of the Women's International League for Peace and Freedom. All of these organizations lobbied for women's equality in the League of Nations and then the United Nations. They were given official consultantship status as nongovernmental organizations that still continue to lobby for women's rights around the world.

4

FRANCES WILLARD
AND THE WOMEN'S CHRISTIAN TEMPERANCE UNION

Many causes the Women's Christian Temperance Union (WCTU) espoused over the past century are still as important as ever, notably alcohol abuse and women's equality. They also continue to oppose prostitution. That and the sexual double standard were often lumped under the rubric of social purity in the nineteenth century. Once the double standard and the impact of venereal disease were openly discussed, Josephine Butler inspired other women to speak out instead of suffering in silence. Today in Asia, the World WCTU actively opposes sex tourism. However, in the United States this oldest and largest women's organization seems archaic as its aging members still perceive God squarely in a Middle-Western Protestant context reminiscent of earlier times. Women's roles as wives and mothers are still seen as primary. To defend the home, members favor total abstinence from alcohol, preferably reinforced by prohibition legislation. Recently, more secular organizations with an updated image such as Mothers Against Drunk Drivers (MADD) and Alcoholics Anonymous (AA) have attained wider publicity. Nonetheless, the WCTU continues to function through both national and international organizations that link predominantly conservative Christian women throughout the world. They raise consciousness and support campaigns for the rights of women and children, not just against abuses of alcohol. Over the past century, the WCTU has contributed significantly to the evolution of women's awareness of their needs and rights, including suffrage.

Many temperance efforts were well underway before the Women's Christian Temperance Union began with a "Woman's Crusade" in Western New York State in 1873-74. Bands of praying, singing women entered saloons to try to force their closure through public pressure.[1] Soon Middle-Western women took up the cause. In Hillsboro, Ohio, on December 23, 1873, seventy women responded to the plea of Dio Lewis, a visiting lecturer from Boston, that they be willing to "go out from their homes and pray in the places where their husbands, sons, and brothers were tempted to their ruin."[2] Lewis had been influenced forty-three years earlier in Auburn, New York, by a crusading band of women led by Delecta Barbour Lewis. When Dio Lewis became a public lecturer, he

Frances Willard, founder and leader of the Women's Christian Temperance Union, World WCTU, and ICW. Reprinted with permission from the World Women's Christian Temperance Union.

remembered his father's drinking and recalled his mother as both the family provider and a victim of abuse and violence.[3]

In Ohio, Elizabeth Thompson was chosen to lead the crusade against alcohol. In 1836 (when she was twenty) she had gone with her father to the National Temperance Convention in Saratoga, New York.

She claimed to have been the first woman who ever entered a National Temperance Convention.[4] Thompson did not attend Lewis's lecture in Hillsboro, but her sixteen-year-old son told her how Lewis had called on the women of the town to unite against the liquor sellers. Thompson was appointed to a committee scheduled to meet at the Presbyterian Church the next morning. Her son encouraged her to go, and her husband overcame his objections as she turned to prayer to guide her decision. After Thompson was unanimously chosen as president, the minister asked the men to leave, and she took over leadership of the meeting.[5] After that, the women went to drug stores, hotels, and saloons where they held prayer meetings and asked the liquor dealers to sign a pledge against alcohol. Caught off guard, many of them initially signed.

The WCTU adopted its name at a convention held in Cleveland, Ohio, from November 18 through 20, 1874. The first national president, Annie Wittenmyer, stressed moral suasion, religious conservatism, and cautious, paternalistic reforms.[6] Frances Willard was elected corresponding secretary, and she wrote the initial statement of principles.[7] In 1876 and 1877 she worked in Boston with the evangelist, Dwight L. Moody. At that time, Willard hoped temperance and gospel work might be united.[8] Indeed, the WCTU had a strong gospel quality even before she was elected the second president at the sixth convention at Evanston, Illinois, in 1879. Willard became president at age thirty-seven and served in this capacity until her death in 1898, nearly two decades later. Through her far-reaching vision, the WCTU evolved into a world organization. Her "Do Everything" policy gave members an opportunity to work for all sorts of causes besides alcohol reform. Under her guidance the aims were broadened very early to include labor reform, social purity, and women's suffrage as well as peace. Willard saw the WCTU as a vehicle to give women political clout to achieve equal rights and a higher quality of human life.

Ross Paulson contends that "It was the historical role of the WCTU in the 1870s and 1880s to create a 'respectable' alternative for middle-class women to the existing women's rights and suffrage organizations that had been 'tainted' by their attacks on marriage and the hint of free love. The WCTU's social purity campaign stayed within the limits of Victorian rhetoric and stressed the theme that a woman's inherent purity was the warrant for her concern about public morality."[9]

Frances Willard is now remembered primarily for her opposition to the use of alcohol, but she was a staunch advocate of women's rights before the WCTU was formed. Her associations with other professional women's organizations trained her for leadership. She joined Sorosis, a professional women's club founded in 1868, and supported their call for a women's congress.[10] Mary Livermore, a fellow temperance worker, was elected president, and Willard was chosen as vice president.[11] Twenty years later, through the leadership of Jennie June Croly, Sorosis was also the genesis of the General Federation of Women's Clubs.[12] When the Association for the Advancement of Women was founded in 1873, Willard joined that, too. The AAW was the progenitor of the International Council of Women and "was the first National body of women devoted to general culture and an inclusive social service."[13] Mary Livermore was president only one year. Then Willard followed her into the American Woman Suffrage Association. After Livermore, Maria Mitchell was elected president of AAW.[14] In 1876 at the meeting in Philadelphia, peace advocate Julia Ward Howe became president. As she held that office for nineteen years, Howe guided the members on a conservative course of home preservation.[15]

Willard was active in the Women's Congresses of 1874 and 1875, but after that she was primarily occupied with the WCTU. Willard knew her conservative Middle-Western audience and proceeded very carefully. She wove in the theme of the coming position of "womaninity" when she first started lecturing in missionary and church groups around Chicago in 1870.[16] She publicly declared her support for the women's movement in a lecture at the Centenary Methodist Church in Chicago on March 21, 1871. As Willard had recently traveled in Europe, she illustrated women's need for greater political power because of their degraded position in Germany, Italy, and Turkey (especially in Damascus where she had observed a young girl who awaited sale in a slave market).[17] Even so, as president of the new Evanston College for Ladies, Willard proceeded cautiously when a local woman suffrage organization was formed. It generated so much opposition that Willard's mother said, "you cannot afford to have your name associated with any such thing as the suffrage movement." So her mother went instead.

But Willard continued to support woman suffrage. When they were in Boston, she and her secretary, Anna Gordon, frequently visited the office of *The Woman's Journal* to converse with Lucy Stone, Henry Blackwell, and their "white ribbon daughter," Alice Stone Blackwell. The white ribbon was and still is the symbol of the WCTU. Opposition to alcohol abuse was the chief drawing card of the WCTU, and the leaders tried not to antagonize conservative women who opposed suffrage. At the national convention in 1875, the following carefully worded resolution was passed: "Since women are among the greatest sufferers from the liquor traffic, and realizing that it is ultimately to be suppressed by means of the ballot, we, the Christian women of this land in convention assembled, do pray Almighty God, and good and true men, that the question of the prohibition of the liquor traffic should be submitted to all adult citizens irrespective of race, color or sex."[18] This proposal does not suggest women's right to the ballot except to control alcohol. Even so, at the 1876 convention in

Newark, New Jersey, some members were bitter that Willard had gone too far.

But she soon went even farther. Although she was not allowed to appeal for woman suffrage at the first International Temperance Convention of Women held in Philadelphia in June 1876, or at the Chautauqua Temperance Conference in July, at Old Orchard Beach, Maine, in August 1876, Willard proclaimed her woman's rights doctrine in a national forum. Then she also saw a way to integrate the temperance and suffrage campaigns when a pioneer Canadian temperance worker, Letitia Yeomans, used the term, "Home Protection." That became Willard's battle-cry.[19]

The first WCTU leader, Elizabeth Thompson, later said she accepted "our woman's suffrage resolution away back in 1877 . . ." although other accounts indicate that the WCTU was not won over to support suffrage until after Willard became president in 1879.[20] The organization had a substantial structure by then. A monthly publication *The Woman's Temperance Union* had been initiated in 1875. The name was changed to *The Union Signal* in 1883 during the transformation into a world organization.[21]

Because Willard was reluctant to antagonize conservative members, she remained cautious in public statements on woman suffrage. In 1877 the Chicago WCTU Convention passed this conservative resolution with a majority vote: "As the responsibility of the training of the children and youth rests largely upon woman, she ought to be allowed to open or close the rum-shop door over against her home." Then Willard requested that legislators in the District of Columbia and the territories permit the sale of intoxicating liquors "only when the majority of the men by their votes and the women by their signatures, should ask that such sale might be legalized."[22] This wording avoids a call for woman suffrage altogether. Also in 1878 at the WCTU convention in Baltimore, Willard called for a Home Protection Petition, the ladies' traditional weapon. Later, Maria Mitchell invited Willard to speak at a National Woman's Congress where Hannah Whitall Smith of Philadelphia also stepped carefully around the suffrage issue as she spoke of "a weapon in the warfare of women against the liquor traffic."[23]

In 1881 a committee on franchise was finally appointed in the WCTU. It consisted of Frances Willard, Mary Livermore, and J. Ellen Foster. In 1882 the Department of Franchise was formally adopted with Mary Clement Leavitt as national superintendent. Zerelda Wallace succeeded Leavitt in 1883, and she was followed by the Reverend Anna Howard Shaw.[24] They worked to convert the broad base of women members from all classes of society. "Working in its own way, but in cooperation with other women's organizations, the WCTU brought conviction on this controversial subject to many conservative home, church and

missionary women who had turned their backs, as well as their consciences, on the seemingly 'bold advocates' of 'woman's rights.' "[25]

Sometimes high-handed treatment by men won them converts.
When the Indiana WCTU appealed to the state legislature for a law that
would protect the young from the ravages of the liquor traffic, a petition
was presented signed by 20,000 influential women. In response, the
youngest member of the House said, "but gentlemen, the signatures of
20,000 women in this state mean no more to us than the signatures of
20,000 mice."[26] To buttress their case, the WCTU observed that women
had a more direct voice in public affairs in Western states where they
had the vote. And conservative women were influenced positively when
prominent men and women came out for suffrage. They were encouraged, for example, when in 1880, at the invitation of the Brooklyn
WCTU, the Reverend Henry Ward Beecher made his first speech in
favor of woman suffrage. In 1883 the Reverend Joseph Cook of Boston
also declared his support.[27]

The WCTU network of influence also expanded in other ways.
From an early stage, Willard eagerly formed alliances with other groups
that might help the causes of temperance or women's rights. One natural
alliance emerged between the WCTU and the newly organized National
Prohibition Party. They subsequently endorsed woman suffrage.[28]
Willard's commitment to the WCTU's home protection policy was evident in 1880-81 when she persuaded the National Prohibition Party to
change its name to the Prohibition Home Protection Party. Ross Paulson
contends that "the political alliance between the WCTU and the National
Prohibition Party did not bring spectacular results for either cause. Yet
thousands of women had gained experience in organizational discipline
and practical politics. Women's suffrage had been restored to the pan-
theon of 'respectable' causes that middle class men and women could
support."[29] On the other hand, the early association with temperance
impeded suffragists because the brewers organized against them. Nonetheless, Willard maintained a positive, well-mannered respectability
that helped contradict the negative image of extremists like Elizabeth
Cady Stanton and Susan B. Anthony.

Not all of Willard's affiliations were so conservative, however. She
also extended the influence of the WCTU by forming liaisons with other
groups such as Terence Powderly's Knights of Labor.[30] They helped
Willard work for state and municipal suffrage, convinced that it was necessary to aid women workers. Jane Addams also subsequently championed labor in Springfield and Chicago, Illinois.

Willard adeptly maintained church and press support as she promoted women's political power to enforce temperance for home protection. Encouraged to broaden their horizons, homemakers rallied to the
slogan, "For God and Home and Native Land" when they joined the

local, state, and national WCTU. A national legislative department was established in 1874, and the first national prohibition law was introduced in the United States in 1876.[31] A social purity committee formed in 1875 was dedicated to opposing prostitution, government-regulated vice, and the double sexual standard of men and women. Labor and suffrage committees were in place by 1881 and peace and arbitration committees by 1887.[32] A Department of Medical Temperance was introduced in 1897. They campaigned against fraudulent patent medicines, especially the ones that contained large amounts of alcohol.[33] Eventually, women could choose among activities in up to thity-nine departments besides temperance, all socially acceptable under Willard's "Do Everything Policy."[34]

Even very conservative Southern women joined their Northern sisters. In 1883 they officially became part of the women's prohibition movement, and in 1887 the National WCTU met in Nashville, Tennessee, south of the Mason and Dixon Line for the first time.[35] Southern women were reluctant to work for suffrage, and no southern states gave them the franchise until the federal amendment was ratified in 1920. However, the conservative women were much more willing to work for temperance, and sometimes southern states more readily passed prohibition laws. Through the WCTU, then, southern women also attained experience in organizing and in lobbying state legislatures. Furthermore, in 1883, the year southern women joined, the Women's Christian Temperance Union expanded into a global mission.

5

MARY CLEMENT LEAVITT AND THE WORLD WCTU

When the WCTU was organized in Cleveland, Ohio, on November 18, 1874, representatives of seventeen American states attended.[1] Soon after, women in Canada and Great Britain began to organize local unions and prepare for a national union.[2] Margaret Parker of Dundee, Scotland, founded the British Women's Temperance Association at Newcastle-on-Tyne. She was influenced by "Mother" Stewart (Mrs. E. D.), also of Ohio, and other American crusaders.[3] Members recognized the need for greater international cooperation as church missionaries and even some heads of state asked the WCTU for aid in organizing a temperance movement. In 1876 at the International Temperance Congress in Philadelphia, Pennsylvania, women met to initiate an International Woman's Temperance Union, and Margaret Parker was chosen president. Her ill health and a lack of funds for proper promotion caused this initial plan to be abandoned.[4] Frances Willard subsequently developed the World WCTU out of the already established American organization. Her global mission emerged after she saw the opium dens and brothels in San Francisco's Chinatown in 1883.

But for the intervention of the sea, the shores of China and the Far East would be part and parcel of our fair land. We are one world of tempted humanity; the mission of the white ribbon women is to organize the motherhood of the world for the peace and purity, the protection and exaltation of its homes. We must sound forth a clear call to our sisters across the seas, and to our brothers none the less. We must be no longer hedged about by the artificial boundaries of state and nation.[5]

After she was moved by this compelling vision, at the national convention in Detroit, Michigan, that same year, Willard proposed a World WCTU. The members endorsed a six-point plan that outlined the organization's methods. A tentative program included an hour of prayer at noon around the globe. All of the national leaders of WCTUs would be vice presidents of the new organization. This format was later adopted by other major women's organizations such as the International Council of Women.

Willard also initiated the WCTU Polyglot Peace Petition on behalf of what she called the physically weaker sex. Women would petition

Mary Clement Leavitt, first world missionary of the World WCTU. Reprinted with permission from the World Women's Christian Temperance Union.

world leaders to eliminate indulgence in alcohol, opium, and other vices. The petition was translated into many languages and circulated world-wide over the next twenty years. It ultimately collected millions of signatures, seven and a half million according to WCTU historian, Elizabeth Putnam Gordon.[6] Willard's biographer, Mary Earhart, gave a larger figure—between fifteen and twenty million.[7]

Preliminary recruiting began after the idea of the world organization was introduced in Detroit. Much of the credit belongs to one woman, Mary Clement Leavitt. Past middle age and granite faced, she had what biographers described as an unfortunate family resemblance to George Washington.[8] In 1884, somewhat hesitantly, she set out on what became a virtual odyssey. Her journey of 150,000 miles over eight years, sometimes under extremely arduous conditions, fulfilled Frances Willard's charge to cinch the white ribbon of purity around the world. The time was right as the World WCTU soon became the largest women's organization in the nineteenth century.[9]

As a teacher in Boston, Massachusetts, Leavitt had become interested in temperance through the "Woman's Crusade" of 1873-74.[10] Leavitt met Frances Willard while she was visiting evangelist Dwight L. Moody in 1877. Then Leavitt organized the Boston chapter of the WCTU and was its president in 1879-80.[11] After she gave up her private school and went to work full time for the WCTU in 1881, Leavitt traveled around New England on behalf of temperance and woman suffrage.[12] She became the first superintendent of the Franchise Department of the National WCTU and also represented the New England Woman Suffrage Association.[13]

Leavitt's recruiting trip began unofficially in July 1883, when she left Boston to honor Frances Willard's request to undertake organizational work in California, Washington, and Oregon. After Leavitt decided local women could accomplish more, Willard suggested that she travel abroad as a temperance missionary. Not surprisingly, Leavitt accepted this awesome assignment somewhat reluctantly. Doubts about the possible success of Leavitt's venture were also evident in the way its announcement was phrased in *The Union Signal*. She was initially designated as "Superintendent of Reconnaissance for World's W.C.T.U," assigned to go to the Sandwich Islands (Hawaii), Australia, and perhaps India, China, and Japan.[14] She would be "visiting missionaries of those countries and endeavoring to introduce the W.C.T.U. methods and to provide for a helpful interchange of sympathy and work by which the gospel temperance movement shall eventually belt the world."[15]

With little money and no assurance of future financial support, in November 1884, Leavitt departed for Hawaii. Willard's sendoff in *The Union Signal* said Leavitt "has no capital save her faith. . . . She receives not a penny from our treasury and went to the Sandwich Islands with $35.00 in her pocket." Therefore, Willard appealed to readers for money and "let me affectionately urge you to pray definitely for Mrs. Mary Clement Leavitt and her embassy, the most distant echo of the great Ohio crusade, the farthest outreaching of the gospel temperance wave."[16] Leavitt soon demonstrated that she merited the members' faith.

She sent extended accounts to *The Union Signal* of the places she visited, local people and customs, and her organizational efforts. These letters from the WCTU's first Round-the-World Missionary, as she was soon designated, were usually published about two months after they were mailed. Often they were split and published in two segments, one per week. Her descriptions of places, people, and events often comprised one of the longest pieces in the WCTU newspaper. Occasionally, some letters were lost or arrived out of sequence. Then Leavitt tried to summarize them, but much detail was often lost and the tone differed. In hindsight, she was able to inject a slightly more humorous tone and restrain the bitterness and sense of being slighted that often permeated her correspondence.

In Hawaii, Leavitt encountered what was to be the pattern for much of the remainder of her world venture. Missionaries often competed instead of helping each other while government officials were courteous and sometimes helpful, but turned a blind eye to traders who brought in liquor and encouraged the degradation of women. In a frequently repeated theme, Leavitt blamed the colonial powers for forcing alcohol on the natives to enhance their own power and profit. She reported that the natives had prohibition before the French forced a treaty that allowed the importation of wines and brandies. "Now native men may buy, but not native women."[17] Leavitt was not always charitable toward the natives either. She concluded that they were simple people who were victimized by their colonizers and needed to be protected.

Leavitt rushed to end her mission in Hawaii because a well-known English evangelist was arriving from Australia, and she knew her audience would soon be diverted. The newly formed Hawaiian WCTU paid her way to New Zealand. After she left, the new organization flourished. Their first annual report pays tribute to Leavitt. The first meeting of about forty ladies is recalled and their subsequent labors recounted, particularly among the indigenous people.[18]

Meanwhile, Leavitt sailed off to a much less cordial reception. As she always trusted to the Lord to provide, her salvation in New Zealand came in the form of another well-known British missionary, R. T. Booth. Leavitt had met his wife in Boston four years earlier.[19] Booth introduced Leavitt and let her speak during his mission. Then local pastors invited her to large and small communities.[20] Even so, after she had visited Auckland and Wellington, Leavitt noted that "neither of these places have [sic] given me the welcome I had reason to expect from the letters received."[21] She attributed the problem to "The bondage to medical drinking, to the sacramental use of fermented wine, to occasional social drinking which is far stronger and more universal than in any part of the United States that I have yet visited." Tourists also undercut the missionaries' efforts and encouraged drinking when they offered the indigenous people money to dance.[22]

Despite local resistance, Leavitt had formed ten WCTU chapters after six months in New Zealand, and about 2,000 people signed the pledge not to drink alcohol. She had traveled 2,000 miles, attended 126 meetings, and had spoken at over 100.[23] She promoted both social purity and temperance. After Leavitt left Wellington, Mrs. Dudley Ward founded a WCTU and work began immediately to try to rehabilitate prostitutes.[24] The next year, the New Zealand WCTU held their first national convention at Wellington and resolved not only to oppose the Contagious Diseases Acts vigorously, but also to ask the Premier to support a bill in the House of Representatives to confer federal suffrage on women.[25] They were allowed to vote in local liquor licensing board elections in 1883.

As the movement for women's suffrage expanded, the Liberal Party was formed in 1887, and new legislation enabled women to vote in school board elections. But they were still denied the national franchise.[26] Most municipalities extended the vote to women by 1890. Jessie Ackerman, a WCTU missionary who followed Leavitt, mistakenly sent word back to *The Union Signal* that national woman suffrage passed in 1891.[27] Based on this premature report, when the World's Congress of Representative Women convened in Chicago, Illinois, in May of 1893, New Zealand (like Wyoming) was a rallying spark for the cause. On September 19, 1893, New Zealand did become the first nation in the modern world to extend the federal vote to women.[28] In the wake of the strong prohibition movement led by the New Zealand Alliance and the WCTU, woman suffrage passed the Upper House by two votes. Ross Evans Paulson contends that the Conservatives supported women's suffrage to embarrass the Liberals by strengthening the power of the prohibitionists, but some men voted out of conviction based on arguments derived from John Stuart Mill.[29]

Leavitt had finished her trip around the world by then. After she left New Zealand, her next port of call, Australia, also received her reluctantly despite some favorable recommendations. A newspaper in Dunedin, New Zealand, praised her speaking style and said she should be welcomed in Victoria as well as Sydney.[30] Although a WCTU had been formed there three years earlier, even they and the local YWCA were not especially enthusiastic to sponsor Leavitt. However, as her press improved, her invitations increased. Leavitt wrote back to *The Union Signal* that she spoke on social purity and was often asked to address "the woman question" as well as temperance.[31]

Leavitt was always conscious of the widely varying restrictions on local women. In Australia as in England, men could sue for divorce based on adultery alone, but women had to have an additional charge such as "want of support" or "gross cruelty."[32]

Leavitt was very sensitive to women's limited opportunities, both her own and those where she traveled. En route to Tasmania, she defended herself as a female. "If I am doing what many here consider unwomanly, in speaking in public, and on governmental themes, etc. they surely should also bear testimony that I have done all that was considered womanly, for I have crocheted on every sea and knitted on every land."[33]

After Leavitt traveled through New South Wales, Queensland, and Tasmania, WCTUs proliferated. As of 1891, they united in a national organization that also actively promoted woman suffrage.[34] Catherine T. Wallace, another American, reported that "A stranger might almost have supposed that the Australian WCTU was a meeting for the advancement of woman suffrage."[35] A Women's Suffrage League was organized in 1888, and women were accorded municipal suffrage in all of the Australian colonies except Queensland by 1890.[36] Their efforts were reinforced by support from English suffragists, and the women of South Australia got the franchise in 1894.[37] As other colonies followed, more women leaders emerged. One of these, Vida Goldstein, organized the Women's Political Association to support her candidacy for the Australian federal senate.[38] On a trip to London in 1914, she persuaded Adela Pankhurst to come to Australia. By then, the militant British branch of the women's movement had halted their activities in order to support the war effort.

While no one would credit Leavitt individually or even the WCTU alone with the implementation of woman suffrage in New Zealand and Australia, she made a marked contribution. Even so, Leavitt had some trepidation as she embarked for the Orient, and she requested support from home. As the success of the new chapters was regularly reported back in Evanston, Willard established a Leavitt Fund. Later, most of this money became a world fund to support other missionaries because Leavitt continued to collect enough donations to maintain her own efforts. Fortified with contacts and recommendations, she arrived in Yokohama, Japan, on June 1, 1886, and continued on to Tokyo with a Mrs. Seidmore who had been in the Washington, D.C. WCTU. Leavitt's confidence increased as she observed that many Japanese wanted their children to learn foreign ways, and substantial numbers were willing to accept Christianity and the WCTU.[39]

In Tokyo Leavitt founded a union of missionaries to work on "education, on scientific and Biblical lines, tobacco and chastity at least." In Kyoto the missionary women did not hold office or vote, so responsibility rested on the native women. This subsequently became the pattern in Tokyo where leaders of the WCTU also were active in the women's suffrage movement. A Japanese government official told Leavitt, perhaps ambiguously, "your mission here is doing for Japanese women what Commodore Perry did for the country." As Frances Willard paraphrased this in a presidential address at a WCTU convention, she concluded that "when our pictures are in Japanese papers and the W.C.T.U. of Tokyo send us their photographs, we know that the World's W.C.T.U. is getting on."[40] The Japanese subsequently developed foreign as well as home missions; and they sent representatives to China, India, and Turkey.[41] Today, they continue to honor Leavitt as the founder of their WCTU.[42] Sometimes Leavitt was praised effusively as new WCTUs sent accounts of their progress back to *The Union Signal*. Lizzie Nelson Fryer wrote from Shanghai that it was new for a woman to occupy a pulpit there, and she gave thanks for "dear Mrs. Leavitt."[43]

As she traveled, Leavitt spoke to any group that would gather to listen, and she tailored her speeches to fit the audience. She liked to spend Saturday afternoons with children, among whom Leavitt organized Bands of Hope and tried to extract pledges of lifelong abstinence. She also worked vigorously for social purity and formed White Cross Societies among men. They took the pledge of chastity and fidelity in this organization originally founded by the British. Leavitt opposed tobacco, opium, alcohol, and sex outside marriage. She often spoke to soldiers and especially sailors if the captains of ships were temperance-oriented or at least willing to let her provide a diversion for the men. Sometimes she spoke to the same crews more than once, as they all went from one port to another. Her letters home reported presentations that varied to reflect her opposition to local customs such as concubines in Japan, foot binding in China, child brides in India, polygamy in Moslem countries, and slavery in Africa.

A few examples demonstrate her diverse activities. In an account sent to *The Union Signal,* she wrote that a Miss Bradley was on hand to meet her in Bangkok, Thailand, although Leavitt had not received an invitation to go there.[44] Usually missionaries took her into their homes (as in this case) but not always. Nor was Leavitt timid about approaching national leaders, including royalty. In a personal interview she urged the king of Thailand to support temperance and the White Cross.[45] King Chulalangkorn had contributed money for an old women's home. Perhaps because of this, Leavitt did not think the fact that he kept a harem reflected such debased character as she saw in Europeans.[46] In Thailand, as in many other places, she blamed the British for forcing opium on the natives. Leavitt also often followed her missions with recommendations to assist the new WCTU chapters. After she left Bankok, the new organization wrote to the American WCTU and asked for literature she had suggested. *The Union Signal* headlined the letter, "The Ends of the Earth."[47]

In Singapore, she got on well because "The press gave more space than was expected and said no offensive things." She addressed men on a ship, formed a small WCTU, and visited the Sultan of Johore. He pleased her as he told how the natives amused themselves at parties by watching the foreigners get drunk.[48] In Rangoon, Myanmar, her letter home chided the British again for "letting drink loose upon these simple people." She observed that every place she went "is a fresh illustration of the worldwide influence of England. . . ."[49] Coeducation was said to be impossible among the Burmese; but one local ethnic group, the Karens, managed it successfully.

Some missionaries strayed occasionally, too. A Miss Haswell in Amherst, Myanmar, had rescued an illegitimate English baby, the child of two missionaries, who had been "tossed to a Burmese brothel keeper." Leavitt did not moralize on this. Instead, she concluded that "In all Asiatic countries that I have visited the looseness and insecurity of marriage makes [sic] a woman's lot wretched in the extreme." She opposed child marriages in China and matches made by parents in Japan. Women in Thailand and Myanmar could choose their spouses, but "no woman is secure in her position unless her husband is a Christian." Leavitt said girls preferred unwed life with Christians to marriage with other men because they received better care.[50]

By the time she got to India, Leavitt was showing signs of burnout. She reported that a mission in one town was much like that in another. She usually spoke to several groups: (1) Europeans, English officials, American missionaries; (2) native Christians, mostly of humbler classes; (3) nonChristian native gentlemen, some who had been of high rank; and (4) soldiers. After relaxing with hospitable missionaries in a mountain resort over the hot summer, Leavitt announced in September 1887 (when she had already been traveling three years), her plans to go to Africa, the Cape, Madagascar, Western Asia, Asia Minor, and North Africa if her health would permit.[51] And she did.

Although she was often asked to speak on "the woman question," suffrage was seldom her main topic. Even so, Leavitt was sure that if women had the right to vote, they would advance the cause of temperance. Education and legislation could raise morals by limiting alcohol consumption. In contrast, Leavitt supported Josephine Butler's contention that social purity could not be legislated. She spoke out against the Contagious Diseases Acts that were still enforced around military establishments. Primarily, though, she called on her congregations to follow their individual consciences to pledge abstinence and a single standard of chastity for men and women.

As a former schoolteacher, Leavitt believed strongly in education to effect change. She wanted what she called "scientific" temperance instruction introduced in school curricula, and many missionaries welcomed her as a guest speaker. Although they were able to educate the natives, the missionaries often lost the battle to convert them to Christianity and abstinence. Leavitt reinforced the missionaries' values and shared their imperialism toward the natives. On her way to Smyrna by steamer, Muslim women displaced her in First Class. With some sarcasm she noted that "Fortunately, one of these Moslem widowed concubines considered that she would be polluted by sleeping in the first class saloon with Christian ladies. A place was found for her in some other corner, thus making room in first class for me."[52]

In other instances, Leavitt was not treated with the respect she thought she deserved. Between Alexandria and Cairo, Egypt, she reported "a few hours by train during which I experienced more of the disrespect felt here for the unveiled, unprotected women than I ever did in my ten months in Hindustan. . . ."[53] At Durban, South Africa, women appeared on the street, which Leavitt reported had been somewhat unusual in Asia. Polygamy was also common in parts of Africa, as it was in Egypt where she said Muslims had four wives and as many concubines among the slaves as they could support.[54] Despite Leavitt's efforts to introduce change, the native women often were not ready to step beyond their restricted roles. In Israel,after Leavitt spoke to a few Muslim women, she declared that "I have never found it so difficult to get the attention of women, not even the half-naked ones of Zululand and the Congo."[55]

Frequently, Leavitt was denied cooperation because of her gender. Wesleyans refused her permission to speak in church in Jaffna, Sri Lanka. At Harrismith, South Africa, both the Wesleyans and Presbyterians refused to let her preach in church, but they opened the Sunday schools to her. Leavitt's frustration was more apparent in Sierra Leone as she noted opposition by clergy: "But hush! It is wrong, all wrong! She is a woman and must not speak in churches. So did not Paul say of such as she but only of babblers, chatterers."[56]

Leavitt received a warmer welcome in Scandinavia. "In 1886 the WCTU was introduced to Sweden at a meeting of the *Fredrika Bremer-fürbundet* (Fredrika Bremer Society) by Mary [Clement] Leavitt and Natalie Anderson-Meijerhelm." Leavitt claimed that scientific temperance education was made compulsory in the schools throughout Scandinavia after her visit. That same year, the American Blue Ribbon Society and White Ribbon Society also established local circles. The White Ribbon Society, which was supported by the WCTU, spread to Denmark in 1888 and to Norway in 1892 as a result of visits by Charlotte Grey and correspondence between Birgitte Estmark (veteran of the social purity campaign) and Frances Willard.[57]

In Florence, Italy, at meetings of the Evangelical Alliance, Leavitt could not get permission to speak, so she had to content herself with leaving WCTU literature. When she finally did persuade the Evangelicals to let her give a temperance talk, she asserted that it was the first by a lady in Florence. Methodist Episcopal churchmen resisted her efforts, but she praised them because they did not let men in polygamous countries come into the church with a harem of wives. She observed that the Italians were most reluctant to give up their wine. After Leavitt spoke at Miss Hall's School for Girls in Rome, she reported that "I never met young girls so obstinately prejudiced in favor of wine. Many of them seemed to miss the wine more than they do their mothers."[58]

Throughout her travels, Leavitt demonstrated great courage, determination, and initiative, although she always insisted that she only followed God's will. She also exhibited major growth in her outlook during her long and arduous travels. Leavitt's journey was a remarkable accomplishment in an era before airplanes and automobiles when, besides ships, trains, and horse drawn carriages, much of her travel was in various conveyances propelled by human beings. The notion of having others transport her made Leavitt uncomfortable when she first encountered the jinrikisha in Japan, but she adapted.[59]

In her early days in India, she traveled by rail, horse, an oxcart pushed through a stream by an elephant, by horse drawn gari, and via a "dandy" carried by human beings. To get to Amdagasgar, the capital of Madagascar, she required fifteen men to carry her and her belongings. They included a camp bed, chair, and table. Her party went part of the way in a canoe paddled by singing slaves.[60] From Antananarivo to Tamatave, Madagascar, she was carried by men for eight days, a journey she said was "not to be coveted, certainly if it is to be passed in solitude."[61] In Japan, half way around the world, Leavitt informed the readers back home that "the globe is bigger when you *go* than when you look at it on the map."[62]

Leavitt made an impact on those she addressed and left some organizations that continue today. She also influenced the readers of *The Union Signal* back home. American women from Palm Beach to Peoria to Portland became more internationally oriented as they shared Mary Clement Leavitt's travels through her letters. She finally returned to Boston more than eight years after her departure, a well-seasoned world traveler whose adventures were not ended. She had one continent left.

Leavitt was welcomed as a hero at the first convention of the World Women's Christian Temperance Association in 1891. Frances Willard had negotiated the politics to form that organization in 1885. Margaret Bright Lucas, President of the British Women's League, was named president. She brought in Canada and England.[63] Mary Clement Leavitt was named Secretary and the first appointed missionary. A Canadian, Mary E. Sanderson, became Treasurer.[64] The women were experienced at national organization by then, and they quickly established a system of dues and made plans to recruit members. The motto of the national organization, "For God and Home and Native Land," was changed to "For God and Home and Every Land" to reflect the world organization's objectives.

After Margaret Bright Lucas died in 1890, Frances Willard called this first international convention in conjunction with the annual American WCTU meeting. Her election as president distressed the British. Although Lady Henry Somerset was elected First Vice President, they felt that the Americans had usurped the organization.[65] Perhaps to reinforce its American origins, Willard contended in her presidential address that the World WCTU had been conceived as early as 1876.[66]

Willard carried over her "Do Everything" policy from the national to the World WCTU, as she stressed "the blessed trinity of movements—prohibition, woman's liberation and labors' uplift." Everything was not in temperance reform, but temperance reform should be in everything, Willard declared. The primary objectives of the World WCTU were to "educate, legislate, organize and agitate for public sentiment in favor of purity, prohibition and peace."[67] Therefore, the Committee on Peace and Arbitration was initiated, and *The Pacific Banner,* the national peace publication, was widely distributed. Willard was well ahead of her time as she promoted this issue among women.

In 1891 the first World WCTU convention was a homecoming for Leavitt in her native city, Boston. Leavitt reported to the membership that she had organized eighty-six unions in twenty-six countries. She had also collected seven and a half million signatures on the Polyglot Petition. Often heads of state were the first to sign. Even those who kept their people enslaved could see the advantage of overcoming the vice of alcoholism. These signatures carried influence with school administrators and legislative bodies who then often passed measures that required the inclusion of temperance instruction in school curricula.[68]

The Great Petition was mounted on white muslin and draped the hall. It had initially been presented at the International Temperance Congress in Antwerp, Belgium, in 1885 and again that same year at the National WCTU convention in Washington, D.C.[69] The petition was also presented at the 1895 convention in London and the 1897 World WCTU meeting in Toronto, Canada.[70] It was likewise displayed in the WCTU exhibit at the Panama-Pacific International Exposition in San Francisco in 1915 and at the Methodist Centenary Celebration at Columbus, Ohio, in 1919. Parts of the petition signed by representatives of various states and nations were also presented to the American president, Grover Cleveland, to Queen Victoria of England, and other heads of state.[71] It was finally housed in Rest Cottage, Frances Willard's home in Evanston, Illinois, where it remains on display.

In 1891 Leavitt was named World WCTU honorary president for life.[72] When Frances Willard recognized Leavitt's contribution, Willard recalled the origins of the World WCTU during her presidential address at the convention in Detroit, Michigan, in 1883. After that "Mrs. Mary Clement Leavitt started on her wonderful journey, resolved to fasten the white ribbon, emblem of purity and peace, above the heart of the world's womanhood." Nearly forty countries had formed world WCTU chapters since Leavitt had begun her travels in 1884. Willard also gave due credit to missionaries as "our steadfast allies."[73] They "opened the way for Mrs.

Leavitt in every nation she has visited and have been her staunchest friends and supporters."[74]

Indeed, Leavitt would not have gotten far if various Protestant church missionaries had not supported and recommended her from one to another. They had already established a bond of language as well as social conditioning. While many were British, Leavitt claimed she received more support from Americans. For example, in Evanston, Illinois (headquarters of the WCTU), The Northwestern Branch of the Woman's Foreign Missionary Society of the Methodist Episcopal Church had commended Leavitt to the hospitality of their missionaries in Japan, Korea, China, India, Bulgaria, South America, and Mexico.[75]

At the Boston meeting, Willard also praised Leavitt's frugality. "In eight years of constant journeying this devoted woman expended but eight thousand dollars, of which all but $1,600 was contributed by those for whom she labored. For though in response to our appeal the local unions raised $3000, Mrs. Leavitt drew on our treasurer for but about one half that sum, and has practiced an economy as unusual as her missionary exploits are unexampled."[76]

When a reporter from *The Boston Daily Globe* asked what was the most remarkable circumstance of her trip, Leavitt replied, "Nothing, I think, was more interesting and remarkable than my traveling alone and unprotected, as I did from San Francisco to Boston, among the coolie class of Japan, China, among the Zulus, the Malagasy of Madagascar, the natives of Sierra Leone, and the Hindus, where, without exception, I was treated as kindly as if I had been their mother, and as respectfully as if I had been their queen."[77] At that point she had not yet visited South America.

That was the only continent not represented at the 1891 world convention. Leavitt left shortly after to try to form WCTUs there, but this trip was not nearly as successful as her earlier venture, largely because the Catholic religion had such a firm hold on the people. Leavitt went to Argentina, Uruguay, and Brazil and managed to establish some unions. Without the strong Protestant missionary base she had had in other countries, however, recruitment was considerably more difficult. After Leavitt was actually stoned in Bahia, she primly noted that Protestants were not approved. Not afraid, she recalled later that as the stones and clods of dirt flew, "I knew the Lord was just there by my side." She thought the mob was mostly students incited by the Bishop. Despite such hostility, three ladies agreed to form a WCTU.

Even where Catholics did not incite violence against her, missionary work by a woman was very reluctantly received.[78] In Buenos Aires, Argentina, Dr. Drees' congregation was willing to hear a woman speak, provided it was not in the regular services.[79] In Caero, Brazil, she complained that she received her only assistance from "a young man who does not allow a woman to speak in the church although the church is only a hired hall, has not been consecrated, and is used for a day school all the week."[80]

But Leavitt was very experienced and did not give up easily as she assessed the customs in the context of her by then very cross-cultural perspective. In Argentina, the ideas of family life were described as being similar to those in the south of Europe. "A married man who should attempt to be faithful to his marriage vows would be the laughing stock of his companions." Women were often secluded, and those who went out or traveled alone were liable to experience unpleasant treatment and remarks. There, as in other parts of the world, however, women were becoming better educated. More of them could read, whereas in the past "Men thought that reading and writing only helped women carry on intrigues." But most of them were married too early to get a good education.[81]

Leavitt returned to the United States within six months, but she no longer attracted as much attention. Later, she had a falling out with Frances Willard and ended her association with the WCTU altogether. Even so, she had made a remarkable contribution not only to that organization but to the development of the international women's movement. At the end of her initial journey, a biography in *The Union Signal* reported that "She has traveled one hundred thousand miles in forty-three different countries; crossed the equator eight times, held over 1600 meetings; had the services of 290 different interpreters in forty-seven languages and formed 130 temperance societies, eighty-six of them WCTUs, and twenty-three branches of the White Cross."[82] They left out the Bands of Hope she had formed for children.

Leavitt was able to accomplish what she did because of the distinctive era at the end of the nineteenth century. By then Western missionaries had entrenched themselves around the world, but were still often isolated enough so that a freeloader from home was welcome. Unlike today, they also lacked any qualms about tampering with native cultures. The missionaries were convinced that they had a higher calling to convert the "simple" natives to Christianity, if possible, or at least to educate them in western ways. Leavitt shared these views, and the far-flung British empire provided a foothold, although she usually perceived of American missionaries as more congenial and more apt to share her abstinence values.

Although Leavitt's detractors charged that some WCTU chapters later floundered, many proliferated. Today they continue to work for peace and abstinence and against prostitution. At the end of her journey, despite the priorities of the WCTU, Leavitt did not cite temperance reform as her greatest accomplishment. Instead, she said: "The greatest value of my years of work lies in the impetus the labors of a woman have given to development among women in remote places."[83]

6

LATER DEVELOPMENTS IN THE WWCTU

From that first World WCTU convention in 1891 until the WWCTU was accorded consultantship status as a nongovermental organization at the United Nations, new chapters were added and the membership expanded. Their numbers enabled the organization to exert substantial political influence. Both the world organization and national chapters worked for social purity and other causes as well as temperance. They scored what they perceived as their greatest victory when national prohibition was enacted in the United States in 1918. This victory proved to be both temporary and illusive, although it helped pave the way for woman suffrage.

In other parts of the world Leavitt's efforts were so successful that more WWCTU missionaries soon followed. The first of these, Jessie Ackerman, went to Australia. Then Mary Ellen West was posted to Japan. She worked zealously with the Japanese until death cut her mission short. In thanks, the Japanese had a large temple bell cast, and it was displayed at the 1893 Chicago World's Columbian Exposition.[1] Increasingly, not only the missionaries but also the native women took up the WCTU cause. Dr. Pandita Ramabai lectured for the WCTU in India and established a college for High Caste Indian widows funded by White Ribboners.[2] While missionaries labored to form WCTU chapters among colonial and native groups throughout the British empire, the members bonded and gained visibility through international conventions. The second was held in Chicago in association with the World's Columbian Exposition in October 1893. Lady Henry Somerset stood in for Frances Willard who was ill in England.[3] Willard was back in charge in London in 1895 when more than a thousand delegates and visitors represented twenty-two countries. The meeting in Toronto in 1897 was Willard's last before she died in 1898.[4]

Lady Henry Somerset became president, and the members worked for voting rights and education, especially temperance instruction in the schools. Between 1881 and 1902, every state in the United States enacted some kind of legislation to require temperance instruction. The WCTU program received a technological boost in 1913 when Thomas A. Edison produced 102 temperance and moral films. He also invented a portable projector that could be carried from school to school. In Japan the women prevailed on the Emperor to appoint a National Director of

Scientific Temperance Instruction. Government grants supplied WCTU materials and promoted temperance education in Sweden, Norway, and South Africa.[5]

WCTU members Elizabeth Wheeler Andrews and Kate Bushnell worked together in South Africa and England.[6] In India they exposed the legalized vice system and the surreptitious opium trade in both India and China. While much of the international work was accomplished through the world organization, the American WCTU also had an international dimension. A National WCTU office was established in Washington, D.C., in 1895. Then national representative Margaret Dye Ellis lobbied to raise the age of consent from ten to sixteen years in the District of Columbia. "There were hearings before the house Judiciary Committee, and Mrs. Ellis, with fear and trembling, went to the Capitol to speak for the voiceless girls."[7] Nevertheless, Mrs. Ellis soon overcame her fears, and the WCTU began to flex some less ladylike political muscle, particularly with regard to women's rights in American-controlled territories.

In 1898 Ellis received a book that described a sixteen-year-old Filipino girl who had been certified to be free of venereal disease. She and others paid fifty cents for fortnightly examinations and two dollars for a cure. Ellis gave this information to Senator Gallinger of New Hampshire, and the WCTU began to publicize it. They applied political pressure in a massive campaign wherein members were called on to protest to President Roosevelt. They published a circular that said American women were splendidly protected by their country's flag and demanded the same for women in the new possessions, Hawaii and the Philippines.[8]

In the face of this onslaught, the chief of the Insular Division told Margaret Dye Ellis that he thought the WCTU was a million strong rather than the half million Ellis claimed. "These letters, if piled up, would reach above my head, and I am six-feet-two." Then he plaintively asked, "Mrs. Ellis, can't you call off your women?" She told him that it was not easy, and he assured her that President Roosevelt had already ordered registered prostitution to be suppressed in the Philippines. The WCTU subsequently worked to secure a new clause in the Chinese Exclusion Bill that would prevent girls who came to the United States from being sold as prostitutes. This had happened to ninety-two who came to the Omaha Exposition.[9] Nor did the WCTU neglect their abstinence roots as they lobbied against the illegal sale of liquor in American Samoa.[10]

Among groups in other nations, Muslims, Buddhists, and Christians in Sri Lanka cooperated to oppose the government when plans were announced to establish 1,300 toddy shops. Processions of floats and elephants were followed by marching children who chanted their disapproval and waved banners that said "Don't Drink Toddy" and "Don't Touch the Evil Thing." They went through the village streets interspersed with devil dancers who intended to keep the evil spirits away.[11]

The WCTU became stronger in the United States as support for prohibition increased. Five Southern states went dry between August 1907 and January 1909. Meanwhile, Finland, Ireland, and the Canadian Prince Edward Island enacted total prohibition. The United States had gained twelve dry states by 1913 when prohibition forces lobbied for a federal amendment. This paralleled the woman suffrage movement, which had been more slowly making gains on a state-by-state basis. But a win for one cause did not assure victory in the other. The prohibition forces won five states in 1914, five more in 1915, and four in 1916. Woman suffrage won only two states in 1914 and was defeated in five. In 1915, woman suffrage was defeated in four eastern states.[12] Abroad, although woman suffrage had been won earlier, prohibition failed in New Zealand and Australia in 1913. Iceland and Newfoundland passed prohibition in 1915, but defeated woman suffrage.

In the United States, women were more apt to receive the vote in municipal elections. Therefore, prohibitionists could restrict the liquor traffic by local option. Women who worked for both suffrage and temperance intensified the struggle for state and federal legislation. Under their "Do Everything" policy, the WCTU also often sent petitions to request a variety of new laws to limit child labor, abolish sweat shops, and establish juvenile and criminal probation courts as well as to abolish white slavery and the trade in opium.[13] In this way, home protection led to social reform, and the numbers of female participants continued to grow. Three thousand women from thirty-four countries attended the Ninth World WCTU Convention in Brooklyn, New York in 1913. Since their last meeting, membership had increased by 46,036. That brought the total to nearly half a million around the world.[14] In 1914 the World WCTU also supported a treaty signed by forty-five countries against the opium trade. Then World War I intervened, and they did not meet again until 1920. But prohibitionists in the United States benefitted from the war against Germany.

Although supporters of prohibition made gains on a state-by-state basis before the war, the German-American Alliance had received substantial financial backing from the U.S. Brewers' Association to campaign against them. They were able to defeat federal temperance legislation until the Alliance was weakened as America drew nearer to war with Germany.[15] Wartime prohibition measures were quickly passed after Congress declared war on April 2, 1917. On April 4, a war resolution called for prohibition as "necessary to the efficiency of our manpower and the conservation of our resources" to protect the soldiers and conserve the food supply.[16] Wartime prohibition was also promoted in Australia, New Zealand, Norway, South Africa, and Sweden.[17]

During the war, the WCTU saw new opportunities to reinforce prohibition and zealously adopted the slogan: "Every white ribboner, a prohibition patriot." Their special concern was to protect the soldiers and sailors from liquor and vice. In the United States, the liquor traffic was prohibited in the District of Columbia as of September 8, 1917. In addition, the WCTU wanted to protect young girls in communities with military camps. Therefore, the social purity goal, a "white life for two," was encouraged as a patriotic appeal and also for religious and "scientific" motives.

When the Reverend Doctor Anna Howard Shaw was appointed chairman of the Woman's Committee of the Council of National Defense and of the Advisory Committee of the Women's Liberty Loan Committee, the WCTU rallied to support her as one of their own.[18] Shaw was a pillar of the WCTU and the ICW as well as the NAWSA. She was outspoken in arguing that if the men could not make the streets safe and clean without women, "then the women under God are bound to go out and help the men to make them clean, for if there is any right which a woman has under God, it is the right to protect her children from any form of degradation and vice, legalized or not legalized."[19] When the war ended, Shaw received a medal from the government and publicly gave the WCTU women credit for their contribution to the national defense.[20]

The WCTU also supported the war effort in other ways. Belgian refugees were assisted and funds raised to supply and maintain twenty ambulances and fourteen kitchens for the battle front. As war industries expanded, the National WCTU cooperated with the National Council of Women to establish employment bureaus for women who replaced men called up for military service.[21] The WCTU Committee of Women in Industry concerned themselves with clean and sanitary working conditions. The previous emphasis on temperance education was also thought to be paying off, as former child temperance advocates took their places in prominent positions. As in the United States, "Students from other lands have felt the impress of our work and are now pushing these principles in the Orient and elsewhere."[22] Like the overseas movement, the Americanization Department attempted to inculcate prohibition among the new immigrants and to help them adjust to life in a new land.[23] This Department professed to offer a "woman touch." This tradition of assisting foreigners to assimilate into the culture began well before Jane Addams founded Hull House.

The prohibition movement was also accelerated during wartime because foodstuffs were needed for the war effort more than for distillation. As the WCTU office in Washington pressured vigorously for federal prohibition laws, they monitored Congressional voting records and passed on the information to local organizations in all forty-eight states. Their war effort culminated in the passage of the federal temperance law. The high point of the prohibition movement, the Eighteenth Amendment, was ratified by two-thirds of the states by January 1919. Ultimately it was rejected only by three: New Jersey, Rhode Island, and Connecticut.[24] As Margaret Dye Ellis savored the victory, she recalled that when she started work in Washington, only three states had prohibition. The number had then extended to twenty-eight along with the District of Columbia, Alaska, Hawaii, Puerto Rico, the Canal Zone and the Virgin Islands.

When the Nineteenth Amendment was ratified in 1920, the WCTU perceived federal woman suffrage as another victory for their cause " . . . for it passed Congress at the psychological moment to aid the enforcement of the Eighteenth Amendment."[25] Jeannette Rankin, the first woman elected to Congress, introduced the Susan B. Anthony bill for the fortieth time (the first time by a woman). At the end of the long campaign, Carrie Chapman Catt, Susan B. Anthony's successor, paid high tribute to her fellow WCTU members, Frances Willard and her loyal legions.

There is something that we women who never did aught to bring prohibition should do now. Some of you, like myself, were busy along other lines perhaps, or perhaps you were indifferent; but at the same time, while we were at work elsewhere, there were women who were working night and day with a sacrifice, with a power of which we of this time have little idea. Some of you may perhaps be old enough to remember, as do I, the time when churches did not work in fellowship with each other; and the greatest cause that brought their union about was the Woman's Christian Temperance Union. There never has been a woman leader in this country greater nor perhaps so great as Frances Willard.[26]

After woman suffrage was passed in the United States, the franchise committee of the national WCTU was merged into the Christian Citizenship Committee. Then the WCTU called upon its members to "make American citizens of our foreign-born women." Even those who had initially opposed woman suffrage understood the power of the ballot. Julia C. Lathrop, first director of the Federal Children's Bureau, said: "Not so-called anti-suffragists, but the liquor interests are the worst opponents of woman suffrage. Over forty years of education and agitation by the WCTU helped to give this nation a Federal Child Bureau."[27]

Even during World War One, the WCTU added 153,930 new members between 1913 and 1920.[28] Afterwards, the WWCTU embarked on a world crusade to ban alcohol.[29] One unifying aspect was "World Temperance Sunday" when temperance sermons were preached in many countries. As more missionaries were sent out, local women also became organizers and received funds from the world organization. When the League of Nations was being formed, these women exerted some international pressure. By 1923, they were comprised of fifty-one national organizations.[30]

The American WCTU commemorated Frances Willard and their fiftieth anniversary at their convention in Chicago, Illinois, in 1924. After four years of woman suffrage, even the most conservative had become aware of their potential political clout. The opening day featured a procession that commemorated "the Marching Mothers of the Crusade of 1873, ballotless women kneeling and praying, despised and rejected by all but the spiritually discerning."[31] Elizabeth Putnam Gordon's history of the first fifty years of the American WCTU, *The Torch-Bearers,* concluded that thousands of marching, enfranchised women "resolved that their possession of the ballot meant that never again would there be a return to the old days when the home was despoiled, children defrauded, and women's hearts broken."[32]

The American WCTU was currently engaged in twenty-five kinds of social, economic, and moral service "in city and in town, among women of all creeds, classes and color. . . ." The goal of the Jubilee membership campaign was to mobilize a million women. This national meeting was followed by state conventions that also celebrated the various departments. Willard's "Do Everything Policy" meant that committees were added, eliminated, or combined as interest waxed and waned. Gradually, forty departments were adopted under six general lines: Preventive, Educational, Evangelistic, Social and Legislative—besides the department of Organization. Two branches were also formed: the Young Woman's Branch and the Loyal Temperance Legion.[33]

As woman suffrage became more widespread, the World WCTU adopted a memorial resolution for women's rights at the Twelfth Convention in Edinburgh, Scotland in 1925. The text of the "Memorial to the Women of Every Land" called for women to oppose alcohol and protect the home. It still carefully avoided feminist language. Women of every nation were urged to unite to enact legislation that would grant equal rights and privileges to all women.[34]

While women were winning more political rights, the WWCTU saw their goal of world prohibition steadily recede. Sometimes the cause was international agreements. For example, Iceland allowed Spanish wine to be imported in exchange for fish. In Canada the dry provinces reversed prohibition and established Government Liquor Control. The biggest defeat came in the United States, the birthplace of the WCTU, when the Eighteenth Amendment was repealed in 1933. Despite such reversals, where prohibition could not be achieved or maintained, the WCTU worked to limit the sale of alcohol and regulate penalties for its abuse. They also struggled against the opium trade, as Asian national unions requested legislation to deny farmers the right to grow opium poppies.

With the repeal of prohibition, the worldwide depression, and the faltering League of Nations, the World WCTU needed bucking up when they met in Stockholm, Sweden in 1934. Still, thirty-one countries were represented by 766 delegates. They reaffirmed their opposition to the three great evils: war, impurity, and alcohol. The failure of national prohibition in the United States had been less than total, they reassured themselves, as fourteen states retained prohibition and thirty-one restored local option laws whereby counties and towns could vote to remain dry. Because more alcohol was being consumed, however, crime had increased along with the hazard posed by inebriated drivers on the highways and in aircraft. Consequently, the WCTU reinforced their resolve and appealed for legislative action to establish penalties for drunk driving. Radio and motion pictures as well as youth camps and temperance meetings carried their message.

The high standards of the WCTU were acknowledged in 1936 when organizers of the Olympics invited the German White Ribboners to be responsible for the rooms and meals of the 500 women competitors, all of whom were required to be total abstainers. And a Japanese village chose to remain dry after a five-year prohibition trial. Drinkers contributed their *sake* money to build a school, and the general health of the community improved. In China the membership pledge was changed to vow not to drink, gamble, or smoke when WCTU missionaries realized that some women did not drink but favored the other two vices. Members were also requested not to have bound feet.

Despite the severe economic depression that was being felt around the world, attendance rebounded at the 1937 meeting in Washington, D.C., the Sixteenth World Convention. The 3700 delegates and visitors who represented thirty-seven countries appealed to the League of Nations to study the effect of alcohol on nutrition. In order to feed the malnourished, they advised a ban so grain and other foods would not be made into alcohol. As the Second World War became imminent, the members honored Frances Willard's memory with a "Great Peace" meeting. They held prayer vigils, rallies, and demonstrations for peace. However when war was declared, as in World War I, the WCTU worked for the war effort. This time twenty of the fifty-six national unions were directly affected, and the 1940 meeting scheduled for London was canceled. From her bombed-out home, World WCTU secretary Agnes Slack struggled to maintain communication between 1937 and 1947 while the organization did not meet.

At the end of the war, representatives attended the peace conference and presented resolutions on peaceful arbitration, cessation of war, and arms limitation. Then in 1945, the World WCTU was one of the fourteen world organizations granted NGO consultative status in the United Nations. Despite this recognition in the postwar period while many national WCTUs expressed a determination to rebuild, others were eliminated in countries like Estonia and Latvia where the Communists banned all Christian temperance work.[35] As of 1948, the World WCTU continued to support world peace through a Court of Arbitration in the United Nations. Although forty-eight countries had accorded women suffrage, that cause remained a priority along with social purity and prohibition. While the WCTU continued its campaigns, other women's organizations were formed with suffrage as a higher priority.

7

THE INTERNATIONAL COUNCIL OF WOMEN

As the WCTU expanded internationally, other suffragists also promoted international cooperation. At the 1878 Paris "International Women's Rights Congress," a permanent international women's committee was created. Representatives were included from both the National Woman Suffrage Association and the American Woman Suffrage Association of the United States.[1] However, ten more years elapsed before the International Council of Women was formed. In 1882 Elizabeth Cady Stanton decided an international woman suffrage association was needed, although she was sure the vote alone would not achieve women's equal rights.[2] She conceived the idea on a trip to Europe, and Susan B. Anthony agreed. Then the two embattled old suffragists promoted the idea as they went around the continent.[3]

At a women's suffrage meeting in Liverpool, England, in November 1883, the participants passed a resolution in support of an international woman suffrage association.[4] The United States, England, Ireland, Scotland, and France were represented on a committee appointed to carry it out, but they never convened. At the Sixteenth National Woman Suffrage Association Conference in Washington, D.C., in March of 1884, letters from the Liverpool group expressed continued support, but still no action was taken.[5]

Finally, at the National Woman Suffrage Association meeting in 1887, Susan B. Anthony proposed the new organization. The participants supported the idea, but the women were divided on what its goals should be. The older women wanted it to be limited to woman suffrage, whereas younger women wanted to include "workers along all lines of human progress. . . ."[6] They would even include antisuffragists.

One of the founders, May Wright Sewall (1844-1920), was the principal of a Girls' Classical School in Indianapolis, Indiana. Sewall had participated in founding the Indianapolis Equal Suffrage Society in 1878. She preferred Stanton and Anthony's more radical National Woman Suffrage Association over Lucy Stone's conservative American Woman Suffrage Association. At the 1887 NWSA meeting, Sewall introduced a resolution to convene the new International Council of Women with the NWSA in 1888 to celebrate the fortieth anniversary of the 1848 convention at Seneca Falls. In its revised wording, this resolution proposed a broader spectrum of goals, not just suffrage. The resolution

Ishbel Aberdeen, first president of the International Council of Women. Picture from *The World's Congress of Representative Women* edited by May Wright Sewall. Chicago and New York: Rand McNally and Company, 1894.

stated that "all associations of women in the trades, professions and moral reforms, as well as those advocating the political emancipation of women, shall be invited."[7] By June 1, 1887, the women publicly announced their intention to form an international combination to support their various causes. The possibilities were perceived as very far reaching. They proposed an interchange of opinions on the great questions that agitated the world. They wanted to rouse women to new thought, intensify their love of liberty, and give them a sense of the power of combination.

The initial conference was scheduled to last eight days, long enough to report on what was known of women's progress around the world during the past forty years. Much of the preparation fell to the American conveners: Susan B. Anthony, May Wright Sewall, and Rachel G. Foster (later Avery). Sewall collected names of organizations in the United States, and Foster did the same for foreign countries. Like her predecessors and mentors, Stanton and Anthony, Sewall was enthusiastic about increasing women's self-esteem and political clout by banding together around the world. To do that, women needed to overcome class and other differences to relate to broader interests. As Sewall wrote later:

The correspondence showed that what was needed to broaden the minds and the sympathies of women was to bring them together under conditions which would show them that however different in traditions, in wealth, social position and in religious and political opinions they might be, they all were equally related to larger interests: that indeed the likenesses existing among the most different classes of women were larger than the differences among the same classes.[8]

By 1888, associations for women's suffrage or civic education had been founded in Canada, Finland, France, Germany, Great Britain, Norway, Sweden, and the United States. Municipal or school board suffrage had also been obtained in many localities. Opportunities for education and employment had been extended. In addition, women's societies for temperance, social purity, and missionary work (notably the WCTU) had been established and representatives sent to China, India, and Africa as well as other parts of the world. As Anna Garland Spencer noted, associations "for penal reform, prisoners' and orphans' aid, for the rescue of 'fallen women' and help to friendless girls, were active on the local and national level in countries from Canada to Australia, Russia to the Argentine, Scandinavia to the Cape."[9]

Susan B. Anthony chaired the first ICW meeting in March 1888, while Elizabeth Cady Stanton gave the welcoming and closing addresses. The founder of the American women's movement had been reluctant to return from England for the occasion, but Anthony reported in her journal that she sent Stanton a letter that "will start every white hair on her head." Stanton soon cabled that she would attend, and Anthony sequestered her at the Riggs House in Washington until her addresses were prepared.[10] The eloquent Stanton described women's progress over the last forty years. Even so, she reminded participants that men were still allowed more freedoms, and "Thus far women have been the mere echoes of men."[11] She called the true woman a dream of the future and heralded a new age of internationalism, "Now that our globe is girdled with railroads, steamships, and electric wires. . . ."[12]

As the leaders were aging, they mended some of the rifts of the past forty years. Lucy Stone once again joined Susan B. Anthony on the lecture platform. The two old leaders were already planning to merge their suffrage organizations. With low attendance at the 1887 American Woman Suffrage Association, a resolution had been passed in favor of unification with their old rival, the NWSA.[13] In 1890, the two merged as the National American Woman Suffrage Association (NAWSA).[14] Meanwhile, in 1888 a session billed as a "Conference of the Pioneers" began with a silent tribute to Lucretia Mott. Forty-eight years later, Elizabeth Cady Stanton reminisced about walking home arm-in-arm with Mrs. Mott at the 1840 World's Anti-Slavery Convention in London. She recalled declaring, "It seems to me high time to call a Woman's Convention. Here are these men from all parts of the globe to discuss the rights of negroes to freedom, and yet they have no idea of any rights of freedom for women."[15] Another old friend and sometime adversary, Frederick Douglass, recalled hearing Mrs. Stanton speak of her women's rights objectives six years before the Seneca Falls convention.[16] Perhaps his memory was also failing.

Forty-nine delegates attended from England, France, Denmark, Norway, Finland, India, Canada, and the United States.[17] Temperance was well represented, not only by Frances Willard but also by Hannah Whitall Smith on behalf of the World WCTU. Among foreign participants were Alexandra Grippenberg of Finland, Isabele Bogelot of France, Laura Ormiston Chant of Great Britain, and S. Magelsson Groth of Norway. Altogether, of the fifty-one associations represented, seven primarily supported temperance, ten suffrage, and six social purity.[18]

Enthusiasm was high as the delegates cheered Stanton's assertion that women's internationalism would triumph over all other ideologies. Like the WCTU, they agreed to work for a wide variety of causes from politics to religion, social purity, education and philanthropy, as well as temperance. The participants drafted a constitution that guaranteed the autonomy of the national councils of women that would comprise the international membership. How much Sewall contributed to the proposed organizational structure is difficult to establish. Anthony's biographer, Ida Husted Harper, credited Sewall with proposing the ICW and related National Councils of Women (NCWs).[19] Anna Garland Spencer credited Willard with designing the format.[20] As president of the national WCTU, Willard had founded the World WCTU. She chaired the organizing committee and starred at that first meeting of the International Council of Women. Willard addressed five sessions: temperance, organization, social purity, political conditions, and the religious symposium.[21] Most the participants shared Willard's faith in the potential of the organization to expand women's quest for equal rights.

First: We (Mrs. Scatcherd dissenting as to The International) are strongly in favor of such federations—National and International—believing that it will incalculably increase the world's sum total of womanly courage, efficiency, and *esprit de corps;* that it will widen our horizon, correct the tendency to an exaggerated impression of one's own work as compared to that of others, and put the wisdom and experience of each at the service of all.[22]

While the international representatives were enthusiastic about the new organization, only the Americans were able to unite organizations and establish a National Council of Women to affiliate with the ICW at that time. Frances Willard was elected President of the NCW. Stanton and Anthony had won the battle for a new international organization, but the planners soon experienced another disappointment. Millicent Garrett Fawcett was elected president of the ICW *in absentia,* but she subsequently refused to serve. Fawcett said she was too busy with the British suffrage movement. When May Wright Sewall was sent as a special envoy to persuade her, Fawcett declared that "it was quite impossible that English and American women should have anything in common, the conditions of their lives and the purposes of their societies being so different."[23] Therefore, the American NCW was *de facto* the ICW until other national groups could be formed.

Undaunted, Frances Willard took control of both organizations and sent Sewall as the American NCW delegate to an International Congress of Women held in connection with the Paris Exposition in July 1889. When Isabelle Bogelot attended the meeting in 1888, the French were already moving ahead to form their own NCW; but they were further inspired by Sewall's stirring address. She cited the principle of equality as a basis for combination and quoted Frenchman Alexis De Tocqueville on organizing in the United States. They were reminded of other international groups such as temperance headed by Frances Willard, the Red Cross led by Clara Barton, and the Universal Peace Society founded by Lucretia Mott and Julia Ward Howe.[24] In a well-tuned speech that Sewall would also deliver at other expositions in 1891 and 1892, she contended that the good work of organizations could be "checked" by ignorance of one another unless they learned the advantages of cooperation.[25]

With this international nucleus, national councils began to be formed in other countries. At the same time, the founders of the American NCW (Frances E. Willard, Susan B. Anthony, M. Louise Thomas, Mary F. Eastman, and May Wright Sewall) called for local and state women's societies to join the national and international organizations. One new affiliate was the General Federation of Women's Clubs. It was established in 1889, a year after the ICW. On the twenty-first anniversary of the founding of Sorosis in New York City, its founder, Jennie C. Croly, called for a convention "of all the women's clubs known to be in existence." The conference call was sent to ninety-seven clubs, and delegates from sixty-one assembled to form the GFWC.[26] As vice president, May Wright Sewall promoted close cooperation with the ICW.[27] She also represented another organization she helped found, the Association of Collegiate Alumnae (later the American Association of University Women).[28]

As the leaders of the ICW strongly promoted Willard's "home protection" theme, they declared that "their combination means a dominance of peace and spiritual power, the purification, the protection and coronation of the home; the home is the shrine for whose sacred sake all that is good and true on earth exists."[29] Although Willard rejected marriage for herself, she had learned in the WCTU that protection of the home was a noble (or at least not controversial) basis on which to attract women members and ward off criticism. The conservative ICW followed the same pattern.

The participants agreed that the NCWs would meet every three years and the ICW every five. They planned to hold the 1893 ICW Quinquinial in London. But when Millicent Garrett Fawcett refused to accept the presidency, the Americans were left to prepare for that meeting. As plans were underway for the Chicago World's Columbian Exposition, what better occasion to bring together women leaders of the world? Planning thus began for what became a World's Congress of Representative Women, a week in May 1893, when the old guard of the women's movement fired the enthusiasm of the next generation and carried women's struggle for equal rights to new levels of respectability and global activity.

8

FROM MAY WRIGHT SEWALL TO ISHBEL ABERDEEN: THE WORLD'S CONGRESS OF REPRESENTATIVE WOMEN

The Chicago World's Columbian Exposition of 1893 has been credited with winning more favorable attention for the woman suffrage movement than any and perhaps all previous efforts. More than a decade after the 1876 Centennial celebration, Susan B. Anthony was still mindful that women had been virtually ignored. Not allowed on the platform inside, they had read their protest against women's lack of rights in the public square in front of Philadelphia's Independence Hall. Anthony resolved not to allow such treatment at the Chicago World's Columbian Exposition.

However, several officials had declared that "those suffrage women should have nothing to do with the World's Fair," so Anthony kept a low profile. She also had to be careful because some prominent women were likely to be frightened off if suffrage were in any way connected with the occasion. Even so, Anthony started plotting and conferring with other distinguished women when the plan for a World's Fair was first publicized in 1889. Ladies whom she trusted in official life were invited to organize World's Fair meetings at the Riggs House where Anthony lived in Washington, D.C. Then they invited other influential women, and a committee was appointed to ask Congress to place women on the National Board of Management of the Fair. Anthony's biographer, Ida Husted Harper, contends that if Anthony "had not been on the field of battle in Washington and acted at the very moment she did, the bill [to create a Board of Managers] would have passed Congress with no provision for women."[1]

As various cities competed for the role of host, Anthony did lobby publicly to hold the Exposition in New York. Simultaneously, some prominent Middle Western women like Myra Bradwell, Secretary of the Illinois Woman Suffrage Association, and Emma R. Wallace, a member of the Chicago Woman's Club, lobbied the Chicago Corporation. As the men labored to bring the Fair to Chicago, the women called for a female auxiliary. Myra Bradwell and Margaret Isabella Sandes also lobbied in Washington to have the Fair site awarded to Chicago. Emma Wallace suggested an official Women's Department, and a Women's Auxiliary Executive Committee was formed. They resolved to erect a Woman's Pavilion to exhibit women's industries. Audience rooms would also be available for an international convention of "reformatory" and charitable workers.

Long before Chicago won the bid, the local women's goals were divided. A group of suffragists and others who worked for women's equal rights, including many professional women, decided they wanted to celebrate Queen Isabella, not just Columbus.[2] Dubbed the Isabellas, their headquarters was in the office of Dr. Frances Dickinson, a cousin of Susan B. Anthony. Another major point of dissension was whether or not women's exhibits should be segregated from men's. The Auxiliary women wanted their displays housed in a separate women's building. The suffragists did not oppose this, but they wanted women's work recognized right along with the men's.

At the national level, the issue was similar. The debate was whether women should be on the Board of Directors or have a separate women's committee. When Chicago was finally agreed upon as the site and the World's Fair Bill was brought before the House of Representatives in January 1890, Anthony prepared a petition to request the appointment of women to the Commission. To support this, influential women obtained the signatures of one hundred and eleven wives and daughters of judges of the Supreme Court, the Cabinet, Senators, Representatives, and Army officers.

The women's petition was initially ignored. But before the Bill passed the House, Representative William Springer of Illinois managed to have it amended to call for the creation of a Board of Lady Managers. This amendment was not included when the Senate returned the Bill to the House. According to Jeanne Weimann, author of *The Fair Women,* "Mr. Springer called attention to this omission, and the chairman of the Committee replied that it was unintentional—the amendment having been left out because the Committee considered it of no importance whatever, but that if desired it could yet be restored to the bill, and this was consequently done."[3]

All Springer's amendment called for was the creation of a Board of Lady Managers who would participate in judging and giving prizes for work done by women. Both the Women's Department or Auxiliary and the local suffragists, the Isabellas, interpreted this as authority to organize. Although the men's committee structure was carefully spelled out, no provision had been made to appoint women. Congress had established a World's Columbian Commission of 108 members: two each from every state and territory and the District of Columbia, and eight commissioners-at-large, appointed by the President upon nomination by the governor. Thomas Palmer, a former senator from Michigan, was elected president. The Commission oversaw the local Chicago Fair Corporation which had forty-five directors, including Potter Palmer, a Chicago businessman, as second vice president.[4]

The competing women's groups vigorously lobbied the Chicago Directors for the unspecified number of appointments to the Board of Lady Managers. The ladies sent flowers. Under this pressure, the local directors referred the women to the National Commission. Then they received flowers. With no guidelines at all in the original mandate, the men followed their own model. They appointed 117 lady managers and their alternates with nine members-at-large from the Chicago area, more members than the National Commission itself. All were appointed by September 1890. Although the women were not appointed by organization, some local members-at-large like Frances Dickinson were Isabellas. Others like Myra Bradwell and Emma Wallace came from the Auxiliary. Matilda Carse, a suffragist, represented the WCTU. Frances Willard was a third alternate.

The disputes were innumerable among a Board of Lady Managers composed of a variety of women who had made some mark on society in their individual states. Some saw a chance for national and even international recognition with expenses paid by the federal government. Some cited themselves as "domestic executives," others were widows, and several were successful business women. No factory workers or African American women were included.[5]

When the Board of Lady Managers convened in November 1890, Bertha Honore Palmer, a.k.a. Mrs. Potter Palmer, a Chicago socialite and antisuffragist, was elected President. The ladies rejected the term "Chairman" because it sounded too masculine. The Isabellas saw Palmer's selection as a defeat, so they regrouped and recruited until they were able to get one of their own, Phoebe Couzins, elected Secretary.[6] This appointment later caused much dissension. Phoebe Couzins had been in Philadelphia with Susan B. Anthony in 1876, and her first complaint was that Anthony had not been appointed to the Board.

Palmer was accustomed to giving parties, but she was new to parliamentary procedure. A native of Kentucky, she believed strongly in womanly virtues such as tenderness, sympathy, and intuition. She believed that women should always be gentle and womanly as they sought to obtain what they wanted, and that what women wanted should be limited by traditional expectations. However, Palmer's iron fist was gradually exposed as the velvet gloves wore thin amid differences of opinion between the suffragists and the antis. Another complicating factor was that a suffragist, Isabella Beecher Hooker, a half-sister of Harriet Beecher Stowe and one of the founders of the American Woman Suffrage Association, led the Committee of Permanent Organization. This group defined the structure of the Board—its rules, committees, and officers.[7]

But Palmer was equal to the fight, as the men also soon learned. She talked the Springfield legislature into giving $80,000, and she charmed the federal Congressional Investigation Committee of the Fair out of a $200,000 appropriation for a woman's building.[8] When the official directors of the Exposition objected to giving awards to artisans as well as manufacturers, she went over their heads and appealed to Congress. Even though the directors told her it could not be done, Congress passed a law that supported Palmer. She also got Washington to approve a female architect to design the Woman's Building.[9]

Although she was not a suffragist, Palmer was sure that if women did the work of men, they should be paid equally. Even so, she turned down the $5,000 salary offered to her as President of the Board of Lady Managers. The daughter of a wealthy Chicago family and the wife of successful business man Potter Palmer, she never worked for pay. Nevertheless, she was financially sophisticated. Years later, after Potter Palmer died, she managed to double his estate by investing in Florida real estate.

Palmer had enough battles to fight planning the Woman's Building (literally from the ground up), and overseeing construction and exhibits. Therefore, she left planning the Congresses to be held in the Woman's Building and the auxiliary sessions in the hands of her friend, anti-suffragist Ellen Henrotin, a member of the Chicago Woman's Club. One of their common tasks was to try to reign in the radical suffragist, May Wright Sewall, who was already arranging the Quinquennial meeting of the International Council of Women.

Before Palmer was appointed, Judge Charles C. Bonney had suggested to the Directors that auxiliary congresses be held in connection with the Exposition. Then he had been appointed cochairman of the World's Congress Auxiliary. When May Wright Sewall approached him, Bonney agreed that the ICW First Quinquennial could be adopted as one of a series of congresses then being organized.[10] Bonney specified, at least after the fact, that the scope of the congress should be enlarged to the greatest possible extent. It should take the name of "The World's Congress of Representative Women," and it should be subject to the same rules and enjoy the same privileges as the other congresses convened by The World's Congress Auxiliary.

Bonney appointed Sewall (by then president of the American NCW) as chair and Rachel Foster Avery (NCW corresponding secretary) to hold those same positions on the Organizing Committee of the women's congress. After Sewall was given this authority, she began to plan for the ICW meeting in Chicago. A prospectus mailed around the world announced that they would address "great themes" such as language, literature, domestic life, religion, insanity, and crime.

Sewall was well established in her position before Palmer was elected President of the Board of Lady Managers of the Exposition. The trouble started after Palmer's authority was extended to encompass the auxiliary women's programs as well as those planned for the Woman's

Building.[11] Sewall's peremptory strike and her determination to further the International Council of Women virtually assured a clash with Palmer. However, both wanted the women's part of the Exposition to be as distinguished as possible. Consequently, both went off to Europe to solicit support—Palmer to drum up appropriate displays for the Woman's Building, Sewall to attract speakers for the World's Congress of Representative Women.

In a way the two women complemented one another. As president of the Board of Lady Managers, Palmer was sure women should receive the best possible representation at this World's Fair. The Department of State did not move quickly enough to establish her European contacts, but Palmer later decided she had done better on her own anyway. Her sister was married to former President Grant's son, and they introduced her to the court in Austria. Abraham Lincoln's son, Robert Todd Lincoln, introduced her in Paris. Elizabeth Cady Stanton's son, Theodore, did the honors in London. Consequently, Palmer was able to persuade female European royalty to display priceless laces and other treasures. At home she also sought exhibits of women's work. Palmer tried to be tactful as she weeded out the mediocre and the hustlers, which was by no means an easy task. After the Executive Committee of the National Council of Women met in Chicago in May 1892, Sewall promoted the ICW Quinquennial in Europe for three months. The call to participate was distributed to "every country of the civilized world." The leaders were asked to present "the woman's view upon every issue affecting humanity—upon the home, the church, the state, and her own function in these institutions. . . ."[12]

The conservative antisuffragists, Palmer and Henrotin, considered Sewall to be a radical feminist; and they regarded the budding International Council of Women as too extreme in its views on the place of women in the world. Jeanne Weimann wrote, "It is not surprising that Mrs. Henrotin should be suspicious of all these organized, dedicated suffragists working busily, supposedly under her direction, but without her actual supervision. They were promoting the International Council of Women; it would not have occurred to them not to do so."[13] Henrotin became alarmed after Mary Logan, a leader of the Woman's Relief Corps, reported that she had received a letter from Sewall on National Council of Women stationery. According to Sewall, this would be a good time to join the NCW because their newsletter, *The Call,* was going to publish a list of member organizations. These organizations would be given space at the Exposition, probably in the Woman's Building.

Palmer and Henrotin especially resented that Sewall said she had "really been given charge of the World Congress," and they were angry at what they regarded as coercion of women's organizations to join the Council in return for special treatment at the Fair.[14] Henrotin and Bonney agreed that only the Women's Congress Committee should send out circulars and letters to women's clubs. They wrote to all officers of large American women's clubs and told them not to be intimidated or coerced by the NCW. The clubs were assured that they had a right to representation at the congresses without having to be members. Even so, Palmer still feared that Sewall would take over the congress, and Sewall thought she already had. Indeed, the National Council of Women paid the costs for foreign women speakers to participate. In the summer of 1892 while Sewall was in Europe, Rachel Foster Avery continued to recruit for the NCW nationally and still sent much correspondence on National Council of Women letterhead. Avery, a favorite of Anthony's, also kept the older woman informed.

When Henrotin decided to reign Sewall in, she sent a letter that said the National Council of Women was most unpopular throughout the East and the South and that the International Council of Women had "an existence only on paper." She called for all correspondence about the women's congress to be sent out by a secretary in Chicago. Palmer also wrote to tell Sewall that she would make no new allies and no new friends by giving the impression that the Congress of Representative Women was only the meeting of the International Council of Women under another name.[15] Palmer requested that Sewall send copies of official letters to her along with the replies. She was going to monitor the mail.

At Henrotin's request, Palmer also demonstrated her overall authority by chairing a meeting called in December 1892, by the Committee of Arrangements for the World's Congress of Representative Women (Sewall's committee). Palmer and Henrotin spoke first and stressed their expectation that women would address their roles in society. Henrotin wanted the women to speak as lawyers, teachers, or even voters, but not on the "Woman Question." Sewall wanted the opposite. In calls for participation, Sewall had informed the European women that the object of this congress was to discuss, "not the subject *per se,* but the relation of the women of the world to the subject."[16]

By the time Palmer had her showdown with Sewall, she had already fired Phoebe Couzins as Secretary of the Board of Lady Managers. Because the Board had no guidelines from the National Commission, Couzins and her supporters contended that she could not be fired. But Palmer did it anyway. With this background, Sewall defended herself for using National Council of Women stationery. She said she had not received any from the World Congress. However, women in the East were still writing to complain that they continued to receive National Council of Women circulars. In the confrontation with Palmer, Sewall blinked first. She agreed not to use the Council's letterhead for Congress mailings.[17] One reason the militants backed off was that the National Council of Women did not want to antagonize the General Federation of Women's Clubs. This group did not support suffrage yet.

If Palmer could not eliminate the suffragists, she could at least dilute out their influence. She and Henrotin broadened the objectives of the conference to include what they called, "a more comprehensive and complete portrayal of women's achievements in all departments of civilized life than has hitherto been made. . . ."[18] Then Palmer topped off her disapproval by limiting Sewall's space in the Woman's Building to an Organizations Room shared by many groups.[19] Despite their private clashes, the generally gracious Palmer gave Sewall more credit on public occasions. At the dedication ceremonies for the Exposition in 1892 she closed her address by acknowledging the effort to improve women's standing: "Even more important than the discovery of Columbus, which we are gathered together to celebrate, is the fact that the general government has just discovered woman." And Susan B. Anthony wrote enthusiastically after the formal opening of the Columbian Exposition on May 1, 1893, "Mrs. Palmer's speech was very fine, covering full equality for women."[20]

The international conference was scheduled immediately after the Fair opened. It was held in the old Crystal Palace, which was being renovated into the Art Institute, not in the Woman's Building. When the World's Congress of Representative Women began on May 15, 1893, the workers had barely cleared out. They left bits of plaster and wood chips on the floor. The ladies and their foreign guests raised a cloud of dust and swept the debris along with them in their long, trailing skirts.[21] The atmosphere was an appropriate beginning—a conference where many women discussed the need for more comfortable clothing, especially shorter skirts. Dress reform was a popular subject.[22]

When Rachel Foster Avery read the report of the International Council Committee on Dress Reform, the spectators grew impatient at not being able to see her so-called "Syrian" costume. The ankle-length bloused trousers, shirt and vest might remind modern film buffs of Hollywood costumes for women in middle eastern harems. At the time, fair goers were more apt to be reminded of Little Egypt's costume. Her dancing was one the most popular attractions on the Midway. The audience at Avery's session of the World's Congress of Representative Women might have reminded Little Egypt of her clientele as well. As they grew more impatient at not being able to see, they finally started yelling, "On the table." Avery stood on top of the speaker's table to finish her report.[23]

The World's Congress of Representative Women was the first of the special programs held in conjunction with the Chicago World's Columbian Exposition; and it was also one of the best attended, except for the Parliament of Religions in August. Three hundred thirty scheduled speakers and nearly as many unscheduled ones appeared at eighty-one sessions. Twenty-seven countries and one hundred twenty-six organizations were represented.[24] Some of these speakers also gave talks at congresses arranged by Henrotin in the Woman's Building, but crowds packed the World's Congress of Representative Women. A large audience was attracted at least partly because famous suffragists participated and Clara Barton presided. Also, topics such as women's clothing and suffrage were frequently perceived as controversial.

While presentations by distinguished women brought out the crowds, some of the better-known American women did not attend. Frances Willard participated in the dedication ceremonies in the fall of 1892, but she fell ill in England and missed the entire Exposition. Because of this, the WCTU was less able to capitalize on the event than was another enterprising reformer, Jane Addams (1860-1935). She gained international recognition as she invited distinguished foreign guests to Hull House throughout the Exposition.[25] Although one session advertised Susan B. Anthony, Elizabeth Cady Stanton, and Julia Ward Howe, by 1893 Anthony could not overcome Stanton's preference to remain on Long Island. Therefore, Anthony made a trip east, stood over Stanton while she wrote, and brought her paper back to read before the Education Congress.[26]

Chicago was the last lecture trip for another first-generation suffragist, Lucy Stone, who died a few days after the close of the Exposition. She spent five days at the business meeting of the Women's Department and spoke in the Suffrage Department Meeting Room under the auspices of the recently combined National American Woman Suffrage Association. Stone wrote home that she talked with a relative newcomer, Carrie Chapman Catt, about suffrage in Colorado. While Willard and Stanton removed themselves from starring roles in this major meeting, Catt (like Jane Addams) enhanced her national prominence. Then she went on to work for suffrage in Colorado after the Congress.[27] While Anthony expended her time and effort on Kansas only to be defeated, Catt helped the Colorado women achieve another state victory.[28]

At the end of the Chicago World's Columbian Exposition, most of the accolades went to Palmer and Susan B. Anthony. Palmer was acknowledged for her grace and also for her astuteness and ability to coordinate complicated and diverse groups and situations. Despite her opposition to suffrage and all the problems the suffragists caused her, Potter was gracious to Anthony. The old suffragist not only starred at the initial Women's Auxiliary Congress, but also made presentations to other groups. Judge Bonney appointed her to the Advisory Council of the Political, Social and Economic Congresses, and Ellen Henrotin asked her to participate in the Temperance, Labor, and Social and Moral Reform Congresses.[29] Anthony enjoyed the public acclaim. Every time she appeared on the stage, the audience broke into applause. When she arose to speak, they stood on the seats and waved hats and handkerchiefs.[30] She addressed the Congress on Government and participated in many smaller gatherings.[31] Her speech at the Press Congress caused a sensation when Anthony claimed the church and religious press dragged their feet on such reforms as temperance, antislavery, women's rights, and labor.[32]

The Chicago World's Columbian Exposition gave woman suffrage a boost and put the International Council of Women on a permanent footing. Although only one session of the Congress of the World's Representative Women was allocated to the National American Woman Suffrage Association, whatever the subject, the speakers pointed out the disabilities of women without the ballot. Sewall had briefed them well. She also received her ration of glory as she presided over the banquet given by the National Council of Women for the foreign delegates and entertained Anthony at her temporary home in Chicago.

Frances Willard's British friend, Lady Henry Somerset, did her best to represent the WCTU. But without Willard's immediate backing, Somerset did not have the same influence with American participants. She lost the election for president of the ICW to a relatively unknown Scotswoman. However, the choice of Ishbel Aberdeen (1857-1939) proved to be highly fortuitous. Her election resulted directly from the fame she achieved at the Chicago World's Columbian Exposition. Her husband, Lord Aberdeen, had been relieved of his duties as Lord Lieutenant of Ireland and would assume the post of Governor General of Canada in October of 1893. Before they left Ireland, Lady Aberdeen had promoted the development of Irish crafts to provide more employment.

Lady Aberdeen attracted much attention at the Chicago Exposition because she had conceived the idea and raised the money to construct an entire Irish village. Guests were delighted. Besides replicas of fifteen cottages, a twelfth-century gateway faced the tower of Blarney Castle where they could kiss the Blarney stone and purchase Irish crafts.[33] During 1893, Aberdeen was able to oversee the Irish village display personally. This made her very well known among Fair goers. She also gained some organizational experience that summer when she briefly replaced Mrs. Gladstone, wife of the British Prime Minister William Gladstone, as president of the Women's Liberal Federation. That British organization became a forum to discuss such political issues as woman suffrage and factory legislation.[34]

Before the International Council of Women closed their conference in Chicago, twenty-eight vice presidents were nominated to encourage the Council idea in their native countries.[35] Within this nucleus, Sewall envisioned a permanent international parliament of women. She ended the final session with this projection and an appeal for an "international parliament of men and women, wherein will be legislated the questions that concern the world."[36] Sewall's vision would come to pass first in the League of Nations and then in the United Nations.

When Sewall wrote the introduction to the proceedings of the World's Congress of Representative Women, which were published the next year, she tactfully implied that it had been authorized by Palmer before (instead of after) the fact. Sewall also described Palmer as having manifested "fairness of temper, quickness of perception, fertility of resource, soundness of judgment and unfailing tact. . . ."[37] The old and much-used swords were buried, but the international women's movement had received substantial support. The great fair ended, but the ICW would continue.

9

THE LATER ICW:
TOWARD THE LEAGUE OF NATIONS

Ishbel Aberdeen took the reigns of leadership of the ICW and became a major shaping force in its evolution over the next three decades. She proved to be as adept at expanding the international women's organization as at funding and developing an Irish village display. Aberdeen had traveled widely in the British Empire: to India, Australia, and New Zealand. She traveled as well to the United States, where two of her younger brothers worked on cattle ranches. Her position gave the organization a respectable, even elitist cast that attracted women who were still unsure about woman suffrage but were willing to work for other rights.

After Aberdeen assumed her new responsibilities in connection with her husband's post in Ottawa, Canada, she sent her secretary, Teresa Wilson, to Europe in 1895 and 1896 to promote the International Council of Women.[1] But everything wasn't left to her secretary. In Great Britain in 1897, Aberdeen's outspoken support of women caused her to be described as "the unofficial lady leader of the opposition."[2] May Wright Sewall also continued on the recruiting circuit. Among other groups, she addressed a National Exhibition of Women's Work in 1898. These efforts brought results at the Second ICW Quinquennial, which had been postponed a year to 1899. Four new NCWs affiliated. Women from twenty-eight countries attended as well as delegates from the World YWCA and the General Federation of Women's Clubs. But the meeting apparently did not promise the same level of excitement as the Chicago World's Columbian Exposition, as many likely participants begged off.[3]

Marjorie Pentland, Aberdeen's daughter and biographer, recounted the variety of responses to invitations to the 1899 meeting in London. Jane Addams declined because she couldn't afford the trip, and Madame Curie received the invitation too late. Although she had been honored in France for the discovery of radium, the invitation was sent to one university after another only to be returned with *inconnu* scrawled on the envelope.[4] Among the participants were Millicent Garrett Fawcett, Susan B. Anthony, and Marie Stritt, president of the German National Council of Women.

Perhaps the wide range of acceptances and declinations can be accounted for partly because the goals and focus of the ICW were still somewhat uncertain in 1899. This congress in London was organized in part by the Women's Liberal Federation. However, many participants were generally conservative and not all that sympathetic toward controversial topics.[5] Charlotte Perkins Gilman attracted the attention of radical suffragists with her argument that women needed economic independence. Later, her book, *Women and Economics,* was translated into Dutch by Aletta Jacobs and into Hungarian by Rosika Schwimmer.

Among the sixteen issues proposed, meetings were set for five sections: education, professions, politics, industry and social life.[6] As far as the suffragists were concerned, not enough attention was focused on what they perceived to be the critical issue. When they objected to anti-suffragists being included, the ICW refused to sponsor their program. Then Fawcett's National Union of Women's Suffrage Societies (NUWSS) offered independent sponsorship, and the women resolved to establish a new international women's suffrage alliance.[7] For that purpose, they held a separate meeting on political enfranchisement.[8] Even the smaller group had its divisions. A Mrs. Dockrell explained the situation of Irish women who insisted on representing themselves separately from the British.[9]

Although the International Woman Suffrage Alliance was being planned, the suffrage committee of the ICW also continued as many NCWs favored the ballot to influence legislation. Representatives of Norway and South Australia pointed out the advantages for women who had suffrage. In her biography of her mother, Ishbel Aberdeen, Marjorie Pentland glosses over this first major rebellion at the 1899 Quinquennial meeting to concentrate on the accomplishments. The global perspective was represented with NCW reports to the ICW, just as Willard and Sewall had originally envisioned. At this session, reports were presented not only by formally affiliated NCWs, but also by individuals who represented Finland, Belgium, Italy, Russia, France, Norway, India, South Africa, Argentina, Palestine, and Persia.[10] Then the ICW participants identified their international priorities. With less emphasis on suffrage, other women's rights committees proliferated. The members expressed opposition to state regulation of vice and formed a standing committee to support suppression of the White Slave Traffic.[11] This was reminiscent of Josephine Butler's earlier struggle.

The conservative members were delighted to have the chance to see if not actually meet the even more conservative Queen Victoria. The ladies were permitted to stand along the driveway at Windsor Castle while the queen drove by in her carriage. Queen Victoria stopped to exchange a few words with Lady Aberdeen, a greeting to her for the delegates. Afterwards the women were invited to see the State Apartments and drink tea in St. George's Hall.[12] Although Aberdeen successfully managed this conference, organized an NCW in Canada, and encouraged the development of others, she was voted out of office. Her successor, May Wright Sewall, continued to promote the Council at international fairs such as the Exposition Universelle at Paris in 1900, the Pan American Exhibition where they first contacted Latin American women at Buffalo, New York, in 1901, and the Louisiana Purchase Exhibition at St. Louis, Missouri, in 1904.[13]

Aberdeen was re-elected president in 1904 and led the ICW through its major development before she retired in 1936. During the early part of that era, former President Sewall chaired the peace committee. Under Aberdeen's leadership, the ICW continued a broad array of efforts on behalf of women. A Bureau of International Associations was founded at Brussels in 1907, and in 1908 at a Special Council meeting at Geneva, the NCWs were requested to report on unequal laws regarding women. This information was intended to be submitted to various governments with a request for suffrage.[14]

By the Fourth Quinquennial in Toronto, Canada, in 1909, the ICW had twenty-two national affiliates and was recruiting in Asia. Some of their success there was due to a Mrs. Sanford of Canada. She spread the word as she traveled through India and Japan and returned via Siberia and Russia. In Latin America, the first Congress of Women was held in Argentina in 1910.[15] Such organizations prepared the way for Carrie Chapman Catt to organize women's suffrage groups in South America a decade later. By 1913, six million women in twenty-three countries belonged to the ICW. Although the approaching war clouded the 1914 meeting in Rome, the ICW continued and suffering European women appealed to them for support. The National Council of French Women was among them. It included one hundred and fifty societies. One was the French Union of Woman Suffrage (with eighty branches), The Society for the Improvement of Woman's Lot, and the Fraternal Union of Women. More than a million French women were represented during the war when the NCFW appealed to the women of all countries to unite with them and denounce war, "the infamous and sinister attack on the common life of humanity through its womankind."[16]

The ICW was ready to expand its sphere of influence after the war and actively promoted the League of Nations. Perhaps Aberdeen made her greatest contribution to international understanding at the 1920 meeting in Norway, the first after World War I. At this Sixth Quinquennial, more than 300 delegates represented twenty-six countries. Although equal political, industrial, legal, and educational rights were on the agenda, peace was a major concern.[17] As former enemies met for the first time since the war, Lady Aberdeen called on delegates from each country to step forward and say a word of greeting. When the Austrian delegate faltered nervously, Aberdeen "jumped up and went to stand protectingly [sic] by her side until the little speech was delivered. A wave of fellow-feeling seemed to run through the audience; tension eased, reserve melted."[18] The women's international comradeship was restored.

The women could also report a number of larger victories. At this time, there were thirty National Councils of Women. New affiliates were Russia, Ukrainia, Iceland, and Mexico. In twenty-three countries, women had gotten the vote since the last Quinquennial in 1914. And new national organizations joined from Poland and Chile. Recruiting also continued in South America. In 1926, L. C. Van Eeghan visited that continent and helped found NCWs in Bolivia and Brazil.[19] After the ICW switched from quinquennial to triennial meetings, more new member countries affiliated: Peru, Brazil, Bolivia, and Lithuania.[20] In 1933 at the fortieth anniversary of the Chicago World's Congress of Representative Women, that city was the site of another International Congress of Women. There, Carrie Chapman Catt and Jane Addams were among the aging stars honored for their work in 1893 and after.[21]

Aberdeen requested to be released from her presidential duties in the ICW in 1936, at the tenth meeting in Dubrovnik, Yugoslavia. At that time Japan was added to the thirty-five affiliates. At the Golden Jubilee of the ICW in 1938, the Eleventh Council in Edinburgh could report twenty-two NCWs in Europe, six in the Americas, four in Asia, two in Africa, two in Australasia, and three corresponding members: Iceland, Egypt, and Southern Rhodesia. The League of Nations and the ILO were also represented.[22] So Aberdeen could look upon a genuinely worldwide organization before she died on April 18, 1939. She was spared the disappointment of seeing the world again at war, but in 1940 those who were able to leave their countries met in Brussels.

At the next meeting at Oslo, Norway, in 1946, Aberdeen's leadership was recalled by the women who once again had to overcome the enmities of war. Her daughter's biography, *A Bonnie Fechter: The Life of Ishbel Marjoribanks, Marchioness of Aberdeen & Temair, G.B.E., L.L.D., J.P., 1857 to 1939,* describes the executive meeting where Lady Nunburnholme told them how Aberdeen had placed her hand on the shoulder of a delegate from a former enemy country while she spoke. Aberdeen had then remained on her feet during all of their welcoming speeches. Numburnholme reported that "It had a magic effect, especially as I could also tell them that my son had been killed in this war, his brother seriously wounded, and my house bombed. I felt Lady Aberdeen's spirit with us that day."[23]

The United Nations Charter followed the League of Nations precedent and included nongovernmental organization status for the ICW. Then the UN became the world parliament of men and women that May Wright Sewall had foretold. At the 1947 ICW meeting in Philadelphia, retiring president Baroness Boel reiterated that "The position of women anywhere affects their position everywhere." Postwar concern was then focused on underdeveloped nations, and the ICW world network continued, as did its breakaway organization, The International Woman Suffrage Alliance.[24]

10

CARRIE CHAPMAN CATT
AND THE INTERNATIONAL WOMAN SUFFRAGE ALLIANCE

When the International Council of Women refused to sponsor the suffragists' program unless the antisuffragists could participate at the meeting in London in 1899, the conservative English suffragist, Millicent Garrett Fawcett permitted her National Union of Women's Suffrage Societies to offer independent sponsorship of the suffragists' meeting.[1] She must have become more of an internationalist in the interim since 1888 when she refused the first presidency of the ICW. A decade later she stood with the participants as they resolved to establish a new international women's suffrage alliance.[2]

Susan B. Anthony finally stepped down in 1900 and chose Carrie Chapman Catt (1859-1947) to succeed her as president of the National American Woman Suffrage Association. Like Elizabeth Cady Stanton, Catt had converted earlier from a staunch nativist to an internationalist. In her later years, Stanton had also established close connections with British suffragists during long stays in England with her daughter and fellow suffragist, Harriet Stanton Blatch. However, even by 1893 Stanton had been reluctant to travel on behalf of the cause, and Anthony had carried most of the burden. She continued to do so for another four years after Stanton died in 1902, but Anthony recognized that the organization needed new and vigorous leadership. Catt more than filled the bill. She was outstanding among women's rights workers because of her diplomatic skills and her ability to compromise on immediate goals and strategize for the long term. Moreover, Catt went further to formulate a world plan to achieve women's suffrage.

Anthony's close but cantankerous friend, Anna Howard Shaw, was disappointed not to be chosen when Anthony retired from active leadership. Shaw and Anthony had toured and lectured together for years, so long that when Anthony's overworked vocal cords failed, Shaw could easily pick up and continue where Aunt Susan left off. Shaw later claimed the two of them were rarely separated between 1888 and Anthony's death in 1906.[3] But Anthony had seen Catt's political savvy in action when she spoke at the merger of the two suffrage organizations in 1890, and also when she guessed right and supported the Colorado women's suffrage campaign in 1893.

Carrie Chapman Catt, first president of the International Woman Suffrage Alliance. Picture from Mary Gray Peck, *Carrie Chapman Catt: A Biography.* New York: The H. W. Wilson Company, 1944.

Catt proved to be a very able leader, but Anthony must have had some doubts about her choice when the younger woman insisted on pursuing the development of a new international suffrage organization. Anthony was reluctant to start another because she and Elizabeth Cady Stanton had founded the ICW for the same purpose in 1888. However, the dissension in 1899 made it clear that the ICW was attracting many conservatives who would work for other women's rights but not for suffrage, and Catt again overrode her mentor's objections. While woman suffrage was her priority, Catt (like Stanton) recognized that many factors limited women, not just lack of the ballot. Catt developed a strong and steadily growing international network of women over her long and active career.

Catt's leadership skills initially developed in the local WCTU. As a young school teacher in Iowa, the newly married Carrie Lane Chapman attended a meeting of the American Association of Women in Des Moines, Iowa, in 1885. Lucy Stone spoke for suffrage, and Iowa WCTU president, Ellen Foster, disputed national president Frances Willard's commitment to the Progressive Party.[4] Two years later, the widow Chapman joined the WCTU and began to lecture publicly. She was a delegate to the state convention in 1889 when the Iowa Union broke away from the national. Catt learned much from Frances Willard about administration and the devastating effects of infighting.

Catt maintained her ties with the WCTU after she concentrated on suffrage. In 1889 she was invited to organize the Floyd County, Iowa woman suffrage campaign. She began to build her national reputation after Lucy Stone heard her speak at the state convention. Catt made a short speaking tour on the East Coast before she addressed the 1890 convention when the two national suffrage organizations ended their twenty-year rivalry. That same summer, Carrie Lane Chapman married George Catt. Soon widowed a second time, Carrie Chapman Catt then was economically independent and ready to concentrate her efforts first on suffrage and then on peace.[5] She initially worked for state and local legislation and then for a federal woman suffrage amendment. In 1892 Susan B. Anthony called on her to testify before Congress, and Catt became chair of the NAWSA business committee.[6] Then Catt called the first Mississippi Valley Conference in Des Moines.

During the 1880s, Catt's lectures often had a strong nativist theme. She contended that foreigners perverted American institutions, and one of her favorite topics was "America for Americans." Her perspective changed in 1893 when she participated in the World's Conference of Representative Women at the Chicago World's Columbian Exposition. Catt recalled, even forty years later, how distinguished women from many countries trailed wood shavings in their long skirts as they walked to and from the speaker's platform. One biographer, Jacqueline Van Voris wrote, "Catt had never seen internationalism on parade and she never forgot it. It changed her life."[7]

So Catt was well on her way to being an internationalist when she decided to promote an international woman suffrage organization. Over Anthony's objections, Catt sent questionnaires around the world to learn about the circumstances of women. Thirty-two countries responded, and the International Woman Suffrage Alliance was tentatively founded in 1902 in conjunction with the thirty-fourth NAWSA conference in Washington, D.C. Seven of the eight countries with woman suffrage societies sent delegates: Australia, Denmark, Germany, Great Britain, Norway, Sweden, and the United States. Chile, Hungary, Russia, Turkey, and Switzerland were also represented.[8]

At that time, the participants voted to form a temporary organization and make it official at a meeting after the Quinquennial of the International Council of Women at Berlin in 1904.[9] Anna Howard Shaw, a staunch suffragist, headed the ICW standing committee on woman suffrage, and she was designated the first convener of the Alliance for Suffrage in the ICW.[10] Shaw had also chaired the suffrage committee in the WCTU, and in 1904 Anthony's old friend finally replaced Carrie Chapman Catt as president of the NAWSA when Catt became president of the new IWSA. With a constitution and elected officers, the objective of the organization was "to secure the enfranchisement of the women of all nations, and to unite the friends of woman suffrage throughout the world in organized co-operation and fraternal helpfulness."[11] Thirty-three delegates from seven countries affiliated with the new alliance. The structure was similar to that of the ICW. Vice presidents would represent national women's suffrage organizations in affiliations with the international. However, that format was not rigidly followed, as suffragists participated before they had organizations to back them. Catt encouraged reports from representatives of nations that were not affiliated as a way to promote their development.

Stanton had died two years earlier, but in 1904 the eighty-four-year-old Anthony was still able to participate, and she was elected honorary president. However, Catt was the president while Anita Augspurg of Germany and Millicent Garrett Fawcett of England served as vice presidents.[12] Many participants continued their membership in the ICW although the new organization was not admitted as an affiliate.[13] Despite her previous objections, Anthony rallied to support the IWSA, and her presence in Berlin generated great enthusiasm among participants and the press. After a motion was made to exclude all reporters, Anthony reminded the women that they were trying to form a great international organization. Therefore, the reporters should be fully informed in order to give them the widest possible publicity.[14]

As Anthony surveyed their progress, she reported that four more states had granted women suffrage since Wyoming became the first in 1869. New Zealand had given women the vote in 1893 and Australia in 1902. Women also voted on the Isle of Man.[15] Other countries had made varying degrees of progress. Anita Augspurg, president of the German society, was the first woman jurist in that country. As German laws forbade "schoolchildren, apprentices, insane people and women" to take part in political associations, she had had to headquarter the woman suffrage association in the free city of Hamburg. Norwegian women had also achieved some municipal voting rights, a privilege Swedish women had enjoyed at least since 1862.[16]

Leaders of national women's suffrage groups rallied to support one another in this new forum. Millicent Garrett Fawcett headed the British delegation.[17] She was accompanied by Margery Corbett (later Ashby) who would follow Catt as president of the IWSA. Aletta Jacobs represented the Netherlands. The first woman physician in her country, Jacobs had refused to pay taxes and had sued the Dutch government for denying her full rights of citizenship.[18] At the Berlin meeting, Catt met many women who became her staunch international associates. Rosika Schwimmer was an observer, but she returned to Hungary to form a national women's suffrage association.[19] Annie Furuhjelm especially appreciated that Finland was allowed to affiliate with the new IWSA because her native country was then controlled by Russia.

Between the official organizational meeting in Berlin in 1904 and Catt's trip around the world to promote the association in 1911, the IWSA met four times. New member organizations joined each time. The Danish affiliate, Danske Kvindesamfund, hosted the second meeting at Copenhagen in 1906. Twelve countries were represented by delegates from suffrage societies.[20] In addition, Australia, Canada, Hungary, Italy, Russia, France, Finland, and Iceland were represented by fraternal delegates.[21] Susan B. Anthony had died recently, so the first order of business was to pay tribute to the woman who had devoted more than fifty years of her life to fighting for women's rights.[22] Then Catt followed Anthony's example and reported on women's recent triumphs and defeats.

On May 26, 1906 (hardly a year after they joined the IWSA), Finland awarded women universal suffrage, the first European nation to do so. The victory was celebrated in Copenhagen that August. Russian women had not fared as well. Their hopes had been dashed when the Duma was dissolved.[23]

The new IWSA celebrated accomplishments of individual women as well. Marie Curie showed her radium to a packed lecture hall.[24] She had just been appointed to the position left vacant by her deceased husband at the Sorbonne. Also, the IWSA publication, *Jus Suffragii,* was initiated with Martina Kramers of The Netherlands as the editor. In the first issue published that September, they announced that Danish women gained municipal suffrage after the conference.

This colorful meeting was long remembered as women from Iceland paraded in their national costume—long black dresses and white head-veils held in place by golden crowns. Briet Bjarnhedinsdottir had organized the women by riding her pony from one farm to another. She persuaded the solitary women of the need to unite to obtain higher status and full citizenship.[25] She also founded a women's newspaper, and by 1902 the women had gained municipal eligibility.

However, divisive issues also arose at that second meeting, especially between competing English suffrage organizations. The conservative Millicent Garrett Fawcett (whose NUWSS was a charter member) objected when the more radical Women's Social and Political Union requested membership.[26] In England, Fawcett's conservative National Union of Women's Suffrage Societies was being overshadowed by the more militant WSPU founded by Emmeline and Christabel Pankhurst in 1903. The Pankhursts' tactics had been influenced by the Irish activist, Eva Gore Booth.[27] The WSPU also learned from Irish leader Charles Stewart Parnell the tactic of opposing all incumbent government candidates at elections. What became the women's much publicized "keep the Government out" policy was a tactic later attempted in Alice Paul's National Woman's Party campaigns in the United States and by Japanese suffragists.[28] Fawcett reluctantly acknowledged that the WSPU possibly contributed to the advancement of the women's cause by reporting it to a wider public.[29] As a compromise, the militant organization was admitted as a fraternal delegate.

Irish women's militancy began in 1908 when Hanna Sheehy Skeffington and Margaret Cousins founded the Irish Women's Franchise League (IWFL).[30] Rosemary Cullen Owens has chronicled the militant struggles of English and Irish women that led to their being incarcerated in one another's countries on occasion. Some English fled to Ireland to avoid being recaptured under the Cat and Mouse Act. Although this law was also in effect in Ireland, the Irish goals were preferable because the Irish public did not favor forced feeding. In both countries, women campaigned to be treated as political prisoners rather than ordinary criminals. Emmeline Pankhurst made several visits to Ireland during the early years of the militant Irish movement. She was very popular until the relationship soured when the WSPU tried to take over the Irish suffrage movement.[31] Although the British Parliament also regulated the rights of Irish women, they insisted on representation separate from their English counterparts.

When the third IWSA congress was held in Amsterdam in 1908, English delegates reported that women's suffrage organizations continued to proliferate, and Charlotte Despard had founded the Women's Freedom League. Violence was escalating, and the IWSA passed a resolution that condemned "any government which classes the women suffragists imprisoned for agitation for the vote as common lawbreakers instead of as political offenders."[32]

The increasing prestige of the IWSA was reflected as official government delegates came from Australia, Norway, and the United States.[33]

In all, sixteen nations participated. The four new affiliates were: Bulgaria, Finland, South Africa, and Switzerland. Five other countries sent fraternal delegates. Individuals reported on women's rights activities in Greece, Serbia, Turkey, and Japan. This Amsterdam meeting introduced Carrie Chapman Catt to Rosa Manus, who became Catt's loyal follower and friend. In a eulogy written forty years later, Catt recalled how she met Manus early the first day when the young page was waiting to help the representatives who wanted to see the sights of Amsterdam. As Catt recalled, "I went to the hall at an early hour every morning, and always found her there prepared for her special work."[34] Despite a generation's difference in their ages, it was the beginning of a long, close friendship.

Catt's opening speech celebrated the fact that nineteen Finnish women had been elected to Parliament. Also, the limited franchise given to women in Norway in 1901 had been extended in 1907, although a tax-paying qualification was maintained.[35] The members agreed to send a message of sympathy to Russian women in general and a special message to Professor Petrovitchski in particular. She had been imprisoned after she advocated women's rights.

European countries could also report some progress. German law had been revised so that women could join political associations, and Berlin University admitted women students. Austrian and Bohemian women were still legally prevented from forming political associations, but both countries had active women's committees, as did France. Italy had held its first women's congress.[36] Among the new nations represented, the Bulgarian delegates reported that the university at Sofia was again closed to women after it had been open for four years. However, they had objected in a widely circulated publication and sent petitions to Parliament to demand their rights. The South African delegates said they were trying to educate women to the need for suffrage. From Switzerland a Miss Honeeger reported that the Swiss pride in being the foremost democracy in Europe had impeded women's fight for equal rights.[37]

Because Millicent Garrett Fawcett invited the IWSA to hold their Quinquennial Congress in London in 1909, only a year elapsed between meetings. Even so, new suffrage societies were affiliated from Austria, Belgium, Bohemia, and France. Fraternal delegates came from Serbia and New Zealand as well as two men's societies from England and Holland.[38] Catt's opening speech celebrated the bravery of Russian women. Despite government suppression, they had managed to hold a congress in St. Petersburg and pass a resolution against capital punishment. The situation of Finnish women had regressed under Russian tyranny. Women had paraded and petitioned in Canada and some American states, and South African women were campaigning for their rights. The IWSA decided to remain neutral on all questions that were strictly national.[39]

In England, the suffragettes' increasing militancy attracted delegates who wanted to see what the press had been reporting. The highlight of the London Congress was a procession of sixty-three groups of women in various occupations that ranged from doctors and cotton mill workers to a group of chain-makers from Staffordshire. Speakers like Emmeline Pankhurst, Emmeline Pethick Lawrence, and Charlotte Despard told of their prison experiences. Lady Constance Lytton particularly inspired the audience. To avoid privileged treatment, she had given her name as Jane Warton, sempstress, when she entered prison. Another barrier was crossed when a special suffrage sermon was preached at St. Paul's Cathedral, the first time the Church of England had officially acknowledged the movement.[40]

Among the suffragists, Emmeline Pankhurst, Emmeline Pethick Lawrence, and Annie Kenney were invited to speak in the United States and Europe after the congress. According to Schreiber and Mathieson, the militants' speaking skills and gentle appearance on the lecture circuit counteracted press accounts of them as "criminal monsters" and "unnatural beings." Their favorable public reaction expanded the membership of national suffrage organizations and promoted the international affiliation.

Overall, the IWSA doubled its membership between the London Congress and the next one in Stockholm, Sweden, in 1911.[41] Catt arrived for that meeting just in time to hear a male university professor proclaim that the woman suffrage movement had passed its climax. She refuted this in her opening speech. With Iceland and Serbia, a total of twenty-four countries were affiliated. Catt reworded the boast of the British Empire to contend that the sun never set on woman suffrage activity and recounted the progress since the last meeting. Women had received the vote in the state of Washington. In Norway the enfranchised women decided not to form a separate political party. In Portugal one woman had gained the right to vote. Carolina Angelo, a physician, had tried to vote after she discovered that the new constitution did not forbid it. After she was turned away, Angelo appealed to the highest court and was upheld; so she was the only woman in Portugal who had equal political rights with men. A suffrage organization had since been formed to seek the same rights for other women. Serbian women were legally permitted to vote in municipal elections, but they were still being denied on the basis of custom.

Ten male delegates represented six countries, and a Swedish Men's League was established as well as an International Men's League for Woman Suffrage.[42] As the IWSA progressed in the suffrage campaign, like the ICW, they began to take stands on other issues. Even so, the IWSA decided not to pass any resolution because women in the labor force were paid less than men and were widely discriminated against in other ways. They did acknowledge that many women were forced into prostitution because they could not earn a living otherwise.[43] While new participants in the Stockholm Conference demonstrated the growth of the international women's movement, Catt would soon add to the expansion by carrying word of the IWSA to women in more countries around the world.

11

CATT'S WORLD TOUR

Because she was ill and overworked after the Stockholm Conference, Carrie Chapman Catt's physician recommended that she relax. He probably did not have in mind an arduous two-year trip around the world. However, Catt decided "to survey the status of women and to organize NWSA's where non-existent."[1] Aletta Jacobs decided to accompany her to see to Catt's health. Jacobs was a distinguished fellow suffragist and very independent, so some of their close associates expressed doubt that the two could accommodate to one another sufficiently to remain friends and complete the trip. However, Jacobs was a valuable asset in Dutch-speaking countries, and Catt's later correspondence addressed to "my dear little doctor" indicated that they had managed very well.[2] Between 1911 and 1913, the two women's efforts were facilitated by missionaries and representatives of the WCTU as well as by suffragists. Catt circled the world, and Jacobs accompanied her through Africa, the Middle East, and Asia. Both women lectured to any groups that would stop to listen. They showed no mercy for fellow passengers trapped aboard ships.

The two women sailed from Southampton, England, to Madeira, and then on to Capetown, South Africa, a country with a large English-speaking population and an already well-developed woman suffrage movement among descendants of the colonial population. Upon their arrival on August 8, 1911, they stayed at a hotel Catt described as "kept by a woman born in America and a good suffragist."[3] They were royally feted, made many speeches, and patched up differences among women's groups. For instance, Catt soothed members of the Women's Enfranchisement League who thought they had been withdrawn from the Alliance. They, in turn, gave her a reception at the YWCA. Catt and Jacobs also addressed a public meeting sponsored by the Citizens League.

At Port Elizabeth, Catt spoke to suffrage groups and the WCTU. As she tried to cement ties with this organization, Catt was unable to accompany Jacobs to visit the famous South African suffragist, Olive Schreiner.[4] Despite their efforts to be conciliatory, the women were not always well received. At Kimberly the mayor's wife professed to be shocked and horrified at Catt's speech.[5] In Johannesburg, Catt was entertained by the Martha Washington Club, where she tried to lessen the ill will between members of two suffrage clubs. She struggled to get both

Aletta Jacobs, suffragist and birth control leader. Reprinted with permission from the International Information Centre and Archives for the Women's Movement, Amsterdam, The Netherlands.

groups to elect delegates for a national suffrage convention in Durban that culminated Catt's visit to South Africa.[6]

   She also met with Mahandas K. Gandhi, who would subsequently play a significant part in India's bid for independence. In 1911, Gandhi was just becoming recognized. He developed his nonviolent tactics in the struggle on behalf of the Indian minority in South Africa between 1897 and 1914. He claimed he learned these tactics from the British suffragettes.[7] Two years after Catt left, substantial numbers of Indian women became emboldened to join his protest after the Supreme Court of South Africa declared all Hindu, Muslim, and Parsi marriages invalid. In light of rising opposition, the government finally met Gandhi's demands to recognize nonchristian marriages.[8]

Catt kept a journal in which she commented freely on what she saw. She also pasted in postcards and local English language newspaper accounts of their visits. Some of these notes were rough and others more polished, retyped by a secretary years later. As she traveled, Catt also wrote articles for feminist publications and sent accounts to *The Woman Citizen* and *Jus Suffragii*.

Back aboard ship, Catt summarized their eleven weeks in South Africa. They had gone 4,000 miles by train, 11,000 by ship, and visited nine major cities. Catt made a total of forty-five speeches, attended seven receptions and eighteen luncheons as well as fourteen afternoon teas, three morning teas, six dinners, three picnics, and twelve committee meetings. She spent thirty-six days on sightseeing and travel. During the forty days spent with suffragists, Catt averaged nearly two events each day.[9]

The suffragists' next stop was the Middle East: Israel, Syria, and Lebanon. In Jerusalem, they visited an American colony led by a Mrs. Spofford, whom Catt described as a sweet-faced, spiritual woman who feared that woman suffrage "may unsex women."[10] Catt's reputation often preceded her. Mrs. Osterheld, "a good suffragist of Yonkers" also on a trip around the world, brought Catt a magazine printed in Arabic. An article by a young Druse woman described the organization of the International Woman Suffrage Alliance and was illustrated with Catt's picture. Until she reached Cairo, Egypt, Catt did not organize any suffrage associations in that region.[11] Muslim women were hesitant to embrace this western organization, but many were working to improve their own circumstances.[12] Older women bemoaned their lack of education and took pride in the fact that their daughters could read. One said she had been married at ten and had given birth to her first child before she was twelve. She did not know about the movement for women to unveil in Constantinople. But she informed Catt that only custom, nothing in the Koran, compelled women to wear veils.[13]

After they left Cairo, Catt and Jacobs spent eleven days aboard a Dutch ship bound for Colombo, Sri Lanka. En route, the other passengers were thoroughly lectured (by Catt in English and Jacobs in Dutch) on woman suffrage. Although they traveled to the interior of Sri Lanka and back to the coast, they were not able to form any suffragist organizations.[14] In India, as in the Middle East, they were most impressed with the progress being made to educate women despite the restraints of religion and tradition.

They visited Annie Besant's Hindu School in Madras and learned about theosophy.[15] Catt concluded that true feminists must feel a sense of gratitude toward Besant for establishing these schools.[16] Besant had first gone to India in 1893 after she attended the Parliament of Religions at the Chicago World's Columbian Exposition. She was just beginning to assert herself in Indian politics. She subsequently became the first woman president of the Indian National Congress. After Catt left, Besant attracted an Irish feminist, Margaret Cousins, to emigrate to India in 1913. With Besant, she was a founding member of the Indian Women's Association in 1917 and later became the first woman magistrate in India.[17] When Besant proposed a system of education for India, local men helped educate girls and women in some cases. In Varanasi where Besant founded a school for Hindu boys, some of them volunteered their time to conduct a school for little girls. In Bombay, male lawyers, doctors, and teachers taught without pay in an overcrowded girls' school.

Catt was not as popular with missionaries as Leavitt had been earlier. Her feminism had been tolerated because of her dedication to Christianity and abstinence. However, missionaries were often not sympathetic to Catt. Although she also lectured for the WCTU when she was invited, her focus was clearly on women's suffrage. In Bombay, Dr. Benson, head of the Cama Hospital for Women and Children, could tell them little about the women's movement in India. Nevertheless, she put them in touch with important Hindu women and took them to a purdah party given by an English hostess. At a women's club, they met Mrs. S. G. Ranaday, a Hindu reformer whom Catt called "as much of a feminist as I am."[18] They also learned that one Indian woman published a women's newspaper and another, Cornelia Sorabji, was practicing law.[19] Millicent Garrett Fawcett had assisted Sorabji when she came to England to study law,[20] a profession that was not open to English women at the time.[21]

The progress of a few women in India did not prepare them for Rangoon, Myanmar, where women of Hindu, Muslim, Parsi, and Buddhist faiths all voted in municipal elections. The survival of matriarchal customs also permitted them to control their property, conduct trade, have bank accounts, sue in the law courts, choose and divorce their husbands, and keep their own names after marriage. In addition, half the retail trade was transacted by women.[22]

In Sumatra, Catt and Jacobs visited a matriarchal society where women had lost power after they converted to Islam. Jacobs' sister was a local pharmacist and suffragist in Indonesia, and Jacobs outshined Catt in what was then the Dutch East Indies.[23] During their two-month stay, she lectured in Dutch and formed many suffrage groups around Sumatra and Java. About four hundred new members were added to the Dutch Suffrage Association.[24] Catt did not understand Dutch and was bored with the meetings. In Indonesia she also was angered that native princesses educated in Dutch schools would be taken out at age twelve to marry men they had never met. After that, they could not appear in public. Usually opposed to violence, Catt concluded that "If breaking windows could liberate our sex, we ought to smash every one in the world."[25]

They saw women with bound feet for the first time when they stopped at Makassar on the island of Sulawesi. Next they went to the Philippines. Under American control, the women there had no suffrage. Nor had any of them been elected to councils or parliament. After Catt addressed the Fortnightly Club in that warm climate, she wrote in her journal that "If the women went home as full of convictions as my garments were of perspiration, it was a success."[26] The suffragists' visit was well publicized in English language newspapers. An editorial of July 13, 1912, in *The Manilla Times* indicated that the time was not ripe for woman suffrage yet. "However, let not us deter; it would be diverting whether practical or not."[27] Catt concluded that the American women were afraid of organization and the Filipinas were afraid of men's ridicule, so both were "of rather weak fiber." She still was able to found a Society for the Advancement of Women with eight officers, half American and half Filipina.[28]

In Macao, Catt wrote of the good-natured boat women who manipulated little water taxis around the harbor: "They don't care a flip about what anyone thinks of them, least of all men."[29] After a year on the road, the high point of their trip was still ahead of them. At Canton (now Guangzhou, China) when they visited missionaries, Catt noted that "The usual inhospitable air pervaded the place when we asked our questions."[30] In contrast, the revolutionary government assembly called by Dr. Sun Yat Sen was in session and included six women members.[31] The two suffragists were thrilled to look down from the gallery upon women who actually served in this provincial governing body.[32] Catt's friend and biographer, Mary Gray Peck, wrote that to Catt "belongs the honor of having established connection between their movement at this momentous and critical period and the movement in the Western world."[33] At that point the Chinese women were leading the way.

In Shanghai, the American Woman's Club entertained Catt, although they were not enthusiastic about suffrage.[34] On the other hand, the Chinese feminists welcomed Catt and Jacobs royally. Many Chinese had attended college in the United States, and they had formed a Women's Cooperative Association.[35] Catt invited them to join the IWSA, and the Chinese women made a silk banner to present at the next meeting. In large Chinese characters embroidered in white on scarlet satin was the motto, "Helping each other, all of one mind."[36] Catt wrote in her journal, "Really this day has been one of the happiest of my life—now I have shaken the hands of Mohammedan, Hindu, Buddhist and Confucian suffragists, and I've seen many a Christian missionary show contempt for the cause and her own ignorance."[37]

In Nanjing the president of the Women's Tung Ming Hui, Captain Wu Moh-lun, quickly arranged for the visiting suffragists to address the local organization.[38] The Chinese women had proven their bravery when they fought for the revolution. They had formed "Dare to Die Clubs" and demanded the vote.[39] However, after the revolution, only men were permitted to vote for members of the Nanking Provisional Assembly, so The Woman Suffrage Union continued the battle.[40] Although Sun Yat-sen had declared himself in favor of national woman suffrage, not long after Catt left, he compromised it away as various groups united into the National Party, the Kuomintang.

The two suffragists made their last Asian stop in Tokyo, Japan, where they visited Ume Tsuda's school for girls. In 1871 under an Imperial rescript, Tsuda had been one of five Japanese girls sent to study in America. Age seven at the time, Tsuda stayed eleven years before she returned to found a women's college in Tokyo.[41] She became an important liaison between Japanese and American women as time went on. Catt and Jacobs also toured the Yoshiwara quarter. Women had been kept in sexual slavery in this famous old red light district for centuries, and their visit added ammunition for the suffragists to continue the fight against legalized prostitution.[42] They also met with sixteen Japanese ladies who were not ready to "Dare to Die." Catt did get "the promise of a report—and perhaps of a delegate to the next IWSA conference."[43] This promise would not be fulfilled until eight years later. From Tokyo, Jacobs returned to Holland on the TransSiberian Railroad, and Catt sailed for Hawaii. Although she was only there two days, with the help of a descendant of the old Hawaiian Royal Family, she organized a suffrage society composed mainly of indigenous Hawaiian women.[44] On her way to San Francisco, she summed up the trip:

We have made suffrage speeches to audiences on four continents: America, Europe, Africa, Asia, and on the ships of three oceans. Our audiences have included the followers of every main religion, Christian and Jew, Moham-medan, Hindu, Parsee, Buddhist, Confucian, and Shinto, and representatives of all the main human races: Aryan, Semitic, Negro, Malay, Polynesian, Mongolian. We have left the seeds of revolution behind us, and the hope of liberty in many souls. But we have got much more than we gave—an experience so upsetting to all our preconceived notions that it is difficult to estimate its influence upon us.[45]

At the end of her two years of foreign travel, Catt was ready to apply what she had learned and welcome new members to further the goals of the IWSA. She prepared for the 1913 meeting in Budapest, Hungary, the largest meeting to date, but also the last before World War I.

12

THE IWSA:
WORLD EXPANSION

Four more American states had given women the vote by the time Catt returned to the forty-fourth annual National American Woman Suffrage Association convention in Philadelphia. She and Jane Addams both spoke on the need for political power to combat prostitution.[1] Afterwards, Catt observed but did not approve of the British suffragettes' rising militancy when she went to London for the IWSA board meeting.[2] In her call for the Seventh Congress of the International Woman Suffrage Alliance at Budapest, she boasted that "For the first time in the woman movement, it is expected that Hindu, Buddhist, Confucian, Mohammedan, Jewish, and Christian women will sit together in a Congress uniting their voices in a common plea for the liberation of their sex from those artificial discriminations which every political and religious system has directed against them."[3]

Rosika Schwimmer organized the Hungarian congress and was able to attract a large number of prominent women. In addition, meetings were held in other countries to host foreign guests on their way to Budapest. Berlin had become a center of the German movement led by Anita Augspurg, Lida Gustava Heymann, and Minna Causer. Prague was described as a "turmoil of activity." The Austrian government was trying to suppress the right to vote and eligibility to the Bohemian Diet, which the women had possessed since 1861. Mrs. Vikova-Kuneticka had been elected, but the governor had refused confirmation. Viennese women welcomed the visiting international delegates, although they did not have the right to form political associations.[4]

At the 1913 Congress, as Catt reported on her travels, many members of the world's press heard her announce that "With the exception of the Spanish American Republics, there are in the entire world only seven constitutionally organized, independent nations without an organized woman suffrage movement."[5] Twenty-two of the twenty-six member countries sent delegates. Among the new groups were a Polish Women's Society from Galicia and others from Portugal and Rumania. Due to Catt's and Jacobs' recent trip, this was the first Congress to hear reports from some parts of Asia. Women's movements were described in Egypt, Palestine, Turkey, Persia, Sri Lanka, India, Myanmar, China, Japan, Sumatra, Java, the Philippines, and Hawaii.[6]

In her presidential address, Catt described the influence of religion in Asia. The great religions—Brahminism, Buddhism, Confucianism, and Taoism—all denied that seclusion and oppression of women were part of their dogma. They blamed the Muslims. However, Catt cited a Turkish princess, an Arabic scholar, who had studied the Koran and proclaimed that nothing in it demanded women's seclusion. Although Chinese women had long been suppressed as wives and concubines, Catt could report that they were elected members of the provincial assembly in Guangzhou. This bolstered her confidence that the women's movement would succeed in China.[7] Consequently, that nation's suffrage movement was admitted to membership, although no representatives attended the congress.

The meeting generated substantial publicity because a number of well-known women participated. From America came Jane Addams and Charlotte Perkins Gilman plus Anna Howard Shaw. Shaw was already well-known for her preaching and also for being president of the NAWSA. From Great Britain came Helena Swanwick and Kathleen Courtney. Swedish pioneers Anna Wicksell and Ellen Hagen were there as well as Fru Quam of Norway, Briet Bjarnhedinsdottir of Iceland, Tersita Pasita of Italy, Marguerite de Witt Schlumberger and Maria Verone of France, Nina Boyle of South Africa, and Emilie Gourd of Switzerland. The International Men's League for Woman Suffrage also held large meetings and received representatives of the Hungarian Government and Budapest City Council. Georg de Lukacs, Hungarian Cabinet Minister, presided and Keir Hardie, the Scottish labor leader, participated. The delegates described their national women's rights movements. For example, in Rumania Mrs. de Reuss Jancoulesco reported that women had the same rights as men in the universities. Yet even though the country boasted one woman lawyer and three university professors, under the Code Napoleon, women had no right to property or earnings.[8]

Although universal woman suffrage was the primary objective of the IWSA, they, like the ICW, increasingly championed other women's rights causes as well. With the Yoshiwara district still on Catt's mind, social purity was a major agenda item in 1913. Although Millicent Garrett Fawcett had been reluctant to join Josephine Butler's campaign against the Contagious Diseases Acts thirty years earlier, she chaired the session on the White Slave Traffic. In 1927 she even wrote a biography of Butler.[9] Catt called on Alliance members to ask their governments to demand an international inquiry into the extent and cause of commercialized vice and to include women on the committee.[10] Of the approximately 400 delegates, many pledged funding to help the IWSA. They also accepted an invitation by the Italian society to meet with the International Council of Women in Rome the following May and join in a suffrage demonstration.

The good will lasted only a short time during 1913. The impending war and related peace movement created dissension among the members. Even so, the participants remained optimistic about holding another IWSA meeting despite the clear threats of war. Within the organization and at home, the British continued to disagree on tactics. Catt persuaded the IWSA to adopt a special resolution in support of the Pankhursts' militant WSPU. Fawcett and other conservative British suffragists could not have greeted this with enthusiasm.[11] Also in Budapest, the ailing Martina Kramers was replaced as editor of *Jus Suffragii*. The extension of the organization's international affiliations was demonstrated as the new editor, Mary Sheepshanks, soon appealed for translators in Czech, Polish, Icelandic, Norwegian, and Danish.[12] Through Sheepshanks, isolated members were able to maintain some contact during World War I.

With the IWSA in wartime suspension, Catt took back the presidency of the NAWSA from Anna Howard Shaw in 1916. After they lost the New York state suffrage campaign, Catt reorganized and instituted the national plan that finally culminated in the passage of the Nineteenth Amendment in 1919. Even before it passed, Catt founded the League of Women Voters to replace the NAWSA and shift priorities from suffrage to education for more effective citizenship.

The IWSA did not meet again until 1920. Woman suffrage was still one state away from ratification in the United States when Catt took time out to attend the Eighth Congress of the International Woman Suffrage Association that June.[13] By the time she sent out the call for this meeting, the situation of many women had changed dramatically. More countries than ever were represented, and women in ten had been elected to parliaments. Four new auxiliaries were added: Greece, Spain, Argentina, and Uruguay. The last two were the first Latin American countries to join.[14]

Although the Chinese did not arrive in time for the conference, Japan and India were represented.[15] Tsume Gauntlett, a Japanese participant, was married to a British man. She later became the president of the Japanese WCTU and WILPF. At Geneva, crowds enthusiastically greeted Gauntlett and her fellow delegate, Michi Kawai, as they did the Indian delegate, Sarojini Naidu, a friend of Annie Besant's and a leader in the Indian fight for independence from Great Britain. Speeches by the new members demonstrated similar problems among eastern and western women.[16]

In the postwar era, many governments sent distinguished women as official delegates. Marie Stritt, the longtime president of the German Woman Suffrage Society, was one of these. Since the war, Austria and Germany were republics with equal political rights specified in their constitutions. Thirty-nine women were in the National Assembly and 155 in the Diets. The Netherlands had also granted women eligibility to be elected to government posts in 1916, and men had elected two women to Parliament. Suffrage was granted to Dutch women in 1919, as it was to women in Denmark, Canada, British East Africa, Hungary, Iceland, Rhodesia, and Sweden. Luxembourg not only gave women the vote, but fined them if they did not use it.[17] All in all, women in twenty-one countries had been enfranchised for a total of twenty-five. Oddly enough, nothing was reported about Russian women who had received the vote in the 1917 revolution, before the British or the Americans.

Newly enfranchised women came forward to tell their stories. Women over thirty could vote in Great Britain, and Viscountess Astor (an American) was the first woman MP to take her seat in Parliament.[18] Some gains were quite unexpected. The wife of the president of Crimea reported that Muslim women had received suffrage when her country gained independence.[19] The new nations of Latvia, Estonia, and Lithuania also legalized equal suffrage rights, and five women MPs had been elected in each. In Poland, the Ukraine, and Czechoslovakia, women also had suffrage. In the latter country, sixteen women sat in the two houses of Parliament.[20]

Despite the gains, the long years of war had taken their toll on the international spirit of cooperation so evident in Budapest in 1913. The Belgian delegation refused to work with the Germans and did not attend. The French would come only if the German delegation apologized for war atrocities. A peace meeting was arranged by Swiss delegate, Emilie Gourd. Then Adele Schreiber-Krieger, a German member of parliament, pointed out that women in neither country had any political influence on the conduct of the war. The French accepted her declaration as an apology and agreed that women everywhere needed to cooperate to maintain peace.[21] So hostility gradually eased among women from nations formerly at war.

As the delegates restored more cordial relationships, new strategies had to be formulated. Some women from nations with suffrage concluded that their task was finished. However, more resolved to work to enfranchise women everywhere and to promote equal liberties, status, and opportunities. The work was divided into two sections—one for enfranchised and the other for unenfranchised countries. Then a program of reform was drawn up to achieve real equality.[22] Committees were established to collect information on the nationality of married women, women's right to work and equal pay, the care of married and unmarried mothers and their children, moral standards, the restraint of prostitution, and efforts to combat venereal disease.

Foremost among the postwar developments was the initiation of the League of Nations. The women had chosen Geneva, Switzerland, where the new League was being established to hold their first postwar meeting because they recognized the importance of the new world organization. Through the efforts of a newly formed liaison committee of women's organizations and the support of some powerful men, the League of Nations charter stipulated that the Council, Assembly, Commissions, and Secretariat were open to women equally with men, an important international precedent.[23] As women's organizations also received consultantship status as nongovernmental organizations, the IWSA Congress expanded their objectives. They recommended that the League summon a conference of women to consider questions about their welfare and status. Margery Corbett Ashby was appointed special secretary to work for this agenda.[24]

Like the pioneers Anthony and Stanton, the second generation suffragists were gradually being displaced as new vistas were opened. Anna Howard Shaw, former NAWSA president, died in America in 1919, after woman suffrage was passed, but before it was ratified. Shaw had been the first woman invited to preach in a number of European churches, and women paid her special tribute by preaching in Geneva.[25] Catt again tried to resign, but she was persuaded to continue as president. Then she mapped out a world strategy. Women from the countries with the vote would help those without. In this division of labor, the United States would organize women in Jamaica, Cuba, and South America. The latter was the only continent where no women could vote, and Catt resolved to conduct her own campaign.[26] However, three years would elapse before she could make the trip.

First she returned to the United States to rally support for ratification of the woman suffrage amendment in the Tennessee legislature. The Susan B. Anthony amendment became law on August 13, 1920, but the taste of victory was short-lived. When Catt criticized the American government for not joining the League of Nations, a number of women resigned from the League of Women Voters.[27] Less than four months after she was hailed as a heroine for winning the vote, Catt was denounced by former friends.[28]

Millicent Garrett Fawcett knew the feeling, and she stood by Catt. During the IWSA Board meeting in London at the end of November 1920, Fawcett presided over a party to celebrate the American victory. She had stepped down from leadership of the NUWSS in 1918 after British women over age thirty were given the vote. As the two aging leaders savored their success, Catt recalled that the women's movement in Great Britain and America had traveled "along on strangely parallel lines, one country shooting forward at intervals and then the other."[29] British women did not attain equal suffrage with men until 1928.

The international women's movement came into a small monetary bonanza in 1921. Mrs. Frank Leslie bequeathed her fortune to support the woman suffrage battle in the United States in 1914. However, that campaign was won by the time the estate was finally settled. As Catt was named the sole beneficiary, she could award grants to the IWSA to continue the global battle.[30] To arouse South American women to fight for suffrage, a Pan-American women's conference was held just before the League of Women Voters national convention in Baltimore, Maryland, in April 1922. Eighty-five women from twenty-two countries met for three days, and the Pan-American Association for the Advancement of Women was organized.[31] Catt agreed to be president and visit South America to report on the status of women there.[32] First, she returned to London where the ICW and the IWSA held a joint planning session but decided not to merge.[33] However, the IWSA was allotted three voting delegates to the ICW Seventh Quinquennial scheduled for Washington, D.C., in 1925.

In 1923 Catt finally sailed to South America with Rosa Manus and two women from Southampton, England. They were far better received than Mary Clement Leavitt had been thirty years earlier. Not only had delegates from Argentina and Uruguay attended the 1920 IWSA meeting in Geneva, but the International Council of Women had affiliated organizations in various countries. Most important, however, were the contacts made at the Pan-American Conference in Baltimore in 1922. As the deliberately temperate ambassador of international feminism, Catt was well received by government officials as well as conservative women's groups.[34] She was treated almost like royalty as she went from one South American country to another. As she built support for local and international woman suffrage movements, her contacts were divided between resident foreign women and local citizens.

At Rio de Janeiro, their first port of call, they were met by Bertha Lutz, a delegate to the Baltimore meeting. Her Association for the Advancement of Women organized a Congress of Women of Brazil and formed the Brazilian Woman Suffrage Association.[35] It affiliated with the IWSA the next year.[36] Two decades later, Lutz played a major role as a delegate to the United Nations Organizational meeting at San Francisco. When Catt left Brazil after a three-week lecture tour, she was welcomed in Buenos Aires, Argentina, by branches of both the IWSA and ICW.[37, 38] Conservative but competitive women in Argentina were willing to join the Pan American Association for the Advancement of Women, but not to form an auxiliary of the suffrage movement. They wanted to host the 1924 Pan American Congress largely to prevent Brazil from doing so.[39]

Like Bertha Lutz in Brazil, Catt was hosted in Uruguay and Chile by women she had met at the first Pan American Conference in Baltimore. In Montevideo, Uruguay, Isabel P. deVital, another subsequent UN delegate, greeted Catt. Their Council of Women agreed to join the Pan American Association for the Advancement of Women and create a suffrage auxiliary.[40] Catt also addressed the American Woman's Club, was given a reception at the YWCA, and gave a prohibition speech for the local WCTU.[41]

In Santiago, Chile, a Señorita Mandujano interpreted as Catt spoke to several women's organizations, including the Santiago Woman's Club. She persuaded their Council of Women to join the Pan American Association for the Advancement of Women.[42] As they left Chile, Catt wrote that "We have now finished all the countries which are classed as progressive." Even those, she concluded, were afraid of woman suffrage, and "no woman had the flame of reform in her soul." She blamed women's lack of progress and leadership on the fact that South American immigrants came from the noble and upper classes, whereas North American immigrants had belonged to the oppressed classes.[43] Nevertheless, Catt underestimated them. Latin American women advanced the cause of all women when the United Nations was formed in 1945.

Over a period of six days in 1923, Catt spoke at eight women's meetings in Lima, Peru. They included the American Woman's Club.[44] Only one organization, Evolución Feminina, advocated votes for women, but a society was organized to work for civil rights. The women had less feminist sentiment than those in the other countries Catt had visited and also less education and far greater class division. Panama was better prepared. Esther de Calvo had scheduled conferences and a meeting of the new suffrage association.[45] As they embarked for Cherbourg, France, Catt was not prepared for a stop in Caracas, Venezuela. She regretted that she did not have letters of introduction to women's groups. On the other hand, she willingly avoided engagements when they docked at Trinidad because that island was British. As her friend and biographer, Mary Gray Peck, reported, "it wasn't her affair if they were slow in giving women the vote there."[46]

Overall, Catt concluded that in South America most of the chief executives approved women's enfranchisement, and each country had a small suffrage movement. However, women were more anxious to gain liberal laws and economic opportunities.[47] She had faith that women with more education would become informed and demand equal rights. Catt summed up their trip for her loyal traveling companion, Rosa Manus, by stating: "We have interviewed six presidents of Republics, been received officially by committees from two Congresses, visited eight Parliaments, and I have made thirty-four public speeches which have been interpreted into seven different languages."[48] She fondly recalled Lima, Peru, where they met at the University of San Marco, established in 1551. That they could preach women's rights in that old Jesuit Convent, she contended, was the best measure of women's progress.

Even so, Catt told the Leslie Commission she was not optimistic that the caliber of women needed to win suffrage was available in South America. The close connection between religion and politics would impede their progress. Moreover, a successful movement would require frequent meetings, but difficulties of travel and lack of money would hamper the most capable women. Catt had also become sensitized to the fact that Latin women resented the efforts of North Americans to control everything. She adopted the suggestion of the President of the Chilean Council of Women that Brazil, Uruguay, Argentina, and Chile form an association because they were at about the same level of development and connected by a fair transportation system.[49] Paraguay could be added to this group because of its location.

Mexico could join the northern countries of Central America in Catt's plan. Panama could unite the northern countries of South America: Venezuela, Ecuador, Bolivia, and Peru. With this proposal to organize the continent in place, the second Pan American Congress for the Advancement of Women was scheduled in Buenos Aires in May 1924. Because the South American women tended to be conservative, Catt favored the National Council of Women as an affiliate with the United States instead of the League of Women Voters.[50] Although Catt did not achieve her ambitious plan to visit all of the countries of Central America on her first visit, she subsequently traveled to Havana in 1924 as the guest of Cuban women's organizations.[51]

From South America, Catt went directly to Rome for the Ninth IWSA Congress in May 1923. Italy had only recently fallen under the Fascist regime of Benito Mussolini. Therefore, Rome had been chosen for this conference to rally Italian women and try to improve their chances of getting suffrage. The number of countries with affiliated societies had risen from twenty-eight in Geneva to thirty-eight in Rome. That year the IWSA also added thirteen new auxiliaries.[52] With fraternal and government delegates, forty-three nations were represented. At least seventeen new societies joined there. Official delegates came for the first time from Brazil, Egypt, India, Ireland, Jamaica, Newfoundland, and Palestine.

By then, equal suffrage had been granted in Ireland, in the Indian states of Bombay, Madras, Travancore, Jahalwar, and Cochin, and in Myanmar. Among other gains, Danish women received equal pay in government service, and Japanese women had won the right to attend political meetings. The legal profession had opened to women in Argentina, Austria, Belgium, Germany, India, Portugal, and Spain. The United States had given married women the right to determine their own nationality.[53]

In addition to suffrage, much of the business of the IWSA was conducted in four committees: equal pay and the right to work, equal moral standards, nationality of married women, and status of wives and mothers. They agreed on married women's right to work, but the struggle over protective legislation was already underway. The Congress resolved:

That the right to work of all women be recognized, and no obstacle placed in the way of married women who desire to work; that no special regulations for women's work, different from regulations for men, should be imposed contrary to the wishes of the women concerned; that laws relative to women as mothers should be so framed as not to handicap them in their economic position, and that all future labour regulations should tend toward equality for men and women.[54]

The committee for an equal moral standard agreed that sex education was needed for the young and that brothels should be abolished. They were less unified on notification about and treatment of venereal disease. However, the Congress also drafted new resolutions that opposed slavery and child marriage, and they added a new committee on illegitimate children.[55]

Twenty-one countries sent delegates to an Enfranchised Women's Day. Their activities, especially the first woman suffrage procession in Rome, had an impact on Mussolini. His opening remarks were quite supportive: "the Italian public spirit and the tendency of our policy offer no preconceived opposition to the enfranchisement of women." He suggested that if nothing unforeseen happened, women could be extended the right to vote in stages.[56] This was the first breakthrough among Latin nations.[57] Schreiber and Mathieson say that Mussolini at first only hinted that he might grant some political rights to widows and mothers of those who had given their lives for their country.[58] After he heard Catt's opening speech and saw the impressive procession of women, however, Mussolini became more specific and pledged municipal suffrage for Italian women.

Catt had led the IWSA for its entire twenty-one years, and she insisted on resigning in Rome. Her accomplishments had been many. At its founding in 1904, only four of the United States, New Zealand, and the Isle of Man permitted woman suffrage. In 1923 women had equal suffrage in twenty-five nations and six Indian states, the first country in Asia to grant suffrage. Worldwide, women were on the march for equality, and Catt's leadership had done much to bring them together. Like Susan B. Anthony before her, Catt became Honorary President as she was succeeded by Margery Corbett Ashby.[59] But Catt was far from retirement. Freed of the presidency of the IWSA, she concentrated on peace, the cause she regarded as most important of all.

13

MARGERY CORBETT ASHBY AND THE IWSA
THROUGH WORLD WAR II

Freed of her presidential responsibilities in the IWSA, Carrie Chapman Catt maintained her ties and promoted the peace movement within the organization. She attended none of the five meetings held in the twenty years from 1926 to 1946, but Catt sent supportive messages to be read at each congress. And she did return to Europe for an Alliance-sponsored peace meeting in 1927.

Between the worldwide depression of the 1930s and the rise of totalitarian regimes in Germany, Italy, and Japan, the new president and long-standing English member, Margery Corbett Ashby (1882-1981), had a difficult task as the surge of progress after World War I receded. After she accepted the presidency at Rome in 1923, she traveled, lectured, and otherwise worked energetically to expand the membership around the world. Unlike her mentor, Millicent Garrett Fawcett, who never visited the United States, Corbett Ashby eagerly reinforced the IWSA in the United States after the board meeting in Paris in 1924. Corbett Ashby spoke to the American Association of University Women in Indianapolis, Indiana, in 1925. She also attended the annual meeting of the League of Women Voters and represented the Alliance with Catt and Aletta Jacobs at the Seventh Quinquennial Congress of the International Council of Women in Washington, D.C.[1] In New York, Corbett Ashby was greeted by Virginia Gildersleeve, president of the University Women's Association. Twenty years later, Gildersleeve would be the only American woman delegate to the organizational meeting of the United Nations at San Francisco.[2]

Forty-two countries sent delegates to the Tenth Congress of the IWSA in Paris in 1926. Associations from seven more countries became members: Bermuda, Cuba, Luxembourg, Peru, Puerto Rico, Turkey, and Bosnia, "the Kingdom of Serbs, Croats and Slovenes."[3] Delegations of affiliates and fraternal organizations also attended, while Gabrielle Radziwill represented the League of Nations and Martha Mundt the ILO.[4] The name of the organization was changed to the International Alliance of Women for Suffrage and Equal Citizenship (IAW).[5] This reflected the fact that a number of supportive countries had received suffrage, and the organization was expanding its women's rights objectives.

The suffrage movement had passed the stage where politicians debated whether or not women could handle politics. Several prominent men testified to the value of the women's vote in parliament and other public affairs.[6] Even the small number in parliament could exercise a direct influence; but in unenfranchised countries, IAW member societies had to confine their activities to welfare work and winning over public opinion. They had to rely on men's good graces to extend women's rights. That meant they sometimes also regressed. In Belgium women still did not have the vote, but one antifeminist had been elected to parliament.

Where women voted, new legislation often eliminated some kinds of discrimination and raised their status. Between meetings, new property rights laws had been implemented in Australia and Denmark.[7] Czechoslovakian women had gained new laws on divorce, appointment to the teaching profession, social insurance, and inheritance rights for illegitimate children. In Great Britain women had made progress on property rights, guardianship of infants, old age pensions, and assistance to widows and orphans. A corps of women police had been recruited and an improved nationality law passed in Austria.[8] Married women were gaining the same right as men to retain or change their nationalities. Russia had been first to grant this right in 1918. The United States and Belgium followed in 1922; Rumania, Sweden, and Norway in 1924, and Austria in 1925. An IAW resolution supported the Nationality Report of a League of Nations Committee of Experts.[9]

President Corbett Ashby spoke of the diverse causes in which the IAW was active in addition to woman suffrage. Their committees worked to eliminate "superstitions, customs and laws which hamper women's free development." Among their goals were "education, equal pay for equal work, equal responsibility to the home, city, nation, and world through the League of Nations."[10] Under the leadership of Paulina Luisi of Uruguay, the equal moral standard committee issued a strongly worded statement against the double standard and laws on contagious diseases. A resolution passed on free and voluntary treatment of venereal disease, an issue upon which they had disagreed in Rome. Two new committees were also formed, one on peace and the other on the need for women police.[11] The Congress resolved that police and health authorities should be kept separate. They also opposed protective legislation and resolved that all work should be open to women. It was decided that the sole consideration regarding work should be the physical and intellectual suitability of the workers.

National delegations reinforced one another with progress reports and recollections. Egyptian delegate, Hoda Charaoui Pasha, recalled that after her first IWSA Congress at Rome, she took off her veil on the way home and never wore it again. Her association had succeeded in getting the age of marriage raised to sixteen, girls admitted to higher education, and women to the teaching profession on equal terms with men.

The Congress agreed to establish an International Bibliographical Bureau in Paris to index books and pamphlets on the women's movement.[12] They also paid tribute to Mme. de Witt Schlumberger posthumously and to Marie Curie, who was dying from radium poisoning. As they continued the close cooperation with the ICW, Ishbel Aberdeen delivered the concluding speech.[13] After this meeting, the Alliance opened a temporary office in Geneva to lobby delegates when the League of Nations Assembly was in session.[14]

When the IAW met in Germany in 1929, it was the first time it convened in a country where women were equally enfranchised with men. Delegates came from India, Peru, Uruguay, and China. Japan sent a woman lawyer, Kaneko Kitamura. Once again, The League of Nations and the ILO were also represented.[15] Among the eleven new affiliates were societies from Indonesia, Sri Lanka, and Rhodesia. Catt missed that Alliance meeting, too, but she sent a message of faith in the good that women could do.[16] President Margery Corbett Ashby observed that equality in twenty-five nations gave advantage to men, women, and their nations.[17]

As members recounted their suffrage victories, the Alliance passed resolutions on the control of prostitution, education, minimum wage, family welfare, drugs, and peace. They also formed a joint committee with the ICW to plan further cooperation. While the German people who participated were very enthusiastic, the depression was soon felt in the economy and took its toll on women. Within two years, they were relegated to menial tasks and the propagation of the race. With the advent of Hitler's government, women's organizations had to choose between rejecting all "non-Aryan" members and dissolution. The German affiliate elected to dissolve, and many leaders took refuge in foreign countries. Other IAW meetings were smaller. In March 1930, Chrystal Macmillan led a joint demonstration with the International Council of Women at The Hague in connection with the Hague Nationality Convention.

Due to the international depression, the IAW canceled the next congress scheduled for Athens in 1933.[18] Instead, presidents of affiliated societies met at Marseilles to discuss economic and other problems. In addition to the Board meetings, they also held public sessions on suffrage, the traffic in women, peace and disarmament. Delegates from twenty-four countries reaffirmed the policies and supported universal woman suffrage, equality of moral standards, economic, and civil rights. The maintenance of peace was recognized as the necessary basis for effective work. In Brussels that November, the Board agreed to hold the next congress in the Near East. Kadin Birligi invited them to Istanbul in 1935.[19]

Between congresses, the leaders strengthened their Alliance ties by personal contacts. Margery Corbett Ashby visited the United States again and then attended the All-India Women's Congress in Karachi. They discussed child marriage, the traffic in women and children, and the need for free compulsory education.[20] Then Corbett Ashby attended a large suffrage conference in Cairo. Other IAW members visited Syria, Palestine, Lebanon, Bulgaria, and Ishtambul, Turkey, where the women were preparing for the 1935 IAW Congress. When Corbett Ashby met the mayor of that city, she remarked what a pity it was "that women will come from all over the world to modern Turkey, and find Turkish women still without the vote." After President Kemal Ataturk heard about this, he granted equal suffrage. Seventeen women were serving in the Turkish Parliament by the time the IAW Congress assembled there in April 1935.[21]

This demonstrated how the presence of an international women's organization could have at least some temporary influence on local politicians, but Turkey was also experiencing a rapid transformation in other aspects of women's status. Women were given new opportunities in education, social work, and other employment, including the professions. According to Schreiber and Mathieson, their progress "was like a fairy-tale!"[22] This news was particularly heartening among women from depression-ridden nations. In Germany and Italy women's rights were being taken away. Neither nation sent delegates to the Ishtanbul Congress. Despite the depression and rising Fascism, four new societies were admitted: the Union of Patriotic Women of Persia, the Union Feministe Arabe of Syria, the Union Feministe Arabe Palestinienne, and the All-India Women's Conference.

By 1935 suffrage had been attained in Sri Lanka, Thailand, Spain, Brazil, Uruguay, and South Africa. Portugal and Behar (a Province of British India) had initiated limited suffrage. Municipal suffrage had been won in Chile, Greece, Peru, and Rumania. Even in Switzerland, 250,000 signatures (79,000 from men) had been obtained on a suffrage petition. Women had been elected to parliament for the first time in Belgium, Brazil, Sri Lanka, Newfoundland, Norway, New Zealand, and South Africa. In her speech to the Congress, Corbett Ashby listed women senators in Myanmar and Canada as well as equal rights recently won in the Irish Free State, Spain, Brazil, and Ecuador. Women were admitted to the consular and diplomatic services in Chile, Finland, and the United States.

Emilie Gourd's report showed how much Alliance activity had been directed to the League of Nations in Geneva. They had pressured that organization both as a whole and by way of individual committees. Women served on some of them. Corbett Ashby represented Great Britain at the Disarmament Conference. Poland sent Mme. Szelagowska, and Uruguay dispatched Paulina Luisi. Four other officers of the International Alliance of Women had been delegates to the Assembly and the International Labour Organization (ILO).[23]

An ILO publication on women's right to work reflected Alliance principles, but disagreement arose over protective legislation after a convention in Washington recommended that night work for women be forbidden. As a compromise, Belgium, Great Britain, and Sweden wanted to extend the time permitted or remove the restriction on women in higher grades of employment. Where working hours were already too long, however, delegates opposed this resolution. The ILO Convention finally forbade night work except for persons with posts of administrative responsibility who did not normally undertake manual labor.[24] At the same time, because of the Depression, women were particularly hard hit by unemployment. Consequently, the right of women, married as well as single, to work outside the home was reaffirmed.

The Istanbul Congress also heard a message from Eleanor Roosevelt, wife of the American president, and one from former president, Carrie Chapman Catt. She told the women to have faith and lead.[25] Catt proclaimed that the campaign for woman suffrage was about over, but she was mistaken. The current president, Margery Corbett Ashby, was more in tune with the times as she described the reversals women suffered where democracy was under attack. Corbett Ashby pleaded that all actions of the Congress be directed first toward world peace. The participants passed resolutions on the right of all human beings to personal liberty, freedom of thought, and expression. They resolved to support the principle embodied in Article I of the treaty signed at the Seventh Pan American Congress in Montevideo, Uruguay, in December 1933. It said: "The contracting states agree that upon ratification of this treaty men and women shall have equal rights throughout the territory subject to their respective jurisdictions." The IAW resolved to work for peace and collective security. But on a more realistic note that reflected the international turmoil, the Alliance called for measures to assist refugees' settlement and legal protection.[26]

Among the national accomplishments reported, women were allowed to become lawyers in Sri Lanka, Egypt, Japan, Ireland, and New Zealand.[27] Laws had been changed on nationality and inheritance in Yugoslavia. Syria had made advances in public health and prison reform. With the global expansion of the IAW, a session on cooperation between East and West attracted much interest. Speakers came from India, Egypt, Jamaica, Algeria, Syria, Palestine, and Australia. A young Jamaican raised a new issue by describing the Color Bar on students in foreign universities.[28] The standing committees also passed resolutions on child marriage, the position of widows, forced labor, and polygamy in addition to prostitution. For Board members and a few delegates, the Congress culminated in a meeting with President Kemal Ataturk. After the Conference, the Turkish government ironically decided that since women had the franchise on equal terms with men, the Union of Turkish Women was no longer necessary, and it was forced to disband. Because that organization had been affiliated with the IAW, the leader, Latife Bekir, had to resign from the Board.

When the ICW met at Geneva in September of 1935, they again proposed a merger that the board of the IAW rejected.[29] They did agree to delay the next Congress from 1938 to 1939, so as not to conflict with the ICW's fiftieth anniversary.[30] In the four years between IAW conferences in Istanbul and Copenhagen, the movement grew larger. However, women's rights and world peace continued to slip away. The IAW participated in a large World Peace Congress in Brussels in 1936. Catt's old friend, Rosa Manus, was General Secretary. The IAW also continued to offer study conferences between congresses, although these were somewhat curtailed in the late 1930s due to the Depression. At Zurich in 1937, they discussed how nations could maintain their freedom and how women could get the vote and equal employment.[31]

That same year, Corbett Ashby once again visited the United States and received an honorary degree at Mt. Holyoke College. She paid tribute to founder, Mary Lyon, for being at the forefront of the women's movement to obtain education. However, Corbett Ashby also recalled that as "seminaries for the daughters of gentlemen sprang up, many were the tales of elopement by backsliding members."[32] She spoke of strength in education and the accomplishments of women leaders. Simultaneously, Corbett Ashby stressed the delusion of women's equality in employment, pay, and promotion, and made a plea for women to support one another.[33]

Despite the president's efforts to achieve worldwide representation, most of the IAW leadership had been European. At the Board meeting at Geneva in September 1937, Winnifred Kydd of Canada and the American representative, Josephine Schain, resigned. However, the twenty-one board members still included fifteen from Europe and six from the rest of the world.[34] Kydd was replaced by Anni Voipio of Finland. This dominant European representation hampered cooperation later, as the organization struggled to maintain viability during World War II.

The last prewar Alliance Congress met at Copenhagen, Denmark, in 1939. Totalitarian regimes had previously dissolved the societies in Germany, Italy, and Austria, while those in Czechoslovakia, Spain, and Japan were practically immobilized. Nonetheless, twenty-nine countries were represented, and they could report some progress. Women had gained the vote in Bulgaria, Rumania, and Mexico. A Rumanian woman had been elected senator, and in India more than fifty women sat in provincial parliaments. Mme. Szelagowska had been elected to the

Senate in Poland, and Bertha Lutz was a member of Parliament in Brazil. The legal profession had been opened to women in Vietnam, and Argentinean women could no longer legally be dismissed from their posts at marriage.[35]

Corbett Ashby contrasted women's new opportunities in democratic countries with Fascist nations where women were pressured to stay at home and bear children. On the other hand, war industries and civilian defense opened new areas of employment. Sometimes, as men entered the army, women were recalled to work from which they had previously been driven out. Whatever the kind of government, however, women were still subservient. English women, for example (even truck drivers who worked at night and wore gas masks) were paid two-thirds of what men received. However, the IAW claimed some success in getting equal pension benefits for dependents.

While peace continued as a priority, the realities of war had a substantial impact on many of the fifteen resolutions passed at that Congress. The first asserted the sacredness of the human personality as the keystone of the woman's movement.[36] Women's nationality had long been on the agenda, and more nations permitted women to retain their birth nationalities when they married. However, this issue became more pressing in wartime when women classified under their husbands' nationalities could be interned as enemy aliens in their own countries.

An equal moral standard was also an old issue given new immediacy as the military supplied women to soldiers. The IAW called on governments not to provide brothels because men would be contemptuous of women degraded to the level of "things of the Administration." Men were deemed the culprits as Alison Neilans declared that "The number of women who take part in prostitution is practically negligible compared with the number of men who were their partners." One resolution called for more restrictive laws to prevent financial gain from prostitution, and another requested adequate recreational facilities for soldiers in their leisure time.[37]

Among the advances the IAW could count, many universities in western countries admitted women, and more professions were opening to them. The organization had better data to support their claims than in the past. Mme. Thibert reported on an ILO study of the legal status of women workers. However, some advances were already being undercut as the call for protective legislation threatened to undermine attempts to achieve equal pay and job opportunities. The IAW Committee on Work had sent out a questionnaire on protective legislation because that issue had so divided the Istanbul Congress. The Copenhagen Congress compromised its previous stand and agreed that protection should be extended to all workers, both men and women.[38] However, the members continued to support equal pay for equal work. They also wanted family allowances to raise women's status and alleviate poverty and malnutrition. Domestic training was advocated for boys as well as girls because women wage earners could not be expected to do all of the housework.

Although women were losing rights in Fascist dominated countries in Europe and Asia, by 1939 at this last prewar Congress, the International Alliance of Women could count major achievements since 1902. The most significant recent development was the establishment of a working relationship with the League of Nations. That body could collect information worldwide, adopt principles of equality, and recommend them to national governments. Among nations, thirty-three had awarded suffrage compared with two in 1902. Many women also had been elected to national parliaments and more served in local governments.

International friendships were reaffirmed with a sense of nostalgia in July of 1939. Two months before the Second World War began, some members at the Congress were already being oppressed. Rosa Manus returned from the farewell dinner to learn that her room had been searched and some papers taken.[39] She and others knew their lives were in jeopardy when they went home, and in 1942 Manus died in the Ravensbruck concentration camp.[40]

As bombs fell on London and other parts of England, officers of the IAW decided to send copies of vital documents to the United States, Switzerland, and Brazil.[41] They met in Paris in March 1940 to plan for the postwar organization. A second meeting was planned for Geneva at the beginning of June, but by then the war made travel impossible. The members agreed that if Britain were invaded, the office of the Alliance would be transferred to Emilie Gourd in Geneva while Carrie Chapman Catt would once again assume the presidency. *The International Women's News* was loaned to the Women's Publicity Planning Association between October 1940 and December 1945, so it remained viable for the duration.[42]

In April 1945, shortly before the war ended, Corbett Ashby held a Board meeting to prepare for renewal of activities. Then the International Committee (Board and presidents of affiliated societies) met in Geneva in October 1945 to plan for the next Congress. Their loyal Swiss affiliate, Emilie Gourd, had managed to keep some lines of communication open through neutral Switzerland. Survivors held a touching reunion, and several (including Emilie Gourd) died soon after. At this first postwar meeting, the name of the organization was changed again from "International Alliance of Women for Suffrage and Equal Citizenship" to "International Alliance of Women, Equal Rights, Equal Responsibilities."[43] Early in 1946, Corbett Ashby visited Czechoslovakia and Poland to try to revive branches destroyed by Hitler. In Czechoslovakia, the Communists took control at about the same time, and women leaders were persecuted once again. Milada Horakova was murdered by the

Communists just as Frantiska Plaminkova had been by the Nazis. In Poland it was already clear that only a Communist association of women would be authorized.[44]

One bright note was added when the Nobel Committee granted a thousand Norwegian crowns to revive women's organizations. When the Board met in London in March 1946, they agreed to hold the first post-war Congress at Interlaken, Switzerland, in August. Of the twenty-five countries with affiliates, sixteen were represented at that first postwar Congress, and five more countries sent national representatives. Catt, then 87, sent a message of hope both for peace and the ability to achieve it. Women had obtained suffrage in France, Italy, Albania, Yugoslavia, and Japan as the war ended. Corbett Ashby could not say the same for their host country.[45] She asked, "How is it possible that Switzerland should lead the world in engineering and use of electricity and be a 'museum piece' in its attitude to women."

Participants debated whether the Alliance should continue. However, a positive decision was almost inevitable as they recognized how much work remained to be done. Then new resolutions were passed on peace and democracy. The seven committees appointed at the Copenhagen Congress of 1939 were responsible for most of the resolutions at Interlaken in 1946. They included the right of women to suffrage, equal pay and conditions of work, and the right of married women to independent nationality and equal rights with their husbands in marriage. Support for an equal moral standard and opposition to traffic in women were also reaffirmed based on the Fifth Convention drafted by the League of Nations in 1937 and the previous Conventions of 1904, 1910, 1921, and 1933. Refugees were also a priority. By then, the Charter of the United Nations was frequently cited as the basis of the pleas for equality, and that organization was called upon to work for implementation.[46]

In October of 1946, Corbett Ashby accompanied her old friend and successor as president of the IAW, Hanna Rydh of Sweden, to a Conference of the International Assembly of Women held in the Catskill Mountains of the United States. Afterwards, Corbett Ashby paid her last visit to Carrie Chapman Catt. Just as Catt had traveled through the Near and Far East in 1911 to stimulate interest in the women's movement, Hanna Rydh toured the Near East—Egypt, Iraq, Iran, Mesopotamia, and Ethiopia—to interest women in the movement.[47] Consequently, the new affiliates of Ethiopia, Iraq, and Iran attended the Amsterdam meeting in 1949. As before, the IAW continued to expand and work for women's rights through national as well as international organizations. By then much of women's effort to gain recognition and equal rights was being channeled through the UN Commission on the Status of Women.

14

THE PEACE MOVEMENT BEFORE WILPF

While women's rights gripped the campaigners from one generation to the next, one war followed another even more rapidly. The old campaigners came to realize that the underlying requirement to maintain stability was peace, the foundation of all progress. Peace movements have been underway at least covertly as long as war, but women added a new dimension in the early twentieth century. They organized in direct opposition to male militarism before World War I and tried to end the conflict by negotiating between the antagonists. It took a long time to develop this self-confidence, but their third party intervention was a bold move to reinforce the possibility that arbitration could be substituted for war. Peace organizations already had a long history before these efforts led to the formation of the Women's International League for Peace and Freedom at the end of the First World War.

Quakers had formed the London Peace Society in 1816, and by 1829 Female Auxiliary Peace Societies also had been organized in England. After Olive Leaf Circles came into being in the 1840s, peace societies in Great Britain, America, and Europe convened international congresses.[1] However, women were not allowed to be official delegates. Two early British peace activists, Elizabeth Pease and Anne Knight, were denied seats at the London Anti-Slavery Convention in 1840 along with the four American women delegates. This incident influenced Knight, who became an advocate for woman suffrage after she attended the 1849 Peace Congress in Paris. Knight believed woman suffrage would bring peace, and she was frustrated that she was denied the right to speak at the 1851 London Peace Congress.[2] Lucretia Mott was among the four American delegates who had also been denied her seat at the 1840 antislavery convention. A founder of the 1848 women's rights convention at Seneca Falls, New York, she and Julia Ward Howe (1816-1910) subsequently formed the American Women's Peace Society.[3]

Neither male- nor female-dominated peace societies made much headway in the face of the Crimean War of 1854-56 and the American Civil War of 1861-65. Although women were excluded from militarism and male-dominated peace movements, John Ruskin blamed them for causing war. In contrast, when the American Civil War ended, John Stuart Mill contended that the only slavery still permitted was that of

Participants in the 1915 Women's Peace Conference at The Hague. From left to right: 1. Mrs. Thoumaian, Armenia. 2. Leopoldine Kulka, Austria. 3. Laura Hughes, Canada. 4. Rosika Schwimmer, Hungary. 5. Anita Augspurg, Germany. 6. Jane Addams, U.S.A. 7. Mrs. Hamer, Belgium. 8. Aletta H. Jacobs, Holland. 9. Chrystal Macmillan, Great Britain. 10. Rosa Genoni, Italy. 11. Anna Kleman, Sweden. 12. Thora Dangaard, Denmark. 13. Louise Keilhan, Norway. From Records of the Women's International League for Peace and Freedom, Swarthmore College Peace Collection. Reprinted with permission.

women in the home. Mill mistakenly argued that highly civilized nations like Great Britain had risen above war.[4]

In 1872, Julia Ward Howe conceived a plan to hold annual Mothers' Peace Day festivals, so she began the tradition of celebrating Mother's Day. The first was on June 2, 1873.[5] Howe also tried to call an international peace meeting for women in London, but she was not allowed to speak to the English Peace Society. The suffragists were not particularly interested either. Howe's proposal for a Court of International Arbitration fared better. This idea appealed to the British, and in 1874 they founded a Women's Peace and Arbitration Auxiliary of the Peace Society.[6]

Howe and other women were finally allowed to speak publicly at the 1878 Peace Congress in Paris. By 1881, the peace movement had gained respectability, and British women had recruited Helen Taylor, John Stuart Mill's stepdaughter. According to Jill Liddington, Taylor was one of the few women who combined the struggles for peace and woman suffrage after Anne Knight died in 1862. Priscilla Peckover, a British Quaker, combined peace and temperance when she established a Women's Local Peace Association.[7]

In America, Frances Willard identified the WCTU with the peace movement in 1887. She asked the Universal Peace Union to send delegates to the meeting in Washington when the International Council of Women was founded in 1888. When they were given this opportunity, women like Clara Barton, Julia Ward Howe, Mary Livermore, and M. Louise Thomas helped forge the link between the Universal Peace Union and various women's organizations. Willard was elected president of the new National Council of Women at that meeting, and she subsequently persuaded the NCW to adopt a resolution in support of the peace movement.[8] The WCTU also sent delegates to the International Peace Conference at the Paris Exposition in 1889 and to the Universal Peace Congress in London in 1890. As part of this cooperation, Willard was named honorary vice president of the Universal Peace Union.[9] After her death in 1898, the WCTU continued to be active in the peace movement. The Sixth World Convention in Geneva, Switzerland, in June 1903, passed a resolution that urged nations to submit their differences to an international court of arbitration. Then the Seventh World Convention in Boston, Massachusetts, in 1906 passed resolutions "to urge the Brussels Conference to approve a universal treaty to protect all races" and "to urge the Hague Conference to consider means to diminish poverty, distress and injustice."[10]

The peace movement got another boost when Alfred Nobel instituted a peace prize. In 1898 the Russian Czar, Nicholas II, proposed a peace manifesto and called for a conference on disarmament at The Hague in 1899. In London that year, the ICW also agreed to work for international arbitration. Ishbel Aberdeen solicited the Austrian novelist and peace propagandist, Bertha von Suttner, to speak. But von Suttner was ill and could not leave The Hague. Her book, *Lay Down Your Arms*, had been credited with converting the Czar of Russia to the peace cause.[11] Despite her absence, the ICW convention still adopted a resolution in favor of arbitrating international disputes. The members sent good wishes to the Peace Conference and offered the support of women from twenty-eight countries.[12]

At The Hague Conference, a Standing Committee on Peace and International Arbitration was formed with Bertha von Suttner as its secretary.[13] In 1905 she was the first woman awarded the Nobel Peace Prize.[14] In 1912 she toured the United States, invited by the General Federation of Women's Clubs, one of May Wright Sewall's affiliations. By then Sewall was honorary president of the ICW, and she chaired the Committee on Peace and Arbitration from 1904 to 1914.[15] During von Suttner's trip, she met with Carrie Chapman Catt and Jane Addams, both of whom had become immersed in the peace movement by then.

Others were less supportive. Millicent Garrett Fawcett hosted the suffrage breakaway group in the ICW in 1899, but she was very conservative and loyal to the government of Great Britain.[16] For example, Fawcett's patriotism inhibited her interactions with the Irish. While they objected to absentee British landlords, she vigorously opposed Home Rule. Fawcett contended that "the crimes committed in Ireland by Home Rulers stopped Home Rule; and if Women Suffragists embark on crime and propaganda they will stop Woman Suffrage."[17]

The Land League was a distinctly Irish development intended to reform a system in which tenant farmers were forced to pay exorbitant rents. They wanted to own their own land. When the male leaders were arrested in 1881, the Ladies Land League was formed to enable women to replace their husbands and brothers. The women gained leadership experience and sent Fanny Parnell to America to raise funds and establish a branch of the League. Women who participated were more likely to see Irish nationalism as a priority over women's suffrage.[18]

Despite their differences, as leader of the English National Union of Women's Suffrage Societies (NUWSS), Fawcett still interacted regularly with Irish suffragists in the 1880s and 1890s.[19] In Northern Ireland, Fawcett worked with Isabella Tod. She had founded the North of Ireland Women's Suffrage Society in 1873 and was also part of the temperance movement.[20] Because the Irish were determined to keep their suffrage movement separate from the English, nationalism continually complicated the struggle. Irish historian Cliona Murphy contends that the suffrage movement was never truly international because the Irish could not obliterate national differences, particularly with British women.[21]

Fawcett's conservative nationalism was also very publicly demonstrated after the Boer War of 1899 to 1902 in South Africa. The British victors herded the Dutch-speaking Afrikaaners, including women and children, into concentration camps where they experienced miserable conditions and starvation. Bertha von Suttner and Emily Hobhouse revealed this abuse and described how war affected noncombatants.[22] After conditions in the camps were publicized, Fawcett was appointed to a government investigating committee. They supported the British conquerors rather than their prisoners. Fawcett was accused of a whitewash, and her loyalty to her militaristic government generated misgivings among fellow suffragists who worked for peace. The breach widened before World War I.

After the Boer War, Charlotte Perkins Gilman and Olive Schreiner highlighted the relationship between feminism and antimilitarism. They argued that women would need suffrage to influence world affairs because militarism was premised on the old notion of separate spheres for men and women.[23] This reinforced von Suttner and Hobhouse's contention that the brunt of war fell most heavily on women and children. Conservative women were not easy to convince, but the peace movement was growing. More than 400 organizations were scattered around the world even before 1900. In England the movement was especially popular with university women, notably those from Emily Davies's Girton College, Cambridge. One was Helena Sickel (later Swanwick) whose feminism was strongly influenced by reading John Stuart Mill.[24] She was among those who split with Fawcett's suffragists over the struggle for peace.

Another woman who became most closely identified with the peace movement was the American, Jane Addams (1860-1939). While her work with immigrants at Hull House was more widely publicized, she also lectured and wrote on peace at an early stage. Addams was well placed to assume leadership in the peace movement because she had not been as prominent in the suffrage or temperance movements. Although she was a lifelong opponent of the use of alcohol, Addams never joined the WCTU.[25] One reason may have been that they did not initially support Hull House, although Frances Willard had proposed such a settlement house in Chicago earlier.[26]

Personally, Addams may have been stricter in her opposition to alcohol than Willard, who had written home about tasting German beer and French wine during her first European tour. Addams' Puritanical belief in the evils of alcohol was reinforced by the devastating effects on immigrant families around Hull House. She recognized that men needed alternative social opportunities to replace the saloons, not just legislation to abolish them. Willard had shocked some of the WCTU membership when she came to a similar conclusion earlier.[27] Initially, Addams was opposed to national prohibition. Nevertheless, she decided it improved conditions in working-class neighborhoods and so did not support repeal either.[28]

Willard had led the WCTU into the peace movement earlier, and Addams joined before Carrie Chapman Catt. Peace proved to be Addams' cause of greatest dedication and also the ruination of her popularity in the United States. She claimed some natural affinity with pacifism because her father's family had been Hicksite Quakers like Lucretia Mott. Her nephew and biographer, James Weber Linn, contends that her support for peace through international understanding, "was merely an extraordinary extension of her concern with the aliens who were her Hull House neighbors."[29] Her public role in the peace movement began on a small scale in 1896 when Addams asked the boys around Hull House to drill with wooden shovel handles instead of wooden guns.[30] In 1899 she participated in a Chicago campaign against "imperialism" in connection with the annexation of the Philippines, and in 1904 Addams spoke at a convention of National Peace Societies in Boston. In 1906 she lectured at the University of Wisconsin on the ideals of peace and then published *Newer Ideals of Peace*. She also represented women at the first National Peace Congress held in the United States in Boston in 1907.[31] On that occasion, May Wright Sewall summarized the work of the ICW Committee on Peace and Arbitration. Besides the Women's Session of the Peace Congress, a special conference was held for peace workers. Among them were Carrie Chapman Catt and Anna Howard Shaw.[32]

Addams's career as a suffragist as well as a social worker and pacifist was well launched before she joined Carrie Chapman Catt in the national and international woman suffrage movement. Willard and Catt both had scarring recollections of learning that women could not vote when their fathers and brothers went off to cast their ballots. Unlike some of his contemporaries, Jane Addams' father supported woman suffrage and encouraged her from an early age. Even so, she was the last of the three to join the movement. Addams was a declared suffragist by 1881, but she did not join the NAWSA until 1906.

As Addams recognized the needs of the people who lived around Hull House, she campaigned from 1892 on for labor legislation.[33] She thought that if more people had the vote, it would promote social amelioration. So she also campaigned for municipal suffrage for women in Chicago. Suffrage was not a new idea for Scandinavian women immigrants who had (in some cases) been allowed to vote in municipal elections since the seventeenth century.[34] They had lost rights when they came to the United States. Most of all, Addams wanted immigrants, both men and women, to be able to vote to protect themselves from being exploited.[35] In this, she was very unlike such strongly nativist suffragists as Elizabeth Cady Stanton. In later years, she tried to appeal to the biases of middle-class men to promote woman suffrage and counter the influx of uneducated immigrants.

Many suffragists only gradually recognized the importance of the peace movement to achieve women's rights. After Jane Addams joined the NAWSA, she lectured frequently on women's right and responsibility to take a more active role in government and society. In 1911 both state and municipal suffrage campaigns were defeated in Springfield and Chicago. Addams also campaigned against regulated prostitution, and in 1912 she worked for Teddy Roosevelt's Progressives.[36] As Roosevelt won fame as a militarist Rough Rider during the Spanish American War in Cuba, Addams' support for his presidential campaign compromised her image as a pacifist. However, Addams argued that as president, Roosevelt had led the United States to accept arbitration by the World Court of Conciliation and Arbitration at The Hague on a long-standing dispute with Mexico.[37] After Roosevelt was defeated in 1912, Addams extended her efforts to promote peace at the International Woman Suffrage Alliance meeting in Budapest in 1913.[38]

Rosika Schwimmer hosted that Congress where the nucleus of the IWSA peace movement was formed. Schwimmer's uncle had founded the Hungarian Peace Society. Budapest was so near the Balkan conflict that the imminence of war was reinforced and several sessions dealt with disarmament and pacifism. At that meeting, British NUWSS delegate Helena Swanwick argued that woman suffrage could be a bulwark against another international war. But the French and Hungarians were more preoccupied with the immediate danger. The continental delegates heightened the consciousness of British women like Swanwick and Florence Lockwood that political freedom was needed to achieve peace as well as women's rights.[39] A French delegate, Maria Verone, and a German, Regina Deutsch, both ended their speeches with pledges for world peace. When Verone crossed the stage and embraced her German colleague, the audience applauded loudly.[40]

After the congress in Budapest, Rosika Schwimmer, the IWSA's international press secretary, went to England to spread the various messages.[41] After an executive meeting in London in July 1914, an Alliance manifesto pointed out that women were horrified at the prospect of war, but had no political power to avert the disaster. "In none of the countries immediately concerned in the threatened outbreak have women any direct power to control the political destinies of their own countries." On behalf of the IWSA, they called on those in power to try every method of conciliation. This manifesto was given to the foreign ministers in London and to the British Foreign Office.[42] Then the women attracted world attention as they attempted peace negotiations among the warring governments just as the conflict began.

15

JANE ADDAMS:
THE 1915 PEACE CONFERENCE AND AFTER

The women's peace movement could be said to have had its greatest triumph or lowest infamy in 1915. Whereas some women had managed an uneasy alliance between the suffrage and peace causes previously, the war forced an open division. In 1914 Rosika Schwimmer, Millicent Garrett Fawcett, Chrystal Macmillan, and Mary Sheepshanks drew up an appeal for mediation among the warring governments. They proclaimed that this appeal was supported by more than twelve million women who represented twenty-six countries. It was delivered to the British Foreign Office and embassies in London on July 31, 1914. Even as the women planned a major antiwar rally, however, troops were being mobilized in Russia, Germany, and France. One speaker at the rally, Elizabeth Cadbury, convened the peace committee of the International Council of Women.[1] Although the ICW had had a Standing Committee on Peace and International Arbitration since 1899, in England that organization tried to distance itself from the peace movement when the nation came to the brink of war. However, the ICW contended that above all else, women had a fundamental obligation to home and family.[2] Consequently, peace was at the top of the agenda at the 1914 meeting in Rome.

As the ICW struggled to determine their stance toward the peace movement, the leaders of the IWSA soon split along lines of national loyalty. Marie Stritt announced on September 19, 1914, that the war compelled the German Union for Women Suffrage to withdraw their invitation to hold the International Woman Suffrage Alliance biennial meeting in Berlin the next June. This decision appeared in the December 1914, issue of the IWSA official publication, *Jus Suffragii*, along with a letter by President Carrie Chapman Catt that accepted the withdrawal. In the same issue, Aletta Jacobs, President of the Dutch National Society for Women Suffrage, invited the IWSA Congress to Holland.[3] She stressed the importance of bringing women together in an international meeting at that critical time.

At Christmas in 1914 the British women expressed their shared pain and grief in an open letter to their colleagues in Germany and Austria. "Humanity and common sense alike prompt us to join hands with

Jane Addams, first president of the Women's International League for Peace and Freedom. Reprinted with permission from the Jane Addams Memorial Collection, Special Collections, The University Library, The University of Illinois at Chicago.

the women of neutral countries, and urge our rulers to stay further bloodshed."[4] A response came in the spring—warm greetings from 155 German and Austrian women.[5] But with the war actually underway, the suffragists were further divided. In England many of them, militant or not, halted suffrage activities and supported the war effort. Along with Millicent Garrett Fawcett, they included her formerly militant antagonists, the Pankhursts.

In resistance to the war, the pacifists among the European IWSA members cooperated with other organizations to form an International Women's Relief Committee chaired by Chrystal Macmillan. They sent relief supplies to Belgium and helped foreign residents who were perceived as enemy aliens as well as refugees brought to London from Germany and Belgium. Many Irish citizens also resisted military and industrial conscription for what was perceived as an English war.[6]

In support of Jacobs' invitation, Chrystal Macmillan, one of the secretaries of the IWSA, sent private letters to the auxiliaries. She urged that the IWSA business meeting be followed by another session. It would include subjects of concern to peace organizations such as international arbitration, control of foreign policy, and reduction of armaments. This meeting could be convened by individual women if the Alliance decided not to support it.[7] The executive committee of the British NUWSS split on this issue. Kathleen Courtney, Catherine Marshall, Helena Swanwick, and Chrystal Macmillan were in favor, but Millicent Garrett Fawcett opposed it. Still the nationalist, she stated at a public meeting that until German troops were driven back, talking of peace was akin to treason.[8] That meant Fawcett also alienated internationalists who still hoped for a negotiated peace. These included the Dutch Aletta Jacobs and Germans like Anita Augspurg and Lida Gustava Heymann.

Because Fawcett headed the NUWSS and blocked participation, the organizers lacked official sanction to link the special session with an IWSA Congress. Consequently, they decided to call a meeting of peace-oriented individuals instead. Then some younger British pacifists resigned from the NUWSS.[9] Among them were some of Fawcett's closest associates: Kathleen Courtney, Chrystal Macmillan, and Helena Swanwick.[10] Afterwards, in her autobiography *I Have Been Young,* Swanwick insisted that she and Fawcett had remained friends, and Courtney later tried to restore friendly relations although Fawcett's responses were decidedly cool.[11]

So Jacobs went ahead without IWSA authorization. She invited women from both belligerent and neutral countries to a preliminary planning session in Amsterdam in February 1915. Chrystal Macmillan, Kathleen Courtney, Emily Leaf, and Theodora Wilson-Wilson came from England and were joined by Anita Augspurg and Lida Gustava Heymann as well as other German, Dutch, and Belgian suffragists. Macmillan set forth peace proposals, and they planned an international congress at The Hague, the site of the International Court of Arbitration, to begin three months later. Participation would be open to women delegates on an individual basis if they were in general agreement with the resolutions on the preliminary program.[12] Aletta Jacobs insisted that war should not be allowed to divide women on issues that transcended national differences.[13] In the short time between the preliminary meeting in February and the opening of the first session on April 17, 1915, Aletta Jacobs, Mia Boissevain, and Rosa Manus publicized the congress by letter and telegram.

In the United States, Catt and Addams came to similar conclusions about the need for peace and suffrage and how they related to one another. Both women used their prominence to emphasize one cause or the other at various times. Carrie Chapman Catt opposed overt peace demonstrations such as a parade in New York City. However, she recommended that the International Council of Women and the International Woman Suffrage Alliance support President Wilson's offer to help negotiate peace. She also went with Rosika Schwimmer to bring Wilson an international petition endorsed by men and women all over the world.[14] Schwimmer had come to the still-neutral United States to lecture for peace after England took up arms and classified her as an enemy alien.[15] At Schwimmer's instigation, Catt requested that Jane Addams call for more peace rallies.

Addams had previously joined Lillian Wald to organize an early response to the European war. This roundtable conference was held at the Henry Street Settlement House in New York City in September 1914.[16] Because both Rosika Schwimmer and Emmeline Pethick Lawrence were in the United States on lecture campaigns for peace, they vigorously promoted the meeting at The Hague, and they encouraged Addams to help organize the Chicago Emergency Federation of Peace Forces.[17] Catt was reluctant to antagonize suffrage supporters, so she asked Jane Addams to send invitations for a Woman's Peace Congress to be held in January 1915 in Washington, D.C. Catt presided as the Woman's Peace Party was formed with suffrage as a platform plank. However, Jane Addams was elected president, and the national office was established in Chicago.[18]

While Addams was presiding over a meeting of the Chicago Emergency Federation of Peace Forces in February 1915, she received Jacobs' cablegram that invited members of the Woman's Peace Party to The Hague for an international peace congress of women from both neutral and belligerent countries.[19] The participants in Chicago accepted the invitation and formed a National Peace Federation with Addams as president.[20] While much of her popularity as a pacifist had eroded when she supported Theodore Roosevelt for president, Addams was still the most famous woman and most important social worker in America. Therefore, the European organizers were most encouraged when she accepted their invitation to preside over the women's international peace movement at this precarious time.[21]

As these women prepared to take direct action, the theoretical basis for the peace movement was also being tied to women's issues. In Great

Britain, Jill Liddington credits Charlotte Perkins Gilman and Olive Schreiner as well as Fawcett's NUWSS and the IWSA with underpinning the women's international peace movement in 1915. Schreiner linked maternalist feminism and equal rights in "Women and War," a short, influential essay that showed a relationship between motherhood and peace. Gilman's magazine, *The Forerunner,* had begun publication in 1909.[22] In it, she attacked patriarchal institutions. Then even women Jill Liddington calls maternalists, those who accepted women's separate role as mothers, began to recognize how war and the fear of it had kept women in subjection. Some of them concluded that childbearing was part of the problem. In opposition to the widely held belief that "in war time only men matter," they heard arguments that noncombatant women and children suffer most. This raised or reinforced their conviction that women must halt war.[23]

Swedish author, Ellen Key, also linked women and peace, but on a racial and eugenic basis.[24] She argued that if the best and the brightest were killed in war, the human species would be perpetuated by the less competent and intelligent. The defects in this concept became evident after the Germans went beyond what Ellen Key had proposed and implemented a state policy of forced maternity.[25] Frances Hallowes thought on a larger scale when she suggested a World's League of Women organized for peace. In *Mothers of Men and Militarism* she argued that mothers must create international solidarity. It was clear to her that women could not achieve suffrage and other rights in a narrowly defined separate sphere.

Peace congresses were held in England and Holland. Just before theirs, the British published anonymously *Militarism versus Feminism: An Enquiry and a Policy Demonstrating That Militarism Involves the Subjection of Women.* The authors owed much to John Stuart Mill and the liberal tradition as they argued that the level of militarism in a country affected the liberty of its women.[26] However, they believed Mill was too uncritical of the growth of British imperialism.

Upwards of 180 British women wanted to attend The Hague Peace Conference after a National Conference of Women was called in London to discuss the basis for a permanent peace settlement. However, the Permit Office refused permission because "there is much inconvenience in holding large meetings of a political character so close to the seat of war." Then the Home Office was persuaded to allow twenty-four selected women to leave, but the Admiralty closed the North Sea to shipping. Only the ones already out of the country got to The Hague.[27] Emmeline Pethick Lawrence was one of four British women who attended. She had been in the United States, and so was one of Jane Addams' party of forty-seven who sailed from America on April 13, 1915.

Irish women fell under the same restrictions as the English.[28] While twenty-one applied to cross the sea, the British government only gave Louie Bennett, founder of the Irish Women's Reform League, permission to travel. The North Sea closure also kept her from completing the trip.[29] British control of the seas nearly halted the Americans as well. Their ship, the *Noordam,* was held up at Dover for four days. English newspaper reporters loaded the enterprise with ridicule, calling the women "Peacettes."[30] They finally arrived in Holland just in time for the opening reception given by the Dutch Executive Committee.[31]

By then the war in Europe had already been underway for eight months. When Aletta Jacobs opened the Congress, she said that "woman suffrage in all countries is one of the most powerful means to prevent war in the future." Like previous temperance, labor, and social purity campaigns, peace workers recognized that suffrage would give women a stronger voice in human affairs overall.[32] With Jane Addams presiding, the women called for democratic control of foreign policy, woman suffrage, and peace.

This gathering marked a turning point in women's rights activities. The participants adopted a resolution that demanded an end to the bloodshed and a beginning of negotiations for peace based on principles of justice. Whereas the women had argued over and adopted innumerable resolutions in several previous congresses, this time they decided to present the resolutions personally. Emily Greene Balch later recalled that Rosika Schwimmer's dramatic proposal was warmly debated before it was finally accepted.[33] Envoys would make their pleas to the warring governments and report back to what they called the International Women's Committee for Constructive Peace.[34] They were taking a major step. Instead of their usual role as supplicants, the women intended to act as intermediaries—negotiators between national governments.

Addams and Jacobs led one group, Schwimmer and Macmillan the other. They divided up the countries they would approach. Initially, they met with some success. Neutral Swedish officials agreed to call a meeting of the warring governments if one from each side agreed. However, neither warring party would make the first move to negotiate, and the women's effort failed. Even so, they revived the peace initiative. Some principles for a resolution of that conflict were formulated, as well as the idea for a League of Nations to settle future disputes. For women, however, Jill Liddington contends that the most important outcome was an organized, international women's peace movement.

Nevertheless, even that movement soon divided. Addams antagonized Schwimmer and the others by returning to the United States immediately instead of waiting to exchange reports. Back in her still allegedly neutral home country, she was not appreciated for her peacemaking efforts. Her enthusiastic welcome home by Carrie Chapman Catt and

Anna Howard Shaw was not shared by the press and public, especially after Addams was quoted as saying stimulants regularly had to be given before men would engage in bayonet charges. Even though America was not in the war yet, that she was thought to have impugned the soldiers' bravery led to widespread public attacks.[35] The story circulated in Europe as well, and Addams tried to counteract it. In one letter to Aletta Jacobs Addams wrote that she did not know if "that ridiculous bayonet story is still afloat in England." She said she had been defended in some leading papers, and she sent clippings in case they might be useful in her defense.[36]

As Addams' image deteriorated in the United States, she alienated friends there as well. In 1916 she agreed to sail with the Ford peace mission, but she became ill and stayed home. Henry Ford said he had gotten the idea for the Peace Ship from Jane Addams, and she was widely blamed for its failure by foes who opposed the trip and friends who did not believe illness prevented her from sailing.[37] Nevertheless, Addams persevered in the cause of peace. As she still hoped to keep America out of war, she supported Woodrow Wilson for reelection in 1916 and helped form an Emergency Peace Federation. They sponsored a letter writing campaign and held demonstrations at the White House.[38] However, even her longtime associate, Carrie Chapman Catt, did not stand by her.

Catt maneuvered carefully while the United States still maintained a pose of neutrality. Her sympathies were with the peace movement, but she knew this stance could damage the woman suffrage cause in wartime. Therefore, she continued to avoid much of the flack directed at the antiwar activists after she helped organize the New York branch of the Woman's Peace Party. To continue her push for woman suffrage, as part of her overall strategy, Catt decided the American suffragists should maintain their low profile on peace activism. Two years later, when America's entry into the war was imminent, she called a meeting of the Executive Council of the NAWSA in Washington. They agreed to offer the women's services to the government to support the war effort. Pacifists saw this as treachery, and Catt was immediately repudiated by the New York branch of the Woman's Peace Party.[39] She was vilified by the pacifists as Addams was by those who supported the war.

Once America entered the war in 1917, Addams lectured under the auspices of Herbert Hoover's Department of Food Administration. She appealed to women to help conserve food and increase production.[40] Anna Howard Shaw also worked for the government and subsequently was awarded a medal for her efforts. Other women were more ambivalent on whether to support the war or continue their protests, especially when President Wilson called on the nation to make the world safe for democracy. Whereas Emmeline Pankhurst had immediately ceased suffrage protests to support the British war effort, her American protégé,

Alice Paul, and her militant National Woman's Party did not. The NWP lost favor, but they maintained their momentum through publicity generated as they chained themselves to the White House fence, were arrested, and pointed out President Wilson's hypocrisy in fighting for democracy while not supporting women's suffrage. Catt's more conservative NAWSA maintained a supportive or at least neutral attitude and stayed on better terms with the government.

After the war ended, women in good standing with the victorious governments met in Paris. Jane Addams also spent two weeks there, perhaps still in some favor because she had supported President Wilson. Then she called a meeting to revitalize the Woman's Peace Party and the International Committee of Women for Permanent Peace.[41] At the 1915 conference at The Hague, the delegates had agreed to hold their next meeting simultaneously with the peace conference. However, when this was held in Paris, they chose Zurich so delegates from the Central Powers could attend more easily.[42] In 1919, women devastated by the ravages of war were ridiculed by the American press. Despite the hardships, the Peace Congress was attended by about 150 people from sixteen countries. German women sat with English and Irish friends from earlier days.[43] Addams was cheered by the members' respect compared with her previous reception at home. She was elected president of the new Women's International League for Peace and Freedom (WILPF).[44]

This international body had its roots in an organization founded in Great Britain soon after the Hague Conference in 1915. Women who had not attended wanted to hear first-hand reports from the small delegation. Millicent Garrett Fawcett was an exception. Her copy of the program and conference resolutions, annotated with cryptic objections, is part of the Woman Suffrage Collection at the Manchester Central Library. She clearly did not support either meeting. However, the others gathered at Central Hall, London, on May 11, 1915. Some who had separated from the NUWSS founded the Women's International League (WIL) and elected Helena Swanwick as chair with Maude Royden, Margaret Ashton, and Kathleen Courtney as vice-chairs.[45]

A women's peace crusade spread around Great Britain, and the WIL affiliated with the International Committee of Women for Permanent Peace.[46] Within two years, that organization could boast forty-two branches.[47] At Zurich when the WILPF was formed, they agreed to establish their headquarters in Geneva near the new League of Nations.[48] The 1919 Congress also sent envoys to Versailles to protest the terms of the Peace Treaty, but none of the proposals from pacifists were accepted.

As Addams concentrated more on the WILPF, her prestige deteriorated even further in the United States. She spent less time at Hull House, and raising money became more of a problem. Many distinguished residents left, and social work became more professionalized. Audiences were cool to Addams or canceled her lectures altogether.[49] At the National Conference of Social Work in June 1922, she could not muster enough support to gain the presidency.[50] For years after the war, she continued to be attacked as a pacifist, Bolshevik, and a dangerous radical.

Many former antisuffragists joined the propaganda effort against advocates of peace and social welfare legislation. The Daughters of the American Revolution (DAR) vehemently attacked the WILPF despite some embarrassment because they had honored Jane Addams with a life membership previously. Although the two women leaders often differed on goals and strategies, Carrie Chapman Catt wrote the DAR a public letter that defended Addams.[51] Undeterred, the DAR also attacked the League of Women Voters and the International Council of Women.[52] Such attempts at character assassination by super patriot groups were widespread in the 1920s, and they continued through the 1930s.

While Jane Addams expanded the Women's International League for Peace and Freedom, Carrie Chapman Catt founded a new organization—the Committee on the Cause and Cure of War. The two women shared many of the same ideals, although they disagreed on how to attain them. As Catt wanted the League of Women Voters to participate in established political parties and to hold office. Addams, on the other hand, felt that they should concentrate on making their communities better places to live. Addams' biographer, Allen F. Davis, contends that "Mrs. Catt would have women remake political institutions to allow their inclusion on equal terms with men. Jane Addams wanted to remake society over in a pattern approved by women." Her belief in women's special responsibility and qualifications for promoting peace and municipal reform seemed old-fashioned even in the 1920s. Addams deviated further from the feminists because she sided with the social justice reformers. They opposed the ERA because it would nullify protective legislation for working women.[53]

Addams remained more popular overseas than at home. She went to Vienna in 1921 to the Third Conference of the Women's International League for Peace and Freedom and to The Hague in 1922 when the WILPF called a Conference for a New Peace. After that meeting, she traveled around the world. She visited India, the Philippines, Korea, China, and Japan. According to her biographer, Allen F. Davis, "Everywhere she went she was greeted by enthusiastic crowds, entertained as if she were royalty, and treated to the reverence and awe she had once been accustomed to at home."[54] The settlement house organizer was impressed with the concern of educated Japanese and Indians for those who were worse off. However, like Catt before her, Addams was pained by the rigid conventions that often governed women. She was cheered where they had more opportunities. For example, women in Myanmar could vote at age eighteen and in India at twenty-one, but they still had to be thirty in England.[55]

During her tour, Addams made many public addresses. One in Osaka, Japan, on "Women and Peace" was translated in detail by Japanese newspapers. News coverage continued as she was taken ill that night and removed to Tokyo the next day. After she had a tumor removed, Addams remained in the hospital for a month and subsequently convalesced in the mountains for three weeks.[56] While she was in the hospital, Addams received messages from the Imperial Court and heard that a reception had been planned there in her honor.[57] This trip established Addams' prominence in the Far East and also in Europe. By contrast, in 1924 when the Fourth Congress of the WILPF was held in Washington, D.C., Addams was embarrassed by the way the American press and patriotic organizations treated the delegates.[58] They fared better two years later in Dublin where participants staged a pilgrimage and formed the Women's Peace Crusade. In 1928 Addams' international prestige was further enhanced when she was chosen president of the new Pan Pacific Women's Association (PPWA, now the Pan Pacific and South East Asian Women's Association, PPSEAWA) when that international organization was founded in Hawaii.[59]

Much of the peace momentum was subsequently lost in the Depression.[60] At the WILPF conference in Prague in 1929, Addams resigned as president and was designated honorary president for life.[61] She addressed the Sixth Conference of the Committee on the Cause and Cure of War in January 1931. The participants were gloomy over the prospects for peace. However, Addams was finally recognized for her peace efforts when she was named co-recipient of the Nobel Peace Prize later that year.[62] At the Cause and Cure Conference in 1932, the participants were even gloomier. All member organizations reported attacks by super patriots. The WCTU was similarly criticized as was the Women's Trade Union League.[63] However, the peace movement was on a firmer footing in Europe, where peace had become a priority in the League of Nations. During this period between the two world wars, the women's organizations banded together into a liaison committee, a kind of female League of Nations that lobbied their official counterpart.

PART III

BETWEEN THE WARS

Although women had to ask to participate at the Paris peace talks, their lobbying culminated in a declaration of equal rights for women and men in the League of Nations Covenant. They also received some official representation and a system of consultation for nongovernmental organizations. As hope for a permanent peace emerged out of the ruins of war, the United States and Great Britain accorded women suffrage, and a major extension of rights seemed possible. Instead, the peace movement hardly attained social acceptability before the Paris Peace Treaty generated the dissension that culminated in World War II.

Despite the equality wording in its Covenant, the League of Nations began to lose its aura of power almost before it was established. The United States refused to join, and women concluded that they would be better off if nations joined without affording them equal rights than not to join at all. The League could advise and recommend equality laws, but the individual nations carefully guarded their autonomy. They could and often did elect not to comply with the recommendations. To lobby for equal rights, the international women's organizations established headquarters in Geneva near the League of Nations. Their lobbying became more direct when some of them were appointed official delegates as well as consultants. Meanwhile, support for protective legislation split the international women's movement. However, new women leaders emerged in Central and South America, and they later played a significant part in continuing the policy of equality in the United Nations.

In the 1920s, while women's organizations expanded their networks and worked together for a variety of causes, others took more individualistic routes to recognition and the advancement of women's rights. Sex education and birth control were too controversial for conservative club women to support openly, but these causes were too important for women (radical or conservative) to ignore. In Great Britain, Marie Stopes published advice on sexual satisfaction and paved the way for the proliferation of "how to" manuals.

At the same time, Margaret Sanger worked for women's right to birth control information in the United States and other parts of the world. Sanger cooperated with Shidzue Kato, who became known as Japan's leading birth control advocate. Kato also cooperated with the

American scholar Mary Ritter Beard on a project to write a history of women. A staunch internationalist, Beard looked beyond the immediate women's rights movement to encourage the preservation of women's history. She called for the collection of women's papers and other relevant documents and formulated a larger concept of women's role in world history. Overall, the short span between the wars increased women's confidence in their ability to organize in a world forum as well as in their own organizations. The Peace Congress at The Hague in 1915 had been the first step in this bold initiative.

16

PEACE AND THE LEAGUE OF NATIONS

Because of her careful political maneuvers, at the end of World War I Carrie Chapman Catt was still reasonably popular at home as well as abroad, and she soon was back in the good graces of the peace movement. After the Armistice, Catt publicly appealed for women to be represented at the Paris Peace Conference. She wrote to Millicent Garrett Fawcett that the representatives should be European. American women had worked for the war effort too, she said, but not as much.[1] But Catt was out of touch with what was happening in Europe. In a later letter to Fawcett, Catt said she had read in *Common Cause* that women had already asked for representation. Then Catt observed that when any country appointed a woman delegate, it would be a strong inducement for others to do so.[2] Indeed, women closer to the scene did achieve some results.[3]

Ishbel Aberdeen, president of the ICW, asked President Woodrow Wilson in late 1918 for permission to make a presentation at the peace talks. At her initiative and that of Marguerite deWitt-Schlumberger, president of the French branch of the IWSA, the Inter-Allied Suffrage Congress petitioned the Supreme Council of the Allies to ask that women's organizations be heard.[4] Nevertheless, apparently no representation of women or their interests was contemplated when the Peace Conference was scheduled to begin in Paris on January 18, 1919. Consequently, the Central Committee of the *Union Francaise pour le Suffrage des Femmes* resolved to invite delegates of the Allied countries affiliated with the IWSA to Paris to lobby for women's representation. In Britain, the National Council of Women also formed a Council for the Representation of Women in the League of Nations.

After that, President Wilson approved a Special Commission to inquire into and report on questions of international importance that were assumed to be of interest to women. Georges Clemenceau, head of the French delegation and presiding officer, thought it would be better to have women enter directly into the Commissions of the Peace Conference. But the Allied Supreme War Council chose President Wilson's proposal. Consequently, Julie Siegfried, president of the National Council of French Women, was informed that women's organizations would be heard by commissions that occupied themselves especially with questions that touched on women's interests.[5] Subsequently, three delegates and three alternatives were invited from each participating country.

Samuel Gompers, the American labor leader, presided over the first commission to receive a delegation of women. It was devoted to international labor legislation. The women asked that all posts in or connected with the International Labour Organization (ILO) be open equally to women and men and that Germany be invited to join. This request was supported by Marguerite deWitt-Schlumberger, a French delegate who wore several medals for war service. Then Gompers said: "You, a Frenchwoman, ask this?" She replied that "Disease and labour problems know no frontiers," and the request was granted.[6] The women's delegation also submitted resolutions on equal pay for equal work and prohibition of child labor below the age of fifteen.

Although a precedent was set for equal rights in the ILO, a more significant and long-range development was women's participation in the Commission of the League of Nations. President Wilson received a delegation from the Inter-Allied Suffrage Conference (victorious nations only) led by Margery Corbett Ashby and another from the International Council of Women led by Ishbel Aberdeen. They called for suppression of the traffic in women and children, woman suffrage, and the right of women as well as men to decide on the fate of their country. They also asked for a permanent international bureau of education and for women to sit on this commission on the same terms as men. Aberdeen recalled May Wright Sewall's predictions in 1893 when she referred to the International Council of Women as "the mother of the League of Nations."[7] In the same vein, General Smuts later told the NCW of South Africa, "Why, your I.C.W. was a League of Nations before the other was thought of."[8] To continue their input, the ICW established offices in Geneva near the League of Nations.[9] Aberdeen and Margery Corbett Ashby were sure they scored a major coup when the League Covenant opened all positions equally to men and women.[10] Article 7 (3) states that "all positions under or in connection with the League, including the secretariat, shall be open equally to men and women."[11] This declaration of equality set a precedent for the future United Nations.

The WWCTU also participated in the international peacemaking efforts immediately after the war, although the organization did not meet from 1913 until 1920. When they responded to the French suffragists' appeal to attend the peace conference, their support for the allied war effort gave them some standing despite their previous peace efforts. One factor was Anna Howard Shaw's public recognition of their contribution when she received a medal from the United States government for her wartime assistance. The WWCTU's petition to the Peace Council asked that men who violated women in war should be punished and the women so outraged should be considered "wounded in war." This declaration was a cooperative effort with the Committee for the Protection of Women under International Law.[12] At each subsequent convention, the

WWCTU adopted resolutions in favor of the World Court at The Hague. They hoped it would facilitate negotiations between the Great Powers to outlaw war and settle disputes by peaceful methods.

The WWCTU also sent resolutions to two peace conferences in 1920—one in Lausanne, Switzerland, and the other in Washington, D.C. One delegation requested international peace and the second cited the need for an International Court of Arbitration.[13] The 1920 convention also endorsed plans for the League of Nations, and the World WCTU was among the first organizations given advisory representation in the Woman's Section on Peace and Disarmament. They subsequently commended the League of Nations for the appointment of a commission to study the alcohol problem.

Disarmament became the next major issue, and a Conference for the Limitation of Armaments was held in Washington in November 1921. Ninety-year-old Kaji Yajima, still president of the Japanese WCTU, traveled to the United States to present President Warren Harding with a peace petition signed by thousands of her country women. Anna Gordon represented the World WCTU and introduced Yajima. Then Prince Tokugawa, the Japanese delegate to the conference, held a reception for her. He praised American women for their leadership in struggles for peace and temperance, education, and moral purity.[14] He left out woman suffrage, won a year earlier in the United States but not yet on the men's political agenda in Japan. When the World WCTU met in Philadelphia the next year, the delegates resolved to commend President Harding for calling the Conference on Disarmament.[15]

Other women's organizations also had substantial input at the League of Nations, notably the IWSA. In 1921 Anna Wicksell of Sweden was appointed to the Mandates Commission of the League Council. They received the IWSA Geneva Congress resolutions on the regulation of prostitution and control of venereal disease.[16] Corbett Ashby's IWSA committee also established friendly relations with the League Secretariat and the International Labour Office. Altogether, fourteen IWSA members held administrative posts in the various committees, and ten were among the government delegates to the Assembly. The first three selected were Anna Wicksell (Sweden), Christine Bonnevie (Norway), and Henni Forchhammer (Denmark). They were joined by Paulina Luisi (Uruguay) and Clasina Albertina Kluyver (The Netherlands)—all old friends of the IWSA.[17] In the ILO a woman was chief of one section, and the IWSA was able to raise a vigorous protest at a proposal to allow employers to dismiss women from their posts upon marriage.

The issue of whether nations should be admitted to the League of Nations if they did not extend women equal rights foreshadowed the same debate later in the United Nations with the same result. In 1923, the Rome Congress of the IWSA resolved that the League of Nations would have no real value if it did not include all nations. Therefore, they urged that the international body "should secure in the shortest possible time the adhesion of all those countries of the world that are not yet members." However, the League was already weakened because some of the most powerful nations had not affiliated, including the United States.[18]

Despite women's lobbying efforts, few were appointed as official representatives to the League of Nations. Altogether, only seven nations appointed women to serve as technical advisors or substitutes in the eight assembly groups. Great Britain had a better record than most because a council for the representation of women was initiated in 1919. Largely due to their efforts, the British government adopted the practice of sending a woman substitute delegate to each League of Nations Assembly.[19] At the Fifth Assembly, Helena Swanwick served in this capacity on a commission that considered the needs of women and children. Women were not placed on other major commissions until 1929, but their numbers did increase.

In 1929, fifteen women attended the Tenth Assembly as delegates and technical advisors. Seven of them were active WILPF members.[20] Few women were appointed, even fewer were promoted. Only Rachel Crowdy attained a relatively high office, Chief of the Social Section.[21] She persuaded the Traffic in Women Commission to collect information. As a result, the Assembly adopted resolutions and recommended them to individual governments for action. The League of Nations condemned the regulation of vice, licensed brothels, registration of prostitutes, and compulsory medical examinations as exceptional measures against women. Corbett Ashby described this as "an amazing victory."[22] She was a substitute delegate to the League's Conference on Disarmament in 1932. That was a losing proposition as the world once again edged closer to war.

In the United States, Carrie Chapman Catt continued to be active in the Committee on the Cause and Cure of War. Because she was still the honorary president of the IAW, Catt also projected her dedication to the peace campaign through this longtime affiliation. Her resolution to form a permanent peace committee was implemented in 1926 with Rosa Manus as chairperson.[23] When the "Committee for Peace and the League of Nations" was established, Ruth Morgan of New York was selected as chairperson. Under their direction, the IAW developed a stronger educational role. At a board meeting in Prague in 1927, they agreed to hold a study conference on the maintenance of peace. Thus, in November 1927, Ruth Morgan and Rosa Manus arranged an Alliance Peace Committee meeting in Amsterdam. Over ninety representatives came from auxiliary countries, and most of the important women's international organizations sent fraternal delegates. The discussions focused on the economic and political causes of war.[24]

Catt crossed the Atlantic once again for that meeting. Other speakers included Signor de Madariaga, head of the Disarmament Section of the League of Nations, and Clasina Albertina Kluyver of the Foreign Office at The Hague.[25] Ruth Morgan later reported in the *International Woman Suffrage News* that the delegates were sure free trade was the key to peace. However, some of them were convinced that the economic problems of Europe were not important to the United States. Catt disagreed and pointed out that they had to be concerned about Asia and Africa as well as Europe.[26] Other matters also caused disharmony. For example, Nina Boyle resigned over what she perceived as excursions into propaganda.

At an interim meeting in Dresden in 1928, they discussed the Kellogg-Briand Pact.[27] It was proposed by France and the United States and initially signed that August. Under its conditions, forty-nine countries eventually agreed to renounce war. Because they retained the right to defend themselves and the Pact had no means of enforcement, it was subsequently ignored. However, the women saw some hope in this proposal and overcame their disagreements when the IAW met in Berlin in 1929.[28] They also pressed for American participation in the World Court. Although she did not attend, Catt lobbied for the Kellogg-Briand Treaty there and at the Third Conference on the Cause and Cure of War.[29] Two Japanese leaders of their peace movement, Uta Hayashi and Tsune Gauntlett, attended the next Cause and Cure of War conference in January, 1930. They were also fighting a losing battle.[30]

As World War I faded from memory and new threats began to arise, The League of Nations scheduled a world disarmament conference in February 1932. As women's organizations actively planned for it, the WILPF regained respectability, and the Peace Committee of the IAW held a Study Conference in Belgrade, in May 1931, to prepare public opinion.[31] A delegate from the Secretariat outlined preparations at the League of Nations.[32] The IAW passed resolutions on disarmament, international economic cooperation, and women's participation at the forthcoming disarmament congress. The delegates called on women in all countries "to urge upon Governments the necessity for this participation."[33]

In the United States, a peace caravan left Hollywood, California, in June of 1931 and traveled to Washington, D.C., to generate interest. A petition in support of disarmament was circulated in Britain, America, France, Germany, and other countries. Eight million signatures were gathered, and a procession that represented fifty-six countries preceded its presentation to the Disarmament Conference.[34] Women in church groups, students, and organizations like the IAW and ICW paraded in the name of peace. The World WCTU also sent representatives to the Committee on Peace and Disarmament when the League of Nations met in Geneva. The leaders of Willard's old organization declared that international friendship was essential to prevent war. They proposed that "international friendship can be attained by creating goodwill based on the Christian principles of justice and with political and economic cooperation to attain it."[35]

To provide some coordination, the alliance of women's groups arranged for an international committee of women to monitor the proceedings of the League of Nations World Disarmament Conference. After the 1931 IAW Study Conference, eleven women's international organizations united to form a committee. The new Liaison Committee of Women's International Organizations included the IAW, ICW, WILPF, and WCTU as well as the Young Women's Christian Association (YWCA) with a membership of forty million women in fifty-six countries. Like the WILPF, their headquarters was in Geneva. The new committee collated materials and tried to present a united front when they interacted with the League of Nations. Mary Dingman of the World's Young Women's Christian Association was president, and Rosa Manus served as secretary.

The number of participating organizations later increased to fifteen. Among them was another that Jane Addams had helped found, the Pan Pacific Women's Association. The PPWA continued to work for women's rights in Asia. They recommended that governments be asked to send summaries of laws affecting women in colonies, protectorates, and mandated territories as well as information about how native customs affected women and marriage.

Despite innumerable well-intentioned efforts and much popular enthusiasm, the Disarmament Conference was doomed before it started. The war machine was gaining speed faster. Japan invaded Manchuria, and both Germany and Japan withdrew from the League of Nations.[36] Reactions against the rise of Fascism in Germany stimulated peace movements although the WILPF, like everybody else, underestimated the horrors of Naziism. Jill Liddington contends that the women's peace activities were still much shaped by the separate spheres doctrine with its strong emphasis on maternalism. After this doctrine was once again taken to extremes in Germany, many women revised their views, as they had in World War I.[37]

As early as 1933, Rosa Manus brought word that the Jews were being persecuted, and Carrie Chapman Catt was part of a Committee of Ten who asked President Roosevelt to ease immigration restrictions, to no avail. At Paris in 1934, the Women's World Congress Against War and Fascism was well attended, but hope for peace kept diminishing.[38] Even Margery Corbett Ashby finally gave up and resigned from the

League of Nations Disarmament Committee in 1935.[39] But Catt continued the struggle. After the Tenth Anniversary Conference on the Cause and Cure of War, *Why Wars Must Cease* was published. It was comprised of ten chapters by prominent women like Eleanor Roosevelt and Jane Addams (who died that year).[40] In 1936, the IAW participated in a large World Peace Congress organized by Rosa Manus in Brussels.

As the Liason Committee of Women's International Organizations became the Joint Standing Committee of Women's International Organizations, it added a substantial presence to the system of nongovernmental organizations that offered advice to the League of Nations and the International Labor Organization. The Joint Standing Committee reminded the League that their Assembly resolved in September of 1935 that conditions of employment fell within the jurisdiction of the ILO. Then the First Committee of the League of Nations expressed hope that the ILO would look into the question of equality under labor legislation that affected women's right to work.[41]

The First Committee also asked the Council of the League of Nations to appoint a committee of experts of both sexes to study the many questions that related to the status of women. They wanted the League to seek the advice and co-operation of competent scientific institutions as well as international women's organizations. In October 1937, the League financed such a committee of experts. When they were appointed early in 1938, the committee consisted of four women and three men, the first time women were in the majority on a League committee.[42] The Women's Liaison Committee worked with them for publicity and education among women's organizations in many countries. Study groups tried to determine the status of women and propose improvements. Panels of men and women lawyers were recommended to advise on the application of existing legislation and suggest changes.[43]

Besides these international efforts, the women called for action in many individual countries. For instance, in England demands were submitted to Parliament at the same time as the Women's Liaison Committee submitted theirs to the League of Nations in Geneva. The women asked for equal conditions and equal pay in all public services, equal minimum wages under trade board decisions, removal of the marriage bar to employment, abolition of the special laws against prostitutes, and independent nationality rights.

While women pressured for action, the first task of the League's committee of experts was to determine the scope of its inquiry. Because of the many systems of law and different religious influences, they decided to study first the status of women under European legal systems. These included America, Australia, and South Africa. The committee then decided Islamic law was also well enough codified, and parts of

China and Thailand were influenced by German law so they could be included. Women's organizations cooperated to try to ascertain the facts about the laws and the extent of their implementation.[44]

On January 7, 1939, the League's committee of experts invited representatives of the women's international organizations to a conference to discuss the progress of their inquiry. They had decided to include the Hindu as well as Islamic system of law, and they wanted to enlist women's organizations to help ascertain actual applications such as case law and administrative decisions. The committee also wanted to know about pre-existing or subsequent laws that nullified provisions intended to improve the status of women and about concerted refusals to enforce them. This information was requested by January 1, 1940. But by then the Second World War was underway, and the activities of the League of Nations were curtailed, so the committee was disbanded.[45] Once again women's rights were put on hold, and the peace activists had to decide whether to support or resist the war effort.

Not all of them were able to face another world conflict. Because Millicent Garrett Fawcett had died in 1929, that staunch supporter of British militarism missed the acceleration into the Second World War. On September 2, 1939, Prime Minister Neville Chamberlain declared war on Germany. That November, Helena Swanwick died of an overdose of sleeping pills. *Three Guineas,* Virginia Woolf's protest against male militarism and male power, had been published in 1938. A feminist and antimilitarist, she echoed John Stuart Mill but went unheeded. In March 1941, as the Germans approached Paris, Woolf waded into the River Ouse to die.[46]

Between the wars, much world attention was focused on the League of Nations and what now seems like a naive effort to assure world peace. However, a variety of other international activities were also underway to improve women's circumstances. At the same time, women's groups were divided on whether protective legislation would prevent women from being forced into the most menial jobs or out of the better ones.

17

ALICE PAUL AND THE BATTLE
OVER PROTECTIVE LEGISLATION

Protective legislation was not a new issue when opposing views divided international women's organizations after World War I. In 1919, besides the far-flung WWCTU, ICW, IAW, and WILPF, new international women's organizations were formed, such as the International Federation of University Women (IFUW). The National Federation of Business and Professional Women's Clubs also established the International FBPWC. The Socialists and Communists also stepped up their campaigns to attract women. In 1920 Alexandra Kollontai founded the International Secretariat of Communist Women.[1] Like them, many European feminists were very concerned about the restrictive effects of protective legislation on women's economic opportunities. As a result, between 1919 and 1922, seven European nations adopted equal rights clauses in their constitutions.[2]

As European women joined together to support peace and a larger role in the League of Nations, the American woman suffrage movement culminated in ratification of the right to vote on August 26, 1920. But the seeds of future dissension were already sown. The National Woman Suffrage Association and the American Woman Suffrage Association had reconciled in 1890 before the deaths of pioneers like Lucy Stone, Elizabeth Cady Stanton, and Susan B. Anthony. However, more division was caused when Alice Paul's (1885-1977) Congressional Committee separated from the National American Woman Suffrage Association and subsequently became the National Woman's Party (NWP) in 1916.[3] Differences in policy and attitude continued long enough to sabotage equal rights for women even in the formation of the United Nations in 1945.

The militant National Woman's Party worked for a federal woman suffrage amendment throughout World War I. What antagonized the politicians most was the NWP's tactic of holding the party in power responsible for not giving women the vote. Paul adopted this strategy from the Pankhursts. Whether the militant NWP helped or hindered the battle for suffrage is still debated, but President Wilson did come around to support woman suffrage during World War I when he wanted women's cooperation. Carrie Chapman Catt was not quite as conservative as her British counterpart, Millicent Garrett Fawcett; but she still

Alice Paul, founder of the National Woman's Party. Reprinted with permission from the National Woman's Party, 144 Constitution Avenue, NE, Washington, D.C.

cautiously maintained a good rapport with the government. As Catt led the National American Woman Suffrage Association in the final drive for woman suffrage in the United States, she and Fawcett occasionally commiserated with one another. In 1916 Catt wrote to Fawcett that she believed her duty was to stay in the USA where "a very bad and hurtful spirit has got into the National Association greatly stimulated by a gang of young women who were Mrs. Pankhurst's followers."[4]

In 1919 when Catt established the League of Women Voters (LWV) to educate a broader spectrum of women, Women's City Clubs were also founded to educate women for their new political roles. However, many women's groups did not want to extend equality to the workplace.[5] They feared that heavy labor and long hours would harm women's health and detract from their ability to perform the domestic tasks still considered their primary responsibility. Along with other conservative women's organizations such as the National Consumer's League (NCL) founded in 1899, the American LWV worked vigorously to retain and promote protective legislation for working women.[6] Consequently, they opposed the blanket equal rights legislation favored by the NWP. The Women's Trade Union League (WTUL) was initiated in 1903 through the combined efforts of settlement house workers and labor officials to organize women into trade unions.[7] With this impetus toward equal rights, the WTUL did not advocate protective legislation for women for another ten years.[8]

Despite conservative opposition, nearly fifty organizations were represented at the National Woman's Party Convention in Washington, D.C., in February 1921.[9] By then many American women saw that protective legislation inhibited work opportunities, and the National Woman's Party was adamant that the battle for women's rights would not be won until they had full equality in work as well as other areas. The social reformers who surrounded Catt disagreed, and the two groups could not reach a compromise to propose a protective legislation clause in the Equal Rights Amendment (ERA). Then the rift widened, but the NWP was still able to have the ERA introduced in Congress in 1923.[10]

As the battle lines were drawn for and against protective legislation for working women, membership in the NCL and the WTUL often overlapped with that of the League of Women Voters. Eleanor Roosevelt (1884-1962) joined the LWV in 1921 and the WTUL in 1922.[11] She vigorously supported protective legislation and also the peace movement. Roosevelt represented the Federation of Women's Clubs at a 1924 Conference on the Cause and Cure of War (Carrie Chapman Catt's peace organization). To her death in 1962, Roosevelt staunchly contended that women were different from men and needed special treatment. She supported protective legislation, and at the same time contended that women did not need equal rights spelled out because they were not disadvantaged. Her participation in these organizations, backed by FDR's presidency, threw major roadblocks in the path to women's legal equality, despite her eventual support for women's advancement in politics and her concern for human rights.

Although Eleanor Roosevelt had volunteered at the Rivington Street Settlement House between her return from boarding school in

London and her marriage to FDR in March 1905, as a young woman, she had very little involvement with the women's rights movement. Opposed to suffrage when she married, Roosevelt later said her first contact with the women's suffrage movement came in 1919 at a luncheon with Alice Wadworth, wife of one of the Senate's most vehement anti-suffragists, while the Nineteenth Amendment was being ratified.[12] Later, Roosevelt said she had no opinion on suffrage then, but "soon after I undertook work which proved to me the value of the vote. . . . I became a much more ardent citizen and feminist than anyone . . . would have dreamed possible."[13] She became very active in the women's division of the Democratic party, but Roosevelt tended to distrust women who were also members of the NWP.[14] This was at least partly because the New York branch had angered Franklin Delano Roosevelt by its obstructionist tactics when, as governor, he attempted to pass protective legislation for women and children. This alienation would have serious consequences after FDR became president.[15]

In 1923, the NWP also antagonized the IAW. They disrupted the meeting in Rome when they made a bid to become a member organization, just as Catt was bowing out of the presidency. In 1925 Alice Paul and Mrs. O. H. P. Belmont recruited European feminists to join the International Advisory Council of the NWP, and they again applied for membership in the IAW. The LWV, then the only organization that represented Americans, voted unanimously against their admission. Carrie Chapman Catt threatened to withhold American financing unless British President, Margery Corbett Ashby, blackballed the NWP, which she did. However, the confrontation Catt had hoped to avoid occurred anyway at the 1926 convention in Paris. The NWP presented their case for membership, and the European women divided on this and protective legislation.[16]

Although the IAW had generally opposed protective legislation, the LWV had been able to keep the international organization from issuing any statement. The LWV contended that the issue needed further study. In January 1926, the Alliance committee on like conditions of work for men and women weakened their stand. Their preliminary report advocated that future labor laws tend toward equality for men and women, and that married women should have the right to work. The NWP opposed this retrenchment, as did British feminists like Chrystal Macmillan, Emmeline Pethick Lawrence, and Lady Rhondda, but they lost. Then Lady Rhondda's Six Point Group withdrew its application for membership in the IAW, and several European feminist organizations opposed to special legislation and protective conventions for women also withdrew.[17]

In 1927, European feminists like the Six Point Group met to organize the Open Door Council. They subsequently formed new groups such as Open Door International to lobby for complete civil equality between men and women at the League of Nations, World Court, and International Labour Organization.[18] To further cooperation, an international advisory council was established for foreign feminists who might wish to affiliate with the NWP.[19] Some American women who had supported protective legislation also modified their views somewhat after they visited the USSR in 1927. As they became more conscious of how far behind women were in the United States, they praised the Scandanavians for having recently passed social legislation.[20]

As in Europe, Alice Paul's National Woman's Party was well received in Latin America. Carrie Chapman Catt had led the way there, and the IAW continued to interact with various women's organizations. The minutes of an IAW Headquarters Meeting of January 23, 1917, reported a letter and a number of reports on a Women's Congress sent by the governor of Yucatan, Mexico. The IAW delegated a Mrs. Evans to express interest and send leaders of the Mexican Women's Congress copies of *Jus Suffragii* in French and English.[21] The IAW had followed the precedent of the ICW when they established these and German as the three official languages of the organization. However, in a meeting of the Headquarters Committee on October 22, 1918, a Mrs. Ruffin was delegated to contact friends in Buenos Aires to try to interest them in a Spanish column in the *International Woman Suffrage News,* the successor to *Jus Suffragii.*[22]

As Catt became more involved in the peace movement, the League of Women Voters' overtures to Latin American women declined. That set the stage for the NWP to take a more active part.[23] Although the NWP was weakened by a decline in membership and finances after the American women's franchise was won, the leaders decided to revitalize the international women's rights movement.[24] Alice Paul contended that women could not be confined within narrow nationalistic bounds. She insisted that the status of all women was interrelated in all classes and in all countries. At the NWP's instigation, the Fifth Pan American Congress held in Santiago, Chile, in 1923 resolved to discuss women's rights at the Sixth Conference scheduled for Havana, Cuba, in 1928.[25]

Meanwhile, local support for women's rights was growing in Latin America. In 1926 in Panama City, an Inter-American Congress of Women passed an equality resolution. However, no women were included in the American delegation to the Sixth Pan American Conference in Havana in 1928, and the resolution of the Fifth Conference at Santiago was ignored until the NWP sent four women to demand a hearing. They were refused initially; but they staged rallies, gave interviews, and lobbied delegates until they were heard. Then the NWP persuaded six countries to sponsor an Equal Rights Treaty modeled on the American Equal Rights Amendment. It would be on the agenda of the Seventh Conference scheduled for Montevideo, Uruguay, in 1933.

At Havana, a draft treaty was also proposed on the civil status of women.[26] An official Inter-American Commission of Women was created to study women's status, and NWP activist Doris Stevens was appointed chair. After the Havana congress, the NWP immediately announced their intention to promulgate the Equal Rights Treaty at the League of Nations in Geneva.[27] Despite this forward momentum abroad, the NWP continued to lose ground in the United States. In 1928 Democratic presidential candidate, Al Smith, strongly favored protective legislation for women and children. Consequently, Alice Paul supported Hoover. His vice president, Charles Curtis, had introduced the ERA.[28] After Hoover was elected, however, he did not endorse the ERA; and the NWP was left with more enemies among the Democrats.[29]

By the summer of 1929, the largely European Open Door International was convinced that supporters of protective legislation were living in the past. They issued a manifesto that called for equal economic freedom for men and women, and the IAW began to fall back in line. At the Eleventh Congress in Berlin in 1929, a compromise proposal for gradual change was attempted to hold member support, but the immediatists still defected.[30] In 1930 when British feminists organized Equal Rights International to work for the Equal Rights Treaty, the NWP was invited to join. Despite some opposition from their members, internationalist leaders like Alice Paul, Mrs. O. H. P. Belmont, and Doris Stevens were convinced that Equal Rights International could be a catalyst to get the Equal Rights Treaty approved in the League of Nations. Therefore, the NWP affiliated with both Open Door International and Equal Rights International.

Even women's nationality rights became a divisive issue. Like the Inter-American Commission of Women, these new organizations followed the precedent of the ICW and IAW and supported the right of married women to retain their original citizenship. Nationality rights were on the agenda of both the League of Nations and the First World Conference for Codification of International Law. This conference was scheduled to be held at The Hague in March 1930. The Inter-American Commission unanimously agreed that "there shall be no distinction based on sex in their law and practice relating to nationality."[31] Although Emma Wold, NWP attorney, was appointed as a technical advisor to the American delegation, the measure did not pass.[32] The conservative LWV women also favored equal citizenship rights for married women, but they felt obliged to oppose the NWP. Based on this division, The Hague Conference recommended that women's nationality remain dependent on their husbands.[33] President Hoover did support the NWP far enough to authorize the American delegate to cast the only opposition vote.

FDR's election to the presidency reinforced protective legislation in the United States in 1932. Then a number of New York women in the NCL, WTUL, LWV, and especially those in the Democratic Party, received federal appointments. Molly Dewson headed the women's committee of the Democratic Party, Mary Anderson the Women's Bureau of the Department of Labor, and Frances Perkins became the first woman in the Cabinet. In the New Deal, they were the core of the women's political network in Washington. With that power base, they supported protective legislation and slowed the drive for equality.

These Americans made their authority felt internationally, too. At the 1933 conference in Montevideo, the Inter-American Commission adopted an Equal Nationality Treaty for women and recommended equal civil and political rights as soon as possible. Initially, the United States did not sign this treaty, although it had been the only nation to sign at the Hague. The NWP contended that Eleanor Roosevelt had influenced President Roosevelt's appointment of Sophonisba Breckinridge, a supporter of protective legislation, to the delegation to defeat equal rights.[34] Congressional opinion was outraged, however, and FDR was besieged to order the signing. Despite Breckinridge's objection, she signed the document, and it was ratified by the Senate in May 1934. American women no longer lost their citizenship if they married foreign nationals.

In Europe, previously opposed organizations began to support equal rights. One was the Women's International League for Peace and Freedom. At the 1926 American section meeting, conservatives were able to table the ERA. That same year a resolution that supported women's total equality passed at the international convention in Dublin.[35] In 1934 at the Zurich Congress, the Equal Rights Treaty was approved, and the WILPF resolved to ask its national sections to recommend it to their respective governments. By 1935, a WTUL secretary wrote to a friend at the League of Nations that the WILPF, The Open Door International, and the International Alliance of Women all supported the NWP's equality objectives.[36]

With this backing, more than a dozen nations brought an equality treaty to the First Commission of the League of Nations. Although the United States was never a member, NWP feminists used their memberships in international women's groups and their friendships with Latin American representatives to present their equalitarian feminist views. In 1931 the League created a Women's Consultative Committee. It was charged to report on the status of women and make recommendations on equality. However, the members disagreed on protective legislation, and the committee ceased to function in 1932. In 1935 the Juridical Committee of the League of Nations debated the Equal Rights Treaty for five days.[37] By then, thirteen international organizations had approved the principle. In the United States three national organizations endorsed the Equal Rights Amendment while four more placed it on their study programs.

Unfazed by the growing support, the League of Women Voters remained opposed. International protective legislation seemed like an appropriate extension of what they had won in America.[38] However, because the LWV was not an international organization, they could not submit a formal protest to the League of Nations. As the IAW would not annex the LWV statement, they turned to the World YWCA. Despite almost no support outside the American delegation, Mary Anderson led the social reformers in a successful effort to block the progress of the Equal Rights Treaty through the League of Nations. Further study was recommended, and the treaty was referred back to individual governments, women's organizations, and the ILO.[39]

Its women's work division remained a stronghold of those who feared that the international Equal Rights Treaty, like the proposed American ERA, would destroy protective labor conventions for women. Mary Anderson, director of the U.S. Women's Bureau, encouraged her allies to express their objections and was appointed to head the official U.S. observers at the ILO in 1933. Then, any attempt to revise the protective labor conventions was prevented.[40] After the United States joined the ILO in 1934, FDR appointed another conservative, Grace Abbott, as the American delegate.

Despite the Americans' added influence as members, the NWP and its equal rights allies continued to oppose ILO-sponsored protective labor conventions for women employed at night or in hazardous work such as mines and the lead paint industry. Equal rights for women continued to gain more favor even in the United States. By 1937, nine national women's organizations and more than one hundred state and local groups had endorsed the ERA.[41] Despite this support, NWP members in the late 1930s were excluded both from the women's coalition formed to study the Equal Rights Treaty and from the new committee of experts appointed by the League of Nations. They were assigned to consider an equal rights treaty and to conduct a comprehensive, worldwide survey of the status of women. Of the four women appointed, only Kerstin Hessengren of Sweden was slightly sympathetic to women's equality.[42] The Americans appointed Dorothy Kenyon, longtime legal adviser to the LWV and an ardent opponent of the ERA.[43]

Those who favored equal employment opportunities for women lost ground in other ways as well. As American conservatives defeated the drive for women's equality in the United States, major ideological shifts occurred elsewhere. The rise of Fascism in Italy and Germany and the Japanese incursions in China halted women's rights movements in those countries. The National Woman's Party was quick to protest and warn of the danger.[44] However, this group remained a small, militant minority who alienated many of the general public. Their voice went unheard when they called upon American women to help their German sisters and try to prevent similar antifeminist movements in other countries.

Other issues generated more cooperation. The NWP quickly supported the IAW's call for women to resist being recognized primarily for bearing children. The NWP also joined British feminist protests against the imprisonment and execution of European women pacifists.[45] In 1938, Alice Paul invited European feminists to participate in the formation of a World Woman's Party (WWP). They wanted to counter the threats to women's status posed by fascist regimes and broaden the movement for complete equality.[46]

That same year, at the Pan-American Conference in Lima, Peru, the Inter-American Commission of Women submitted their report to a special committee. Also, various delegations presented resolutions that related to the political and civil rights of women. "The Lima Declaration in Favor of Women's Rights" was based on a draft submitted by the Mexican delegation and a treaty suggested by the Cubans. It set forth the right of women to political equality with men, equality as to civil status, full protection in and opportunity for work, and maternity protection. Assistance was also requested for rural women. Another resolution called on the Pan American Union to study the possibility of convening an Inter-American Conference of Women.[47]

Despite these victories, the NWP soon lost its leadership role among Latin American feminists. With the backing of President Roosevelt, the protective legislation proponents planned to eliminate the Inter-American Commission on Women and so depose Doris Stevens as chair. Endorsed by the WTUL, LWV, YWCA, NCL, and the Councils of Jewish and Catholic Women, in 1939 Mary Anderson succeeded in getting her former assistant at the U.S. Women's Bureau, Mary Winslow, appointed to replace Doris Stevens.[48] By 1940 the Inter-American Commission on Women had been reorganized. With their new, conservative outlook, they staunchly supported protective legislation and opposed any overall equal rights amendment or treaty.[49] However, they were out of step with the internationalists, and the groundwork had already been laid to include women's issues when the United Nations was founded after the war.

18

MARY RITTER BEARD:
SCHOLARSHIP AND A LINK WITH JAPAN

In England women like Josephine Butler broke down barriers to protect others from being vulnerable to arbitrary designation as prostitutes, and Annie Besant waged a major lawsuit over the right to publish birth control information. Later, Marie Stopes in England, Margaret Sanger in the United States, and Shidzue Kato in Japan were among the campaigners for women's right to control child bearing. Still active in 1997, Kato survived more than one hundred years and became a living reminder of women's struggle for equal rights. In the 1930s when she wrote her autobiography, Kato also played a part in Mary Ritter Beard's effort to promote the collection and preservation of women's historical documents.

Beard was an American enigma in the international women's movement although she forged connections with women in both Europe and Asia. Beard's ties with women's suffrage, the labor movement, birth control, and the collection of women's history on a global scale mark her as a forerunner of Second Wave feminism. Her contribution will probably never be fully explained, and she certainly did not help when she destroyed many of her own and her husband Charles' papers. Despite her own bad example, women owe much to Beard for encouraging them (especially leaders of women's colleges) to collect women's papers.

Beard wanted to make women aware of their collective history and contribution to social development. She was convinced that the belief that women had been oppressed was in itself oppressive. Instead, she argued that women had always been active, assertive, competent contributors to their societies. To accept the myth of women as a subject sex would undermine their collective strength and sense of self-worth.[1] Ann J. Lane edited a collection of Mary Beard's writings and appraised her contribution to the women's movement. Lane concluded that Beard's fundamental theme was that "women were now and always had been active and engaged participants in the human story."[2] Beard's goal, which Lane described as more of a calling than a career, was to arouse every woman to a new and vital sense of self-worth through an understanding of the past. Within this context, she opposed academic programs designed to enable women to compete directly with men. She said this turned them into male imitations instead of, as the recent women's

Mary Ritter Beard, women's historian. Reprinted with permission of the DePauw University Archives and Special Collections. Roy O. West Library, Greencastle, Indiana.

movement expressed it, "persons in their own right." This viewpoint ultimately isolated Beard from the feminists. She did not attract sympathy or support, according to Lane, because "time and again she attacked college-trained 'professional' women and academics, entrenched within the walls of convention and pseudo-intellectualism, who speak with authority of worlds that she knew they had never seen outside of a book."[3]

While Beard tried to show women's independent accomplishments, her own life (like Eleanor Roosevelt's) in some respects contradicted her beliefs. Mary Ritter married Charles Austin Beard in 1900. By then they had graduated from DePauw University in their home state of Indiana— she in 1897, he in 1898. Then Charles went to study English and European history at Oxford.[4] Mary Beard gave birth to their first child in England and cut her own activist teeth in the women's suffrage and labor movements there. In Manchester, they lived across the street from the Pankhursts.

When the Beards returned to the United States in 1901, both entered graduate school at Columbia University. But Mary dropped out

Shidzue Kato, pioneer in the Japanese birth control movement. Reprinted with permission.

to raise their first child and give birth to another. Charles went on to complete his doctorate in 1904. He remained on the faculty until 1917 and wrote the books and articles that were the basis of his distinguished scholarly reputation. He wrote ten articles for the *Political Science Quarterly* and reviewed approximately sixty-five books, but these were a minor part of his achievement.[5] During that thirteen-year period he wrote nine books alone, collaborated on writing two four-volume textbooks and editing another, and wrote *American Citizenship* with his wife.

Altogether, Mary Beard collaborated with her husband on seven books. These included the distinguished five-volume series, *The Rise of American Civilization,* published between 1920 and 1942.[6] The six books she wrote by herself, the first at age 39, never received anywhere near the recognition of those she coauthored with her already established spouse. Moreover, despite her designation as coauthor, critics always viewed her contribution as secondary. She demonstrated one of women's common problems as she labored for recognition in the shade of her more famous husband. A later acquaintance, Dorothy Hamilton Dick Brush, recalled that Mary Beard told her about a gathering where Charles was honored for their book on the rise of the American Republic. She was invited, but he got the recognition and the medal. Brush compared this occasion with those when Stalin and Mussolini gave medals to fathers, but not mothers of large families.[7]

Mary Beard's collaboration probably resulted in the inclusion of more women's history than would have been the case otherwise. In a 1966 survey of the twenty-seven leading American history textbooks, the Beards' *Basic History of the United States* (published in 1944) contained the most material on women although twenty-five of the total were published after 1960.[8]

As she tended their family and collaborated with her husband in scholarly endeavors during their Columbia University years, Mary Beard also continued her feminist activities. She was a member of the National Women's Trade Union League in 1909 when they supported the shirtwaist makers' strike. By 1910 she was raising funds for the National American Woman Suffrage Association, then presided over by Anna Howard Shaw with Jane Addams as first vice president. Beard became vice chairman of the Manhattan branch; and the next year she edited *The Woman Voter,* the official organ of the New York Woman Suffrage Party. She resigned in 1912 to work for the Wage Earner's League, a working women's affiliate of the NAWSA.

When Alice Paul formed the Congressional Committee of the NAWSA, she chose Mary Beard as one of the members along with Lucy Burns. She and Alice Paul, like Beard, had gained experience in the British suffrage movement.[9] Beard continued to support trade union organizations and work for woman suffrage until the vote was finally won. However, she gradually became less active in the movement even before the suffragists divided over the Equal Rights Amendment. Like many women in the labor sector such as Florence Kelly, Rose Schneiderman, Alice Hamilton, and Lillian Wald, Beard felt that protective legislation was essential for working women. As early as 1914 Beard told Alice Paul that, as far as she was concerned, the rights of labor women came first and suffrage second. Her transition from feminist-activist to histo-rian-observer was well underway before Paul initiated the ERA.[10]

Other interests also diverted Beard away from the American women's rights struggle. In 1922 she accompanied her husband to Japan where he was invited to serve as municipal advisor to the mayor of Tokyo, Baron (later Count) Shimpei Goto. After the great Tokyo earth-quake the next year, Charles was again invited to advise Baron Goto, who had been appointed Home Minister charged with the reconstruction of Tokyo.[11] During these visits, Mary Beard became acquainted with the Baroness Shidzue Ishimoto (later Kato). They formed an enduring and mutually rewarding international association.

When Shidzue Ishimoto met Mary Beard, she was already well connected among activist American women. Ishimoto had visited the United States for the first time in 1919.[12] She was studying English and secretarial skills at the YWCA training school in New York when Agnes Smedley introduced her to Margaret Sanger in 1920.[13] Sanger was already famous for her pioneer efforts to promote birth control, a term she coined, when she encouraged Ishimoto to champion the cause that became her major lifetime preoccupation. Ishimoto returned home to form a birth control league in Japan in 1921.[14]

Ishimoto became known as the "Japanese Margaret Sanger" after she hosted the American original in Japan in 1922. The Japanese govern-ment was reluctant to receive the notorious Sanger, and enormous pub-licity was generated as the officials shifted positions. First, they refused to grant Sanger a visa. She circumvented this by boarding a ship bound for China with a stopover in Japan. When her ship docked, the authori-ties initially would not let her land. Without a visa, the controversial lady cooled her heels on the ship the first few days they were in port. During that time she received many visitors. In her autobiography, Sanger recalled one group of women who represented several labor organiza-tions. The leader said the industrial revolution had put women in virtual slavery in Japan. However, because they were accustomed to sub-servience to men, she thought it would be a long time before they learned to rebel. Nor was suffrage likely to come soon, she predicted, because many women did not see its advantages.

They were not stirred either, she went on, by the thought of eco-nomic independence, because Japanese women liked to have their hus-bands take care of them. Despite this dismal picture, Sanger recalled that the petite, kimono-clad lady then brightened and "with eyes sparkling, she added, 'But when the message of birth control came to us from Hon-olulu (where Sanger had stopped en route amid much publicity), like the lightening we understood its meaning, and now we are awakened.'"[15]

As the pressure of public attention increased, the authorities decreed that Sanger could land but not lecture publicly on birth control.

Then this directive was also rescinded, and her month-long stay became a triumph for Baroness Ishimoto as well. Sanger had been invited by *Kaizo* magazine to give ten lectures of five hours each. Later, she wrote in her autobiography that when she accepted, she thought that must have been a translation error, but it was not.[16] After Sanger's visit, Ishimoto was an old hand at dealing with Western guests when she welcomed Mary Beard on her first trip to the Orient that same year. Beard also received a tour of the infamous Yoshiwara prostitution area, but she was not ready to tackle the social purity cause.

Instead, after the Beards' second trip, she published an article on how Japanese women organized to meet the crisis of the earthquake and fire.[17] She described how forty-two groups quickly affiliated with the Tokyo Federation of Women's Organizations (Tokyo Kengo Fujinkai) in various departments such as Politics, Industry, and Labor.[18] Ishimoto was active in the political department where the suffrage movement was strengthened by the support of the Japanese Women's Christian Temperance Union under Ochimi Kubushiro. This department became the League for the Realization of Women's Suffrage (Fujin Sanseiken Kabutoku Kisei Domeikai) in 1924. Mary Beard concluded her article with an appeal for books to construct a library for Japanese women like the one American men were preparing for their male counterparts. She noted that a separate library for women was necessary because the other donated books "may not be accessible to very many women because they will be shut up in the men's universities."[19] The journal that published her article, *The Woman Citizen,* offered to collect and send any volumes contributed by their readers.

After these two trips, Beard's friendship with Ishimoto expanded with their mutual interests. She saw Ishimoto's autobiography, *Facing Two Ways,* through its American publication by Farrar and Rinehart in New York in 1935.[20] That book followed Ishimoto's stint on the Feakins Lecture Bureau circuit in 1932 and 1933. Her lectures and other contacts brought her many American friends and supporters. Ishimoto also participated in the International Women's Congress in Chicago in 1933.[21] Her broad base of international support came in handy when the Baroness's politics got her arrested on December 13, 1937. Then Ishimoto's son, Arata, notified another American friend, Dorothy Hamilton Dick. She was also an old friend of Margaret Sanger's and had recently met Ishimoto during her second visit to Japan. Hugh Byas, whom Mary Beard described as "the outstanding Western reporter in Japan," also publicized the arrest. Then the publisher of Ishimoto's autobiography as well as Margaret Sanger and other acquaintances protested her incarceration.

Ishimoto's American ties were strong enough to exert pressure on Hiroshi Saito, the Japanese ambassador to the United States; and she was released within two weeks.[22] This episode ended the prewar birth control movement in Japan as the warlords tightened their control. As in Germany, they called upon women for the patriotic exploitation of their wombs to fill the ranks of youths who would inevitably be lost during the battles to come.

As war tensions increased, the international cooperation between Ishimoto and Beard shifted more toward Beard's realm of interest. Beard and Austrian feminist, Anna Askanasy, were part of a group who had begun an ambitious enterprise, an encyclopedia of women. Shidzue Ishimoto was asked to write the Japanese women's history.[23] She enlisted a number of Japanese scholars to write sketches of important women, a difficult task at a time when women were not allowed to enroll in most institutions of higher learning in Japan and could not even avail themselves of library facilities at Tokyo University.

By the time Ishimoto and her associates prepared and translated a rough draft, the Nazis were threatening Austria; and Anna Askanasy was forced to flee. Although she was able to get to Switzerland and then on to Canada, all of her papers had to be left behind and were destroyed by the Nazis. The Japanese manuscript was spared because Ishimoto sent it to Mary Beard for safe keeping in the United States. By then Beard had to give up on one of her major goals—the formation of a World Center for Women's Archives. Beard had envisioned a clearinghouse of information on the history of women when an office was opened in Rockefeller Center to collect money in 1936. Hungarian feminist-pacifist Rosika Schwimmer had influenced her conception of this project.[24] As Director of Archives, Beard had grand plans for a global collection of materials, but a lack of funds forced the World Center for Women's Archives Corporation to be dissolved in 1940.

After that, Beard attempted to persuade presidents of women's colleges to collect materials about women. Beard was very far sighted in that enterprise, but she was also often disappointed.[25] However, archivist Margaret Grierson showed some interest at Smith College, and Beard deposited Ishimoto's manuscript there for safekeeping.[26] Because Beard planned to write a history of women, she also enthusiastically accepted editor Walter Yust's invitation to critique the *Encyclopedia Britannica* for gaps in women's history. When Beard and her associates were finished, Yust expressed great enthusiasm; but the suggested changes were never incorporated and the report was lost.

While World War Two forced the women's encyclopedia project into abeyance, Ishimoto's unpublished manuscript must have rested uneasily on Mary Beard's mind. In a letter dated October 28, 1945, she joyously wrote to Margaret Grierson that an article in *Newsweek* said Ishimoto had not only survived the war but had divorced, remarried, and given birth to a child. Her new husband was labor leader Kanju Kato. Beard told Grierson that she intended to contact General MacArthur to get in touch with her old friend. She was eager to see if Kato wanted to turn her sketches of women into a book in Japan.[27] In the same letter she advocated that all of the Smith College alumnae write books on their specialized aspects of the force of women in history. This subject was probably much on her mind as her most important book, *Woman as Force in History: A Study in Traditions and Realities*, was due to be published by Macmillan Company in 1946. Presumably that also left a gap in Beard's scholarly activities just as the war ended.

Later, Beard wrote to Grierson that she had been contacted by a Lieutenant C.H. Phillips "on his own initiative" to tell her that, under American Occupation regulations, she could write to Shidzue Ishimoto (now Kato) through Lieutenant Ethyl B. Weed.[28] As a lieutenant, Phillips was unlikely to have acted on his own initiative. But whether or not he was responding to orders initiated by the Beards' request or elsewhere is unclear. Most likely, the well-known Beards were the primary force behind this particular bit of women's history.

In any case, Ethyl B. Weed, an unknown American, former director of the Women's Club in Cleveland, Ohio, played a major role in the interactions between Beard and Kato as well as in the Japanese woman suffrage movement. General MacArthur had announced before he arrived in Japan that he would extend suffrage to women. In his Supreme Command Allied Pacific (SCAP) Civilian Information and Education Section under General Kenneth Dyke, Lieutenant Weed was the Women's Affairs Information Officer in the Policy and Programs Branch. She was charged with getting out the Japanese women's vote in their first national election, so her assistance in reinstating Beard's communication with Kato was a small sidelight.

Shidzue Kato did not respond to Beard's query as quickly as Beard might have hoped. For one thing, as Japanese women were about to be awarded suffrage, Kato was among the first group of women who wanted to run for political office. She was elected to the Diet on April 10, 1946. Perhaps Kato's political campaign as well as the chaos of postwar communication delayed her response to Mary Beard's inquiry about the manuscript on Japanese women. At least Beard must have become restless and perhaps a bit competitive. She wrote in a June 6, 1946, letter to Grierson that "we don't absolutely have to get Mrs. Kato's consent" for publication. Beard enclosed a clipping from *Book Notes* that said Ruth Benedict, author of *Patterns of Culture,* had received a grant of $1,000 from Lord & Taylor to work on a new book, *Assignment Japan.* At that time, Benedict was a professor of Cultural Anthropology at Columbia University. Apparently she had looked at Kato's manuscript at Smith College. Beard also may have felt pressured because she had heard from Askanasy that publication of the *Woman's Encyclopedia* was going ahead (at least for the German and Japanese sections) under Ilsa

Langer's direction in Hamburg.[29] Kato solved Beard's dilemma when she sent permission to publish the Japanese women's history.[30]

After this negotiation ended, Beard professed not to be interested in completing the book herself. She expressed pleasure that Margaret Grierson recommended Dorothy Hamilton Dick. Although they had not met before, Dick, a 1917 Smith College graduate, was a fortuitous choice because of her own acquaintance with Shidzue Kato and their mutual ties with Margaret Sanger and the Birth Control Movement. With Beard's blessing, Dick resumed correspondence with her old friend, Shidzue Kato, through Ethyl Weed. They had been in touch as late as 1939 despite Beard's assertion that she could not communicate with Kato after 1935 because of the war. Dick subsequently began to reflect Beard's influence in some ways. As a loyal Smith graduate, she wrote to Ethyl Weed that Margaret Sanger had decided to give her remaining papers to Smith College and she hoped Kato would do the same.[31] Kato did not.

After Beard's death, Dick (remarried with a name change to Brush) professed amusement as she recalled how the project gradually became Mary Beard's. When she donated some of her correspondence with Beard and Sanger to the Sophia Smith Collection, Brush wrote to Margaret Grierson:

One of the things I love about Mary is the funny, thoroughly human quality she exhibited after I had begun this work. She had said that she didn't want to do it, indeed wouldn't do it, wanted me to do it and would help me in every way she could! But after I had shown her the first of my work while she praised it and said it was fine, she concluded that it would be much better for her herself, to write it—not as I had planned it but as examples in a history of Japanese women! Had Mary been nearer my own age, I might have been offended, as it was I was only amused. I admired her so much and really loved her so it made no difference to me.[32]

To complete the book, Beard's letters to Ethyl Weed for Shidzue Kato requested additional information on contemporary Japanese women such as Doctor Yayoi Yoshioka, who was purged by the Americans along with pioneer suffragist, Fusae Ichikawa, for allegedly helping the Japanese war effort. This must not have disturbed Beard particularly because she asked Weed at one point if Ichikawa might write sketches of current women in the Diet. According to Beard, "She probably knows them all and could do this between bouts in her garden."[33] Apparently Kato did not favor this because she provided the sketches herself.

Beard finally met Ethyl Weed when the officer returned briefly to the United States in 1948. Shidzue Kato also visited Beard in 1951 after she failed to be reelected to a third two-year term in the Lower House. On the next round, Kato was elected to the Upper Chamber for a six-year term. In the final chapters on modern Japanese women in *The Force of Women in Japanese History,* published in 1953, Beard pays glowing tribute to Shidzue Kato and Ethyl Weed, whom she describes as "the attractive, sensitive, and persuasive American WAC" who stimulated Japanese women to vote.[34] This gave Weed a great deal of credit to the neglect of the hard-working Japanese suffragists like Fusae Ichikawa. This seems odd in a book intended to recognize the contributions of Japanese women.

Charles A. Beard could take no credit for *The Force of Women in Japanese History.* He died without knowing his wife was working on it. Dorothy Brush said Mary Beard kept it a secret so she could surprise him with a *fait accompli.* Brush wrote to Grierson, "I always felt that feminist Mary resented his greater fame and hoped to prove with this book that she was just as good as he was!"[35] If so, she was disappointed. A cumbersome book initially rejected by several publishers; it never attained the recognition of her earlier book, *Woman as Force in History: A Study in Traditions and Realities.*

While the ghost of Charles A. Beard could not take credit for her effort, the contributions by Shidzue Kato and other Japanese scholars only receive limited acknowledgment also. The Preface states that:

The sketches of Japanese women who appear in this volume, with a few exceptions, were collected by a research committee in Tokyo during the years from 1935 to 1939. This committee was composed of native men and women, most of whom were members of college and university faculties. They had been spurred to undertake this research by Baroness Ishimoto, who had been invited by Mrs. Anna Askanasy of Vienna to prepare Japanese materials for a monumental encyclopedia of women.[36]

But Mary R. Beard's name stands alone as author. Perhaps she relished receiving the larger share of recognition in a cooperative effort for a change. This was Mary Beard's last major publication except for a long essay, *The Making of Charles A. Beard* (New York, Exposition Press, 1955). More information than usual is available about the development of the book on Japanese women, primarily because so many women kept her correspondence and donated it to the Sophia Smith Collection at Smith College. Among these were: archivist Margaret Grierson, Dorothy Hamilton Dick Brush (who donated Shidzue Kato's letters to her as well), and Ethyl B. Weed, who sent Beard much material from Supreme Command Allied Pacific (SCAP) and *The Nippon Times.*

Finally, Mary Ritter Beard has to remain a contradiction. She argued that women should maintain a sense of self-worth and respect for their contribution to history, but she also demonstrated its personal damage. Surely Beard would have benefitted from the intellectual rigor of a doctoral program, which might also have increased her credibility as she worked with Charles Beard. This had to be an ego-diminishing experience. Her destruction of their papers prevented later scholars from evaluating her contribution to their coauthored works. This contradicted her long campaign to collect other women's papers. Nor is it clear how much assistance she rendered to Shidzue Kato in seeing her 1935 autobiography, *Facing Two Ways,* through the American press. However, even a major rewrite would not seem a fair tradeoff for Beard's claim to single authorship of *The Force of Women in Japanese History.*

In some respects, Mary Ritter Beard was a maverick as she rejected the mainstream women's rights movement. However, her concern for the collection of women's history put her in the tradition of Elizabeth Cady Stanton and Susan B. Anthony, as they carefully preserved and published accounts of the women's suffrage movement. In her own way, Beard exemplified the growing internationalism. So did Shidzue Kato. She assisted Beard with the publication of some Japanese women's history, while Kato was a major figure in Japanese women's struggle for birth control and political rights. In the same era, Fusae Ichikawa and legions of Japanese women worked for suffrage only to see it fade away under Japanese militarism and then be realized under American military occupation.

19

FUSAE ICHIKAWA
AND THE JAPANESE WOMAN SUFFRAGE MOVEMENT

Japanese women were ready to cast their ballots in the first general postwar election on April 10, 1946. They came with children in hand and babies on their backs to stand in line to vote, a reaction that could not have been generated simply by postwar education under the Occupation forces. While the women buried the notion once and for all that they were too passive and disinterested in politics to care whether they had the vote or not, this response did not arise spontaneously. Rather, it ended a long campaign fought by a variety of individual Japanese women and organizations over many decades. Many women made significant contributions, but Fusae Ichikawa (1893-1980) is now most vividly remembered because of her long service in the Japanese Diet and the Fusen Kaikan, also called the Ichikawa Woman Suffrage Centre in Tokyo. She is commemorated in this small museum. Comparable to the relationship between Mary Beard and Shidzue Kato, many Japanese women exchanged ideas and participated in the international movement before suffrage was obtained after World War II.

The first wave of western influence ended precipitously when the missionaries were killed or expelled from Japan in the seventeenth century. After that, the country was essentially closed to outsiders for more than 200 years. The modern era began when Commodore Matthew Perry's black ships presented themselves uninvited in Uraga Harbor on July 8, 1853.[1] Under the gun, Japan agreed to open trade with the west. Townsend Harris, the first United States Consul-General, arrived in 1859. The second wave of missionaries was not far behind.[2]

November 8, 1960, marked the one hundredth anniversary of Protestant Christian missions in Japan. After Japanese officials agreed to the American demand to admit missionaries, restoration of Emperor Meiji to power in 1869 added impetus to expand trade and accept more western innovations.[3] From then on, the Japanese were torn between a wish to cling to their old customs and a desire to be perceived as modern by the outside world. This division persists to the present day.

Education for girls remained a much lower priority than for boys, but the return of the missionaries marked the beginning of major

Fusae Ichikawa, pioneer Japanese woman suffragist. Reprinted with permission of The Fusae Ichikawa Memorial Association, Tokyo, Japan.

changes for both genders. A Department of Education was established in 1871. By December of that year, a government edict called for a public school. It admitted both noble and common students who could afford the tuition. Western women teachers were imported to teach English, social dancing, and European etiquette.[4] In addition, under an Imperial rescript, five Japanese girls, including Ume Tsuda, were sent to study in America in 1871.[5]

An influx of western literature in translation also prompted reexamination of traditional views on education. Previously, Japanese women had been trained in Confucian principles.[6] Girls grew up with the expectation that they would be passive, obedient to their fathers in youth, to their husbands in marriage, and to their sons in old age. An exception was their authoritarian relationships with daughters-in-law because senior women commanded households. Concubinage permitted men to incorporate their illegitimate children into the family, and sometimes they inherited the man's estate if the legal wife did not produce a male heir. In fact, under Emperor Meiji, concubines were given the same rights as legal wives in 1870, a step backward for married women at a time when they were gaining property rights in Europe and America.[7]

This reflected old customs. Women's educational objectives had previously been set forth in *Great Learning for Women* by Kaibara Ekken (1661-1714).[8] Government-sponsored schools continued to emphasize the family and women's subordinate role in it—"the good wife, wise mother" doctrine. However, some Christian schools, like the Girls' Academy, stressed mutual respect and the equality of individuals.[9] Based on a translation of John Stuart Mill's *The Subjection of Women,* Koho Dohi published a new educational plan, *Great Civilized Learning for Women,* in 1876. This book and others provoked a spate of Japanese books and debate on the proper course of women's learning, rights, and social roles.[10]

The missionary fervor for educating young Japanese women was such that by 1885 more than fifty mission high schools had been established. The Japanese government had founded twelve teachers' schools for women by 1880. Some of them were combined with men's teachers' colleges in 1885. When Ume Tsuda initially returned to Japan in the 1880s, she taught at the Peeresses' School.[11] Then she went back to the United States in 1889 to study biology at Bryn Mawr. Under President M. Carey Thomas, this college was noted for providing women with an equivalent education to men's, and it has continued to attract Japanese women scholars. Tsuda subsequently established Tsuda College in 1900.[12] It was followed by Japan Women's University in 1901 and Tokyo Women's College in 1918.

While women developed more awareness of their educational capability through schooling in Japan or abroad, they also began to initiate social reform movements that ultimately led to the call for woman suffrage. For example, Fusako Yamawaki (1867-1935) was inspired by western women's movements to organize a women's club in 1890. Dai Nihon Fujin Kyoiku Kai was composed of outstanding women with the goal "to raise the spirit and intellect of women." Yamawaki was instructed by Mrs. Calk, one of the eleven English teachers originally invited to Japan to teach social dancing, etiquette, and the like.[13] Yamawaki also established another society, Taisho Fujin Kai, to aid the poor, rather like settlement work in the west. When a society of young ladies, Dai Nippon Rengo Joshi Seinendan, was organized, Yamawaki chaired the board of directors.[14]

One of the earliest foreign reform movements to take root in Japan was the Women's Christian Temperance Union. A leading male missionary wrote home to his church paper that what Commodore Perry's visit was to commerce, Mrs. Leavitt was to the women of Japan.[15] In *100 Years of the WCTU in Japan,* historian Masako Sato reports that fifty-six women attended the organizational meeting. Kajiko Yajima, who divorced her husband because of alcohol, was president from the organization's founding until 1921.[16] Yajima had attended and subsequently taught in a girls' academy, Joshi Gakuen, run by Chikako Sakurai, an earlier women's rights pioneer. She had attended the WCTU convention held in Chicago in connection with the World's Columbian Exposition in 1893. Japanese suffragist, Fusae Ichikawa, also attended Sakurai Josei Gakuen in 1908 during her first visit to Tokyo.[17]

When Kajiko Yajima attended the World WCTU Convention in Boston in 1906, her translator was a young Japanese woman, Ochimi Okubo. She studied in Oakland, California, where her parents attended the Pacific Theological Seminary from 1904 to 1914. In 1910 Okubo married a Japanese pastor and took the name by which she became well known, Kubushiro. She followed Yajima as president of the WCTU in 1921 and supported the budding Japanese woman suffrage movement.

Another organization of western origin, the Young Women's Christian Association, also was introduced in Japan. *Eighty Years of YWCA in Japan* recounts that at a 1901 meeting, a resolution was adopted to establish a YWCA in Japan. The recommendation sent to the World YWCA was quickly acted upon. Almost eighty missionaries were already there by the time Annie Reynolds, the general secretary, arrived.[18] Modern industry introduced on a large scale had created what Reynolds described as "an appalling situation among women and girls." They needed housing and other kinds of assistance that the YWCA could provide. Consequently, Theresa Morrison was sent to Japan in 1903, supported by the Associations of California, Oregon, and Washington. Among the Japanese on the founding committee were Ume Tsuda, Michiko Kawai, who became the first Japanese General Secretary, and Chio Kazaki, wife of the YMCA leader.

Other women activists also emerged in more secular causes. Raichō Hiratsuka is often described as the first major Japanese feminist. In 1911 she founded a literary society, Blue Stocking (Seitosha), and began publication of a journal, *Seito*. At the turn of the century, all women's political activities had been banned under the Public Peace Police Law, Article 5. Literature was one of the few available legal outlets to voice women's concerns.[19]

Hiratsuka's introductory statement in the first issue of *Seito* suggested more rebellion than literature in her motives, and perhaps more than she intended. Hiratsuka referred to the ancestor of the Japanese race worshiped as the Sun Goddess, when she declared that:

Woman in the primitive age was the Sun, a real and just human personality. Now she is the Moon, dependent on others for a livelihood; the Moon that borrows light from others, pale like a sick patient. We are to restore the hidden Sun. "Find the Hidden Sun which is our genius!"[20]

This journal also published influential western writers like Ellen Key. Some of her views expressed in *Love and Marriage* and *Woman Movement* were similar to Fukuzawa's *Revised Great Learning for Women*. Henrik Ibsen's *Ghosts, The Lady of the Sea, The Weaver,* and particularly *The Doll's House* also attracted considerable interest. As women went on the stage, actress Sumako Natsui (1886-1919) specialized in performing the part of Nora.[21] Readers were attracted not only to Ibsen and Key, but also to the likes of anarchist Emma Goldman as the focus of *Seito* shifted more openly toward feminism. *Seito* was published from 1911 to 1916. The magazine had been discontinued by the time Fusae Ichikawa returned to Tokyo in 1918, but she was attracted by the idea of the "New Woman" (atarashii onna), described by the Blue Stocking Society, and she soon became one of Hiratsuka's cohorts.[22]

While the various women's organizations were initially founded to educate, assist, and inform Japanese women, their suffrage movement also received substantial encouragement as well as some discouragement from Western visitors. For example, on October 7, 1912, Mrs. E. G. Blattner presented an American flag from the General Federation of Women's Clubs to Countess Okuma, an honorary member. On that occasion, Blattner told the Japanese women that "no true modest woman of America would ever resort to the suffrage movement that is so common in European Countries." Carrie Chapman Catt's ship docked two days later. She and Aletta Jacobs were on their round-the-world tour to promote woman suffrage.

In the shipping news from Yokohama, the *Nippon Times* listed the two travelers as men. Identified as women by the time they reached Tokyo, their visit was otherwise unpublicized in that newspaper until they were safely at sea again. However, in her short stay in Japan, Catt did manage to sow a few suffrage seeds and tour the Yoshiwara Red Light District. After she left on October 20, 1912, the *Nippon Times* headline read, "Woman Suffrage in Japan," with the subheading, "Movement Tentative Here though in Full Swing in China and Elsewhere."[23] This article reported that an earlier letter in which women were urged to join the International Woman Suffrage Alliance had met with strong protest among educated men. Although Catt managed not to be too threatening in person, her hostess Mrs. Ichiro Hatoyama, the Prime Minister's wife, still felt obliged to explain how a letter of introduction she had given one of the wives of the American Legation had led to Catt's visit.

Apparently, the reputation of the more militant British suffragists had raised an alarm because Ume Tsuda proclaimed that "Mrs. Catt is a pleasant woman whom none need to be afraid of . . . quite different from Mrs. Pankhurst and her colleagues whose suffrage movement is accompanied by militant forms." Nonetheless, Hatoyama did not accept Catt's invitation to send Japanese women delegates to the International Woman

Suffrage meeting in Budapest the following June. Probably because the Japanese were skilled at maintaining ambivalence, Catt concluded that they were ready to organize. Her memoirs recalled that she had to work hard to persuade the hesitant ladies to take what they considered to be a plunge into great waters, but they finally capitulated. Actually, a few more years were needed before votes for women became a formal movement in Japan.

Christian women like Ume Tsuda often worked for more than one organization. Shortly after Catt's visit, another important pioneer who was active in both the WCTU and the YWCA made the jump into the international suffrage movement. Tsume Yamada married a British journalist named Gauntlett and carried that appropriate designation into the fray. In 1920, Gauntlett accompanied Kaji Yajima to the Tenth World Assembly of the WCTU in London and then went with Michiko Kawai to the International Woman Suffrage meeting in Geneva.[24] Gauntlett later recalled that Carrie Chapman Catt inspired her to return home and work for suffrage.

The period immediately after the First World War, a time when British and American women were finally enjoying national suffrage, marked the first clear campaign for women's rights in Japan. In the spirit of what the Japanese called *demokurashii,* former Blue Stocking leader Raichō Hiratsuka enlisted Fusae Ichikawa, who was active in the International Labour Organization, to form the New Woman's Association (Shin Fujin Kyokai) on November 24, 1919.[25] They also brought in Mumeo Oku, who later led the housewives' association. She was determined to link politics with domestic life and so make women's participation acceptable.[26]

The first issue of *Josei dōmei* (*Women's League*) was published on October 20, 1920. It was more overtly political than *Blue Stocking* had been. Among other things, the founders wanted legislation to protect women from being forced to marry men with venereal diseases. This was prompted by domestic legislation in Norway and Finland. In their December 1920 and January 1921 issues, the journal also called openly for woman suffrage.[27] To organize actively, the women first needed more political freedom, so they wanted to revoke the Public Peace Police Law that prohibited women from participating in political meetings. On July 19, 1920, Tabuchi Toyokichi proposed to amend this law in the Lower House of the Japanese Diet. He noted that women had political rights in England and France that even Japanese men did not have.[28] The changes passed the Lower House, but not the House of Peers where Baron Yoshiro Fujimura said women's participation in political movements was extremely boring and against natural law. He cited Queen Elizabeth as a bad example. According to Ichikawa scholar, Kathleen Molony, "By alluding to Queen Elizabeth, Fujimura contended that the idea of women's political participation was foreign and therefore antithetical to the traditional social order."[29] Like the British House of Lords, the Japanese House of Peers remained steadfastly conservative, oblivious or unconcerned with women's rising desire to participate in politics.

Despite this resistance, advocates like Margaret Sanger and Shidzue Kato raised the consciousness of even very conservative women toward issues like birth control. Also, a nucleus of support for woman suffrage gradually formed as some women saw suffrage as a way to achieve other goals. Fighting the battle against prostitution without woman suffrage, new WCTU leader, Ochimi Kubushiro, declared, was like fighting a war without arms. She represented the Moral Reform Society at the International Women's Suffrage Conference in Honolulu, Hawaii, in December 1920.[30] Then she and Makoto Sakamoto brought several women's groups together to form the Japan Women's Suffrage Association (Nihon Fujin Sanseiken Kyokai) in 1921.[31] However, individual differences splintered the organization. In one of these disagreements, Fusae Ichikawa resigned as director of the New Woman's League and sailed to the United States, in July 1921, to observe American women and the labor movement.[32] At least part of the initial disagreement arose because Hiratsuka continued to favor the traditional "good wife, wise mother" role for most women, whereas Ichikawa wanted them to become more independent and work for political reform.

After Ichikawa left for America, Hiratsuka went home to recuperate from the women's rights struggle. That left Mumeo Oku, leader of the housewives' organization, to lobby for revision of the Public Peace Police Law. When women were given the right to attend political rallies, in May 1922, one prominent political opponent said Mumeo Oku convinced him to support the change. As she campaigned with a baby on her back, some Japanese men apparently became convinced that women could be good mothers and participate in politics.[33] During the same era, the internal dissension that had prompted Ichikawa to resign in 1921 finally caused the dissolution of the New Woman's League on December 10, 1922. On January 27, 1923, several women's groups united to organize the Alliance for Participation of Women in Government (Fujin Sansei Domei).[34]

The Japanese woman suffrage movement split between radical and conservative along lines somewhat similar to the British and Americans. In November 1922, Kubushiro and five others attended the World Assembly of the WCTU in Philadelphia. They then went on to Europe where Kubushiro was impressed with Millicent Garrett Fawcett and the conservative British suffragists.[35] Ichikawa, on the other hand, was most influenced by the American, Alice Paul, who learned her suffrage battle tactics from the militant Pankhursts. Paul promoted the introduction of the Equal Rights Amendment in Congress in 1923, and the Japanese suffragist struggled with whether or not she should join the National Woman's Party.[36] Ultimately, Ichikawa decided not to, perhaps partly because she wanted to maintain her neutrality among American feminists and partly because of concern over the fate of protective legislation if the ERA were passed.[37]

In the United States, Ichikawa worked part of the time as a nanny. While the children played, she practiced her English and talked women's rights with her employer and local birth control advocate, Bernice Guttmann, in Evanston, Illinois.[38] Ichikawa also visited Jane Addams at Hull House in Chicago, met Carrie Chapman Catt, and went to Seneca Falls, New York, in July 1923, for the commemoration of American woman suffrage.[39] By the time she returned to Japan in early 1924, the climate had changed substantially for women's activities.

As in other countries, Socialist women also entered the struggle. They favored reform of the entire system, not just women's rights. In 1921, Kikue Yamakawa founded the Red Wave Society (Sekirankei). She accused the New Women's League of being too bourgeois like the earlier Blue Stocking. Yamakawa had first learned about the western woman suffrage movement as a student at Tsuda College where she graduated in 1912.[40] Attempts to band together continued to be stymied by lack of cooperation among women's groups. The Alliance for the Participation of Women in Government also fell into factions, and no efforts were made to coordinate with the Christians. Kathleen Molony, Fusae Ichikawa's biographer, said the earthquake of 1923 provided the necessary jolt to bring them together. On September 28, 1923, approximately one hundred leaders from forty organizations formed the Tokyo Federation of Women's Organizations (Tōkyō Rengō Fujinkai).[41]

Ichikawa was still out of the country then. However, she had returned to work for the ILO when Ochimi Kubushiro called a meeting of the government section of the Tokyo Federation of Women's Organizations in November 1924. They formed the League for the Realization of Women's Suffrage (Fujin Sanseiken Kakutoku Kisei Dōmeikai). Kubushiro proposed that they work to amend the Public Peace Police Law and also to obtain voting rights for women at the local and national level. All Japanese men over age twenty-five were given the right to vote in February 1925. Two months later, the women changed the name of their organization to the Women's Suffrage League (Fusen Kakutoku Dōmei). The word "Fusen" can be interpreted to mean "universal suffrage" or "woman suffrage," so the women thereby announced their intention to broaden the meaning of universal suffrage to include them.[42]

As men formed proletarian political parties, the women hoped their cause would receive more support, too. However, they disagreed on how to align themselves among male political parties, much like the American suffragists had earlier. Because the women were generally conservative, the tactics of the Women's Suffrage League resembled those of Catt's National American Woman Suffrage Association more than Paul's

National Women's Party. Like Paul and the British, however, they campaigned against the party in power as the ones responsible for not granting women suffrage. In the United States, that strategy had provoked much opposition because it meant that women had to campaign against some prosuffrage men. Catt's group, on the other hand, had campaigned for candidates who supported woman suffrage regardless of party. This tactic was not favored by some Japanese women either. Mumeo Oku said the women would be like prostitutes who went with men from one party in the morning and another in the afternoon.[43]

As head of the Women's Suffrage League, Fusae Ichikawa concluded that their primary task was to educate women to the need for suffrage so they would build a broader base of support. The Joint Committee for Woman Suffrage was formed to try to bring together such women's groups as the Japan Women's Suffrage Association, the Women's Political Alliance, and the Socialists.[44] As they defined their goals, they were encouraged by women's progress abroad. After Fusae Ichikawa met with Jane Addams and both of them addressed the Pan Pacific Women's Association in Honolulu in August 1928, she went back to the United States to see women participate in the national election. Then she returned home to fight for women's rights at the local level. Ichikawa later recalled 1928 to 1931 as the period of hope for woman suffrage in Japan. The first National Women's Suffrage Conference was called for April 27, 1930.[45]

By then, the women enjoyed more favorable press as their cause was reinforced by news of foreign suffrage successes. For instance, in 1927 Shigenao Moriguchi published *A Discussion of Women's Suffrage* in which he argued that, like westerners, Japanese women would use this right judiciously.[46] Nevertheless, the House of Peers would not budge. They rejected a bill passed by the Lower House that would revise the City and Village Codes to give women local political rights. Many other bills were proposed that the women would not accept. One would have given women the ballot, but not the right to hold office. Another would have required that married women have their husbands' permission to accept political appointments.[47]

Nothing passed the House of Peers. While they held out, external events turned public sentiment against women's rights, as it had in Europe. As the Japanese government embarked on military conquest, they became more reactionary. The men wanted to maintain the old, stable family structure based on passive, obedient women dedicated to being good wives and wise mothers. As the pressure mounted, the Women's Suffrage League lost members to such government-sponsored organizations as the Patriotic Women's Association (Aikoku Fujinkai).[48]

With suffrage no longer a politically acceptable cause, Ichikawa then fought for local issues such as garbage disposal, the protection of mothers and children, and the decentralization of the wholesale food market. On September 21, 1940, the Women's Suffrage League voted to disband after a sixteen-year fight.[49] On February 2, 1942, the government established the Greater Japan Women's Association (Dai Nihon Fujinkai), and many women's groups were absorbed into it. Ichikawa was appointed to the male-dominated board in early 1942 and then was removed from it in January 1944.[50] After that, she went to the country to plant vegetables and wait for the war to end. Then things happened fast.

Item Number 10 of the Potsdam Agreement of July 26, 1945, specified that the Japanese government would have to remove all obstacles to the revival and strengthening of democratic tendencies among the Japanese people. Freedom of speech, of religion, and of thought, as well as respect for fundamental human rights would be established. General Douglas MacArthur, America's version of the imperial warrior, listed votes for women as one of his five top priorities for the political reorganization of Japan.

Japan surrendered in August 1945. Ten days later, Ichikawa formed a women's group to deal with postwar problems and request suffrage. Two days after the official surrender, the ceremonial surrender documents were signed on September 2. On his way into Japan, MacArthur told a press conference in Yokohama that he planned to institute woman suffrage. The *Nippon Times* of September 25, 1945, quoted this information from a story by Ted Dealey published four days earlier in the *Dallas Morning News*.[51] However circuitously the news traveled, by the end of that month, Prince Fumimaro Konoye was emboldened to say he thought women lacked the political intelligence and understanding necessary to vote.[52] In October, Countess Satoko Otani spoke out in support of eventual suffrage, but MacArthur did not intend to wait for the issue to gain favor among the peerage.[53]

He called the wartime Japanese cabinet back into session long enough to adopt his proposed reforms and recommend them to the Diet. MacArthur told Premier Baron Kijuro Shidehara that "The regimentation of the masses under the guise or claim of efficiency, under whatever name of government it may be made, must cease."[54] The Cabinet members got the message. Indeed, when Prime Minister Shidehara met General MacArthur on October 10, 1945, he said they had decided on woman suffrage the day before.[55]

On October 12, 1945, the Japanese Cabinet proposed to amend the election law to lower the voting age from twenty-five to twenty and include women, a plan that would be submitted to a special session of the Diet in December. Even before this occurred, however, Shidzue Kato announced her candidacy for the general election then scheduled for January 1946.[56] Under American directives, Japanese women assumed that they would receive the right to run for office along with the right to vote.

Then Emperor Hirohito ordered the Japanese Constitution revised, and in November the Public Peace Police Law was abrogated so Japanese women finally had the right to join political parties. On December 17, 1945, the House of Representatives revised the Election Law and gave the right to vote to everyone age twenty and older. At age twenty-five, women could also stand for election without their husbands' permission.

In this special session of the Japanese Diet, the House of Representatives was still more compliant than the more conservative House of Peers. The Upper House was so slow that Premier Baron Kijuro Shidehara began to talk of extending the extraordinary parliamentary session. However, that proved to be unnecessary after the war crimes list was promulgated. On December 12, Prince Morimasa Nashimoto entered Sugamo Prison, the first prince of the blood to be imprisoned in modern Japan. That same day, Lieutenant General Masaharu Homma and two other officers were flown to Manilla to face war crime trials. Homma was charged with responsibility for the Bataan Death March. The American occupation chiefs were also rumored to be seriously concerned over scattered demands that the Emperor himself be tried as a war criminal.[57] The House of Peers got the message.

As of December 17, all of the proposed reforms had passed. The War Diet was ready to dissolve to allow time to campaign before the proposed January 24 election. The first session of the new "democratic" Diet was then scheduled to begin in early February. In the Diet's semifinal session, a resolution was adopted to extend condolences to the relatives of Prince Fumimaro Konoye, the former President of the House of Peers. He had committed suicide the preceding Sunday after the American authorities listed him as a suspected war criminal.[58] A parallel news story said the Philippine Supreme Court had stayed General Yamashita's execution, although they rejected the argument that he should be tried in the civil courts of the Philippines instead of by American Army officers. Although the Emperor system remained intact, under MacArthur's directives and the threat of being tried as war criminals, members of the Peerage went one step further and scrambled to renounce their titles. Indeed, American-style democracy had come to the Japanese, and the women were ready to make the most of it.

They quickly formed the New Japan Women's Party and presented several candidates for office. Major campaign issues included the prohibition of prostitution and the abolition of all laws and customs that restricted women's rights.[59] Elections were finally set for April 10. After a message was received from the American League of Women Voters on April 8, 1946, seven Japanese women's groups responded that Japan no longer must be a man's paradise and a woman's hell. The Women's League of Japan declared that Japanese women "have begun to taste the joy of being freed from feudalistic fetters."[60]

The Japanese suffragists had been suppressed at least since 1937. With the ballot within reach, leaders like Fusae Ichikawa rallied immediately.[61] However, she was not among the suffragists who went to the polls. According to her old friend, Taki Fujita, former president of Tsuda College, in all of the excitement Ichikawa forgot to register.[62] Afterwards, the pro-American Ichikawa was forced to swallow an especially bitter pill when she was purged by the American occupation forces for allegedly supporting the Japanese war effort. However, Ichikawa was subsequently depurged just as mysteriously. After the American occupation ended, she was elected to the Japanese Diet almost continually until her death in 1980.

Not just leaders, but average women were ready to take advantage of their new rights. On April 10, 1946, sixty-six percent of the eligible female voters went to the polls. They outnumbered men in some places and accounted for more than one-third of the total votes cast. Unlike European women who counteracted fears that they would all vote Catholic and conservative, Japanese women did vote conservatively. This dispelled fears that they would either be completely passive and avoid the political process altogether or vote for the left-leaning candidates. The Socialists still posted a good showing, especially in large cities. Women candidates tended to run ahead of their parties, including Shidzue Kato.[63] This Socialist and two independents led the thirty-eight (thirty-nine according to Barbara Molony)[64] women candidates who won in a field of eighty.[65] When the votes were tallied and the election critiqued, some Japanese felt that the caliber of the women candidates was higher than the majority of males, but winning was only the first step. Their place in the new political structure had yet to be determined.[66]

In a country with such a clearly defined gender hierarchy, the new women legislators had a difficult time. In an attempt to introduce a bill for "peace memorial enterprises" to commemorate Japan's surrender, they were chastised for "unbusiness-like and careless" parliamentary methods. Representative Saburo Shikuma declared that Japan needed food and reconstruction far more than monuments.[67] Later monuments recalled war damage, especially the atomic bomb disaster, but not the military's loss of face. Old customs kept women subordinate in other ways, too. For instance, when the new constitution was adopted, men were given ten cigarettes and a ration of sake to celebrate, while women got three cigarettes, no sake.[68] Nevertheless, Japanese women had the right to vote. While it could be said that MacArthur and the male Japanese Diet had given women their rights, others (like longtime Diet member Fusae Ichikawa) knew the women earned them. Women's rights were also restored or instituted in many other countries after World War II, but the formation of the United Nations held out the most promise for major changes in women's circumstances on a global basis.

PART IV

GLOBAL ADVANCES AND THE UNITED NATIONS

Between the world wars, even as various peace committees worked for agreements like the Kellogg-Briand Pact to end wars, nations were soon arming and beginning more territorial aggressions. Militarists once again summarily abolished equal rights for women. They were sent home to raise the next generation of soldiers or into the work force to replace the fighting men.

The power of militarists to give and take away women's rights is well demonstrated in Japan. Between wars women made some headway, at least by raising their lobbying skills against alcohol and concubinage and also by lobbying for consumers' rights and birth control. They also saw some advances in education and moved away from Confucian principles to more egalitarian ideals, at least in missionary schools. Despite limitations on women's participation in political organizations, the suffrage movement steadily gained momentum. Some aspects resembled American and British efforts, but others were distinctly Japanese.

These organizational efforts were defeated as the Japanese war machine cranked up. Then wartime restrictions forced women into patriotic associations. However, equal rights were accorded Japanese women expeditiously after MacArthur's occupation force arrived. Although the woman suffrage movement had been abolished during Japan's military expansion, the suffragist campaigns had paved the way for a positive reception of *democurashii*. Similarly, women in other countries made some significant gains in suffrage and other rights.

Although the gains were not always so dramatic, the period of reorganization after World War II saw women's rights extended in many countries. Rights were also restored in those that had regressed under totalitarian regimes. As women gained the franchise in countries like Italy, Belgium, and Yugoslavia, they overcame men's fears that they would be too disinterested to vote or so conservative that they would be under the thumb of Catholic priests. More women leaders also became candidates themselves. In other countries, the gains were just as important if less dramatic. Some women gained the right to hold their own gatherings and attend meetings outside their home countries. Then international contacts fueled their enthusiasm.

Overall, the most important development after World War II was the new United Nations. The precedents set by the League of Nations paved the way, as Latin American delegations insisted on similar wording to affirm equal rights for women in the 1945 Charter. In 1946 the Commission on the Status of Women was implemented, and in 1948 the Declaration of Human Rights made clear that it referred to both genders, not just males. In this new era, women had the circumstances to collect information, the forum to air it, and the confidence and experience to conduct the process. Nonetheless, like the League of Nations, the United Nations is only advisory to individual nations. Moreover, where war poses frequent disruptions, men often still have to be convinced that women are entitled to equality. Consequently, the whole process is often put on hold.

20

THE INTERNATIONAL WOMEN'S SUFFRAGE MOVEMENT, 1944-1948

Women saw major gains in political if not social and economic equality in many countries at the end of World War II. Carrie Chapman Catt helped pave the way, although she had turned eighty in 1939 and did not attend the Conference on the Cause and Cure of War that year. She was back in 1942, though, and saw the committee dissolved in the spring of 1943. In the middle of World War II, it was succeeded by the Women's Action Committee for Victory and Lasting Peace.[1] When the war ended in 1945, Catt called for another women's crusade. Once again, she rallied women around the world to work for equality and peace.

On January 10, 1944 (her eighty-fifth birthday), Carrie Chapman Catt told an audience of 650 persons that Hitler had taken the vote away from women in twelve European countries. This wartime reminder marked the beginning of another phase in the struggle. She implored all loyal suffragists to help these women regain the ballot, and she joined with her long-time admirer, American First Lady Eleanor Roosevelt, in a plea for world peace.[2] The elderly Catt continued to maintain some influence as the matriarch of the International Alliance of Women as well as through individual contacts and other international women's organizations.

Public recognition of previous efforts did not help contemporary women, and new rights were slow to be won. Carrie Chapman Catt had learned from World War I that women's rights depended fundamentally on peace. In August 1945, on the twenty-fifth anniversary of woman suffrage in the United States, she pointed out that of the thirty-four countries that had given women the vote before the war, fifteen had robbed them of it since. Catt also promoted the International Alliance of Women as they prepared for their first postwar meeting in Geneva, Switzerland, the following year.[3] At that gathering, Dorothy Kenyon read Catt's final message to the Alliance in which she said:

Let me assure you that the greatest question in the world today is how to get rid of war . . . women must have a higher and more dignified place than ever before, because the largest task they have ever performed lies before them.[4]

184

As Catt again tried to rally women in American and world organizations, similar stirrings were underway in other nations as well. In Central America in 1944, the Nicaraguan Liberal party called for woman suffrage, which was not awarded for another decade. In the Middle East, a bill for woman suffrage was introduced in the Chamber of Deputies in Lebanon.[5] This prompted Iraqi and Egyptian feminists to call for the ballot again in their countries. Egyptian women had been demanding the right to vote since 1919.[6] In December 1944, Middle Eastern women called a landmark meeting to discuss ways to secure equal rights. Delegates came to Cairo from Palestine, Lebanon, Syria, Trans-Jordan, and Iraq. While Egypt's foreign minister, Mahmoud Fahmy Nokrashi Pasha said this meeting was an effective step toward an Arab federation, it meant more to women in that region. At the opening session, Lali Abou Hoda, head of the Trans-Jordanian delegation, tellingly remarked that this was the first meeting the women of her country were ever permitted to attend. Rose Shahfa of Lebanon proposed that women be represented at the forthcoming peace conference.[7] Despite their enthusiasm, suffrage was still at least a decade away.

In addition to such regional activities, International Women's Day gave prominence and publicity to women's war efforts. In Russia women had voted since the 1917 Revolution, before the Americans and the British. Appropriately, in 1944 the Soviet Union paid homage to Russian women's great contribution to the war effort.[8] Also, a March 6 celebration was attended by 2,000 women in the war services in London. Clementine Churchill, wife of the Prime Minister, extended a message of hope for world peace, as did other prominent women from the United States, Russia, and China.[9]

As the war drew to a close, the women's rights movement gained momentum unexpectedly. General Charles DeGaulle added a political grace note to the war effort by according French women in the homeland suffrage long-distance from his exile headquarters in Algiers.[10] DeGaulle did this just when he was going to need the women most, before the Allied invasion. By December when the men were back in their own territory, they raised concerns about the need to educate French women on the use of the vote. The men feared that women would be too conservative and would support only Catholic candidates. They raised the possibility that suffrage enacted under the Provisional Government might not be continued in the new Republic. At that time, sixty-nine percent of the women reportedly wanted the vote while twenty-six percent were opposed.[11] Many of the men's fears were dispelled on April 30, 1945, when more women than men voted, including nuns. The Communists made a good showing after they promised larger food rations if they won. Women retained suffrage, although men continued to fear that they would be too conservative and the Catholic Church would exert undue influence.

Like the French, the Italians began to make democratic promises under wartime stress. In their case, they switched allegiance from the Germans to the Allies before Italy was back under their own control. In 1944, the new Government of National Union promised "a constituent and legislative assembly, to be elected by the people convened in free public meetings and acting under universal suffrage, as soon as the hostilities end." This was interpreted to include votes for women for the first time.[12] Mussolini had never gotten around to it. The Communists and the Socialists also said they favored votes for women.[13, 14]

An American member of the House of Representatives, Clare Booth Luce, was not taking any chances. In an early visit to Rome after the war ended, she took the occasion of a congressional party to do a little arm-twisting. She assured Premier Ivanhoe Bonomi that American women were deeply interested in the vote for Italian women. He promised that it would be legalized as soon as possible.[15] After many Cabinet ministers and their wives pledged themselves to the cause, Luce went home and delivered on her promise, aid for Italians who were starving and freezing in their war-impoverished country.[16] Perhaps the Italian Council of Ministers was convinced that they were trading votes for blankets and food. Within a month they decreed the right of suffrage for women twenty-one years of age and over.[17]

When the registration lists were completed, women comprised fifty-three percent of the Italian electorate.[18] Before they voted, a woman addressed the Parliament for the first time in Italian history. This honor was accorded to the wife of the Vice President of the Consulta.[19] Women did not actually go to the polls until March 9, 1946, and then it was for provincial elections only.[20] These were the first free elections held in Italy in twenty-six years, and the first ever where women could vote. Nonetheless, authorities expressed astonishment at the high proportion of women who cast ballots.[21]

Three months later, when national elections were held on June 2, 1946, even the *New York Times* gave the story front page coverage. That august publication usually sandwiched news about women's political activities between the recipes and fashion advertisements in what was then called the Women's Section. This time the headline read: "Italy Goes to Polls Quietly; Women Glory in First Vote."[22] "First" was not quite accurate, and "quiet" was a relative term in Italy where people waited an average of three hours to vote. As they crowded around polling stations instead of forming lines, many fainted from the heat and malnutrition.

The big political issue was whether the Republicans or the Royalists would prevail. Things did not bode well for the Royalists early on, as even the former King of Croatia was jostled about for more than three hours in the waiting crowd. Moreover, while King Humbert was uncertain whether to follow the example of his father and grandfather (who had not voted while they were on the throne) or the new election law which made voting compulsory, Queen Maria Jose disregarded the king's dilemma and voted.[23] Whatever uncertainties accompanied the initial process, Italy capped off this democratizing phase a year later by outdistancing other European countries. The new constitution gave Italian women equal rights with men in every field and even guaranteed freedom of religion—right on the steps of the Vatican.[24]

Royalty and religion also posed a dilemma in Belgium. In 1945 women were extended limited suffrage to vote in municipal elections, but with the stipulation that they not do so until 1947.[25] The assumption that women would vote conservatively and support the Catholics and the King prompted the Catholic Christian Social Party to protest the delay.[26] While most women were kept from voting, a few already had suffrage. Those eligible to vote in the 1946 election (5,290 women) were the mothers and widows of men who died in World War I and those who had been forced to work in Germany between 1914 and 1918.[27]

Belgian women were allowed to vote in communal elections at the end of 1946. Their new clout and ten percent larger numbers than men prompted last-minute appeals from the politicians.[28] The women finally voted in parliamentary elections in 1948. The last-ditch opponents were Socialist anti-feminists who continued to fear the Catholic clergy's influence.[29] Also in Europe, Yugoslavian women voted for the first time in 1945.[30] British women (who had voted on an equal basis with men since 1928) were finally given the right to sit in the House of Peers.[31]

In the United States, where women already voted, they did not gain as much. Eight American women's organizations with a membership of more than ten million—groups such as the American Association of University Women, the General Federation of Women's Clubs, the National Education Association, and the National Women's Trade Union League —pressured for a plank in both the Republican and Democratic national committee platforms for "equal opportunity for work and equal pay during the post-war period." One-fifth of women workers had been the principal support of their families before the war.[32] By 1947, women would be slightly over twenty-six percent of the 15.3 million workers, and many women were now obliged to work outside the home because their male supporters had become war casualties. Despite women's collective lobbying efforts, equal employment and pay legislation did not pass for decades. Many women's fears about postwar loss of standing in the work force were subsequently realized. Thousands were laid off or fired when the soldiers returned home.

Politicians were more willing to pay homage to safely deceased pioneer women than living activists. President Truman declared Election Day, November 2, 1945, to be Women's Enfranchisement Day.[33] The next day, his political rival, Governor Thomas E. Dewey of New York, proclaimed November 12 as Elizabeth Cady Stanton Day to commemorate the birth of that "distinguished citizen of our State who devoted her life to the emancipation of women."[34]

Despite the advances, the ongoing fight for suffrage and equal rights was not likely to end soon. As the women met in Geneva, Switzerland still did not accord all women the right to vote. Men in one of the Swiss Cantons did not share this privilege for another forty years. Meanwhile, women began to pin more of their hopes on the new United Nations. The American League of Women Voters (LWV) campaigned to persuade the political parties to do what they wanted to anyway, to plan for the United States to take the initiative with other nations to form a new international organization that would be more effective in resolving world problems than the League of Nations. American government officials expected the United States to become a member of the new international organization. They would agree to the joint use of military force to suppress future attempts at military aggression.[35] Secretary of State Stettinius responded to LWV President Anna L. Strauss, "I want to reassure you that the department is completely sympathetic with your concern that the general international organization be established as quickly as possible and that no effort be spared in sustaining public support for this task."[36] Indeed, planning for the UNO had been underway long before the war ended, and the support for women's rights was particularly strong among Latin Americans.

21

THE ROAD TO THE UNITED NATIONS

American supporters of protective legislation temporarily ended advocacy of an equal rights treaty and NWP dominance at the Pan-American Conferences. However, the seeds of women's equality would sprout anew in the ideals of the new United Nations. Leaders of the World Woman's Party took their demands to the 1942 meeting called to lay the foundation of a post-victory United Nations Organization (UNO). They lobbied for equal rights provisions in the UN Charter and consultant status at all sessions concerned with human rights.[1] Two years later, at Dumbarton Oaks, Dorothy Detzer, president of WILPF, was critical because her organization was not allowed to participate.[2] Indeed, no women were included. However, a Social and Economic Council was proposed for the new world organization based on the League of Nations precedent and a 1939 report by Australian, Stanley Bruce. FDR subsequently compromised it away to appease the Soviets. Nor were other attempts to include women's equality successful in this initial planning conference.[3]

However, at the Inter-American Conference on Problems of War and Peace held in Mexico City in March 1946 (a month before the UNO meeting in San Francisco), the feminists were able to gain support in their call for equal rights. They were effective despite the influence of protective legislationists on the delegates from the United States and the fact that, among the six working commissions, none was specifically devoted to women.[4] Instead, the rights of women in the Americas were reaffirmed because of pressure by unofficial advisors from women's rights groups. First of all, they were able to have the Inter-American Commission of Women (created in 1928) accepted as an official agency. Then the Latin American countries where women had achieved political rights were acknowledged. The Inter-American Conference on Problems of War and Peace recommended that all countries of the Americas modify their legislation to abolish any existing discrimination because of sex. This was approved at the plenary session on March 7, 1945.

In the resolution to establish a general international organization, also approved at the plenary session, the governments included Number XXXI, Cooperation of Women in International Conferences. Under this resolution, the governments of the American republics agreed to consider the inclusion of women in the formation of their respective delega-

Bertha Lutz, suffragist and United Nations Organization Delegate. Reprinted with permission from the United Nations Photo Library.

tions to international conferences. The next one would be the UNO at San Francisco. Another outcome was that Mexico suggested some twenty changes in the Dumbarton Oaks Proposals. One was to restore the Economic and Social Council as an essential, major committee. Because Latin American countries would cast twenty out of fifty votes at the UNO, they were able to make their wishes felt. The session in Mexico City also was significant because it transformed Senator Arthur H. Vandenburg, leader of the American delegation at San Francisco, from an isolationist into an internationalist.[5]

The Mexico City Conference also affirmed the precedent of official consultant status for nongovernmental organizations (NGOs). On April 10, 1945, two days before FDR died, a list of forty-two NGOs was designated for the UNO. Each was allowed to send one representative to San Francisco. That meant women were represented by such organizations as the American Association of University Women, the General Federation of Women's Clubs, the National Federation of Business and Professional Women's Clubs, the National League of Women Voters, and the Women's Action Committee for Victory and Lasting Peace.[6] The National Woman's Party was not among them, but such undesignated groups also sent representatives determined to be heard. One hundred ten observers attended the UNO meeting, and when the Economic and Social Council was established, NGO consultant status was formalized.[7]

Besides the NGOs, women were appointed as official delegates to the UNO only from Canada, China, the Dominican Republic, the United States, Brazil, and Uruguay. Minerva Bernardino, who represented the Dominican Republic, was also president of the Inter-American Commission of Women.[8] Isabel P. de Vidal was a Senator from Uruguay, and Bertha Lutz was a former congresswoman and President of the Confederated Association of Women of Brazil. Twenty-five years after the UNO meeting, Lutz wrote an informal account in which she recalled that in Venezuela, on the way to San Francisco, a member of the airline staff tried to take her off the plane to ensure priority to a male friend of his. She wrote, "He evidently failed to realize that a small woman might represent a great country at an International Assembly."[9]

As the leader of the American delegation, Edward R. Stettinius, Jr., had been criticized for leaving women out of the Dumbarton Oaks Conference. The State Department did not make the same mistake as they planned for the UNO meeting. A list of a dozen women qualified to be delegates was drawn up; and FDR selected a New Yorker, Virginia Gildersleeve (1877-1965). This token woman, a dean at Barnard College, was one of the founders of the International Association of University Women and a staunch advocate of women's rights in education. Gildersleeve had been a member of the New York Women's City Club in the early 1920s, along with Eleanor Roosevelt and Frances Perkins.[10] She had also been on the Democratic Platform Committee in 1940.[11] In addition, Gildersleeve had sat for five years on the Commission to Study the Organization of Peace, a research affiliate of the American Association for the United Nations. This commission had considerable influence on the Dumbarton Oaks proposals.[12]

Gildersleeve's conservative political views were much like Eleanor Roosevelt's. Both believed hard work alone would enable women to rise in society. Both also accepted the principle that women should be treated as individuals and receive no special consideration because of their

gender. Additionally, both women had received their own opportunities
to participate in government precisely because of special consideration
afforded their gender and positions (Roosevelt as FDR's wife and
Gildersleeve as her friend).

The Chinese woman delegate, Wu Yi-fang, President of Gingling
College, told Gildersleeve she had been appointed as soon as news of
Gildersleeve's appointment reached China. The Canadian delegate, Cora
T. Casselman, left very soon after the meetings started and so contributed little.[13] Two women from the United Kingdom were alternates.
Venezuela sent one and Mexico sent two women Councilors. The Soviets accounted for the total absence of women in their delegation by
saying the plane trip might have been too much for them. The male delegates were kept informed on women's issues through Jessie Street, a
leading member of Australian women's organizations and a consultant to
that delegation.[14] An Indian woman, Vijaya Lakshimi Pandit, gained
much publicity as she held court outside the UNO and protested India's
colonial status under Great Britain. After her brother, Jahawarlal Nehru,
became prime minister when India gained independence in 1947, Pandit
led the Indian delegation to the UN and subsequently became its first
woman president.[15]

At the UNO, the few official women delegates were often not on
good terms. The radical Lutz and conservative Gildersleeve clashed
immediately. Gildersleeve invited the women to tea and said she hoped
Lutz would not ask for anything for women in the Charter because that
would be a very vulgar thing to do. Lutz replied that the need to defend
the rights of women was the main reason the Brazilian Government had
appointed her. She regarded Gildersleeve's old-fashioned and narrow
views as an embarrassment and later recalled that the LWV also was
afraid and ashamed to work for women's interests. But Carrie Chapman
Catt backed Lutz. She told the LWV that her Brazilian daughter was
right in the matter, however roughly she might have expressed it to
them.[16]

The women who had fought for standing in the League of Nations
previously, as well as their younger successors, lost no time in mustering
support for the inclusion of equal rights for women in the United Nations
Charter. Nine women's organizations, some with consultant status and
others without, asked for wording that called for women's equal opportunity with men.[17] With the aid of some official female delegates and
their well-placed male supporters, they succeeded in inserting many
statements on women's equality.[18] The fundamental provision was set
forth in the preamble, in the statement of purposes and principles, and in
other sections.[19] In her autobiography, *Many a Good Crusade*, Gildersleeve undercut their achievement and credited the Soviet Union with
wording sent prior to the San Francisco meeting. Whatever their origin,

the various articles of the Charter guaranteed "Human rights and fundamental freedoms for all, without distinction as to race, sex, language, or religion."[20]

Dorothy Robins, an NGO representative, wrote later that the provisions on human rights and fundamental freedoms were included in the UN Charter at least partly due to pressures from the NGOs and other consultants. They forced the issue after Gildersleeve informed them that no Commission on Human Rights would be specifically mentioned "to keep the Charter short." Rather, the Economic and Social Council would be authorized to establish commissions later.[21] The NGOs then developed new proposals and got them to Stettinius in time to be included, but the Human Rights Commission still was not initiated until after the organizational meeting.

Whereas the American woman delegate, Virginia Gildersleeve, let down the cause of women at this significant time, other women and some men at least figuratively rang the liberty bell in their behalf. Bertha Lutz later paid tribute to Field Marshall J. C. Smuts, Prime Minister of the Union of South Africa, because he held to the principle of equal rights for men and women and nations great or small. Another supporter was Sir Ramaswami Mudaliar, a British appointee from India. Although Vijaya Lakshmi Pandit contended that he had no authority to represent India, Mudaliar diligently worked for a Subcommittee on the Status of Women. When the women delegates from the Dominican Republic and Uruguay supported this proposal, Lutz reported that Gildersleeve was the only woman dead set against it. After she lost the battle to form a Commission on Human Rights, Gildersleeve opposed the creation of a special Subcommission on the Status of Women. She argued that the proposed Commission on Human Rights would adequately protect women's interests. Gildersleeve saw her chief opponent, Bertha Lutz, "as a militant feminist in favor of what seemed to me segregation of women."[22] Only the Chinese delegate sided with Gildersleeve.

In contrast, some inexperienced American diplomats tried so hard to assist the women that they nearly did more harm than good. Of genuine assistance, however, was Sir Peter Frazer, the Premier of New Zealand. The Australian Premier also defended the proposal for a subcommission on women, as did the Soviet delegate. After the matter was debated, Gildersleeve and Wu Yi-fang refrained from voting on it while the British delegates showed their support by also abstaining because their women alternates were opposed.[23] The motion carried unanimously to form the Subcommission on the Status of Women. Meanwhile, they would be represented under the forthcoming Commission on Human Rights.

When the historic San Francisco meeting ended, Bertha Lutz was one of only four women who signed the UN Charter. On October 24,

1945, the United States and twenty-eight other countries accepted this document that reaffirmed "faith in fundamental human rights, in the dignity and worth of the human person, in the equal rights of men and women."[24] Despite its pledge of equality, women's participation was and still is limited. When Lutz looked back on the twenty-five subsequent years, she recalled that women had not played as large a part as they should have in the UN. They continued not to receive much support from conservative North Americans like Eleanor Roosevelt. President Harry F. Truman appointed his predecessor's widow to replace Virginia Gildersleeve as the token woman in the American delegation to the United Nations.

Although the militant women had managed to prevail at the United Nations Organization in San Francisco, Eleanor Roosevelt did little for their cause. Like Virginia Gildersleeve, she argued that women should participate in all UN functions on an equal basis, but she contended that no special legislation was necessary to insure this. Consequently, Roosevelt also opposed a special subcommission on women's rights. However, armed with the policy of equality in the United Nations Charter, a 1946 resolution from women's organizations in the United States and Great Britain urged the inclusion of women in its Councils. This resolution, presented to the president of the Economic and Social Council, Sir Ramaswami Mudaliar, asked that a permanent commission (not just a subcommission) on the status of women be established under the Economic and Social Council. One of the presenters was Emmeline Pethick Lawrence, a pioneer campaigner in the British and international woman suffrage movement.[25]

The implementation of this resolution was further delayed, although the UNO had already agreed to create a subcommission. When it was initiated in February 1946, National Woman's Party and World Woman's Party leaders (among others) began lobbying to raise the subcommission to full commission status. Eleanor Roosevelt continued to oppose it when she was appointed chair of the Human Rights Commission. The chairperson of the Subcommission on the Status of Women then appealed directly to the Economic and Social Council, and the militants won again.[26] The Commission on the Status of Women was created in June 1946. The General Assembly also adopted a resolution that requested all member nations to accord women political equality. This resolution had to be enacted and enforced by the individual nations. Few complied fully.

At the end of 1946, Denmark presented a resolution that asked the UN Assembly to urge all member states to adopt measures for women's political equality. Former First Lady Eleanor Roosevelt opposed this resolution, too. She said it was "just more words." Roosevelt's only supporter was Warren R. Austin, chairman of the American delegation. He argued that equality for women would be a stricter eligibility requirement for new applicants than that required for current members. Austin contended that the current qualifications specified in the UN Charter were sufficient.

Instead, Roosevelt wanted to refer the Danish resolution to the Economic and Social Council to recommend ways the principles could be put into practice. The Czechoslovakian delegate, Jan Papnek, said this would delay the matter for a year. He and others stood staunchly in favor of the resolution. The *New York Times* reported that "Sentimentally, melodramatically and statistically, delegates paid tribute to womankind and reported on the status of women in their respective countries." Rossura Martinez spoke for Mexico, and Agnes F. P. McIntosh of New Zealand cited Roosevelt herself as a positive role model. Delegates from the Arab states and others where women markedly lacked equality remained silent. At that time, about twenty member nations still denied women the franchise although women represented a dozen of the total fifty-one.[27]

Extended international publicity gave women a stronger weapon to pressure member states in the United Nations. Delegates hastened to correct errors in reports on woman suffrage in their countries, including the host nation, Lebanon. Dr. Charles Malik reported that progress was being made, that Lebanon had "one of the most active women's movements anywhere."[28] Despite this new awareness, Eleanor Roosevelt still needed Carrie Chapman Catt to keep her priorities straight. But that was soon to end. Catt made her last public appearance on January 9, 1947, her eighty-eighth birthday. As an honorary vice president, she attended the American Association for the United Nations dinner. Catt had been a board member when it was founded in 1923 as the League of Nations Association. On the day before her death, March 9, 1947, she joined Eleanor Roosevelt and other prominent women to salute Russian women's efforts to build a peaceful world as they celebrated International Women's Day.[29] By the time Catt died, the WILPF (like the WWCTU, ICW, and IAW) was appointed a nongovernmental advisory organization to the United Nations. All these women's groups continued to work through that organization and also through their own memberships for a multitude of women's rights, as well as the broader issue of human rights.

The liaison committee between the League of Nations and women's international organizations also continued to maintain consultative status to the United Nations. In several presentations to meetings of the Human Rights Commission at Lake Success in June 1948, the liaison committee proposed several amendments that were accepted in whole or part, such as one on equal pay. Eleanor Roosevelt also agreed to accept less sexist wording in the Declaration of Human Rights after Hansa Metha of India said the wording "all men" might be interpreted to exclude women. Roosevelt acquiesced after she declared that American women had never felt omitted from the Declaration of Independence because it said "all men."[30, 31]

When the Universal Declaration of Human Rights was adopted by the United Nations General Assembly in Paris on December 10, 1948, it stipulated equality of all persons and opposition to all forms of discrimination.[32] Hanna Rydh and Margery Corbett Ashby were on hand to represent the IAW. They proclaimed a major victory and announced that from then on the Declaration could be used as the vindication of every demand for equality.[33] Social purity also got a boost in the international forum. During a session on December 2, 1949, the UN General Assembly adopted a Convention on the "Suppression of the Traffic in Persons and of the Exploitation of the Prostitution of Others." This reflected the sentiments of an IAW committee active since 1920 on the Equal Moral Standard, Prostitution and Traffic in Women. United Nations backing could lend credibility and publicity for such issues, but it still could not insure national enforcement.[34]

Ever since the UN Commission on the Status of Women was inaugurated in 1946, that organization has reported on women's circumstances each year and has become an important instrument to pressure for women's rights. However, equality for women continued to be a principle that member nations were quite sporadic in implementing. Many were reluctant or downright unwilling even to provide complete information on the status of women in their countries. Even so, the Commission on the Status of Women ensured that recognition was accorded to those who extended suffrage to women, passed married women's nationality laws, and accepted other equalizing measures. By 1964, this committee could report that 106 nations had given women the vote on an equal basis with men. Six still put some qualifications on women that did not apply to men, and nine did not allow woman suffrage at all. The patchwork progress continues, although the United Nations Decade for Women (1975-85) and the 1995 meeting in Beijing generated much publicity and enabled women to pressure their home countries more publicly for equal rights.

22

CONCLUSION:
LOWERING THE BARRIERS TO AWARENESS

In the century from 1848 to 1948, numerous talented women and men channeled their efforts into extending women's participation and acceptance in public life. Many belonged to organizations that lobbied for changes. While it is now readily acknowledged that the accomplishments of earlier women's rights struggles contributed significantly to the current movement, it is also increasingly apparent how carefully both their efforts and subsequent interpretations have been constructed to reflect the ladies' viewpoint and limit offense to the male patriarchy.

In this long campaign, the first obstacle women had to overcome was the long held belief that they were physically, intellectually, and emotionally weaker than men. Organizations and education gave them opportunities to show their capabilities and stamina. Even so, social customs that segregated women from men have proven to be highly resistant barriers to equal standing. Without the ballot, women initially relied on strength of numbers in petitions, parades, speeches, and personal lobbying. Despite the obstacles, women's organizations promoted the perception that females were equal to men—entitled to hold up half the sky, as Mao Tse-tung later proclaimed.

As encroachments on the male political domain became more common, the pressures were often indirect. Women's organizations defined their objectives by drafting innumerable position papers. These were backed by petitions, sometimes containing millions of signatures. Supportive men like John Stuart Mill gave women some direct access to the political system even from an early stage, and over the long term his theories have been of enduring influence. *On the Subjection of Women* continues to be widely published and anthologized. Despite such support, women had to band together for strength and emotional support to overcome ridicule and to achieve progress. It was a long battle to break down male resistance to equal rights even in limited areas.

As Elizabeth Cady Stanton drafted the Declaration of Sentiments for the Seneca Falls convention in 1848, she crystallized many salient women's rights issues, including the demand for suffrage. Very soon activists in Great Britain and the United States reinforced each other. In this early phase, they benefitted from Mill's prestige and backing. In addition to his accepted standing as an economist, the movement initially gained respectability because of distinguished participants like Josephine Butler, a clergyman's wife, and Harriet Martineau, a writer. In the American struggle, Stanton and Anthony tested the limits of what was socially accepted for mainstream women to strive for. They had to overcome the resistance not only of men, but of middle-class women who were socialized to accept their separate domestic sphere, content in the belief that politics was better left to the men. Working-class women sometimes grasped the implications more readily. Although their limited time and finances restricted their efforts, some of them took more interest and participated more actively than initial studies suggested.

One of the most distinctive features of the individuals and organizations described in this volume is how carefully they aligned themselves with what they perceived to be acceptable to the patriarchy and avoided other issues like prostitution, venereal disease, and birth control. Single and widowed female leaders avoided public antagonism by not challenging male prerogatives related to sex and parenthood. Josephine Butler stands out among the nineteenth-century leaders because she knowingly violated the code of ladies' expected behavior to assist prostitutes and to protest the Contagious Diseases Acts. While John Stuart Mill promoted women's rights and introduced suffrage legislation in England, Butler gave precedence over woman suffrage to personal suffering and helped set limits on how far women's civil rights could be eroded.

Even so, respectable women continued to be reluctant to acknowledge how prostitution affected them. To protect her credibility in the suffrage movement, Millicent Garrett Fawcett distanced herself from Josephine Butler's campaign although she later took up the cause of the single moral standard and wrote an admiring biography of Butler. With leaders avoiding the issue, other women were not easily empowered to act. But opposition to the Contagious Diseases Acts generated public awareness of the sexual double standard and the impact of venereal disease on women and children. Butler's campaign revealed that the line between so-called good and bad women might not be as well demarcated as the former wanted to believe.

That she and her cohorts were able to have these laws rescinded in England marks a small victory based on a peek into the nether world that ladies generally refused to acknowledge. Butler was uniquely situated for this enterprise, well-buttressed by her position in society, a married woman whose husband was a well-placed scholar and clergyman. The perception of prostitution was altered from a moral to an economic issue deserving public scrutiny in the nineteenth century. Stanton and Anthony also pushed the envelope on what was socially accepted and were quickly castigated when they went too far. Stanton particularly spoke out for domestic rights such as divorce and supported Victoria Woodhull's carefully coded campaign for eugenic improvement, which the press immediately decried as free love. The cause of rehabilitating prostitutes was taken up in New Zealand where suffrage and temperance were quickly linked. More often, however, women leaders almost instinctively compromised to avoid intimate taboos and cultivate male approval.

Alcohol abuse more directly raised women's consciousness in the nineteenth century. Although conservative women wanted to avoid crossing the line into controversial behavior, desperation drove many into the temperance movement. Hard drinking was socially accepted among men. Women paid the penalty with less money, more children, and frequent physical abuse. Unlike suffrage, women of all classes, races, and nationalities could see the immediate benefits of abolishing alcohol. They readily banded together, and some like Carry Nation picked up stones and axes to attack saloons directly.

Frances Willard's primary gift as a leader was to establish an organizational tone that suited conservative women. Willard capitalized on their concern with a gospel-like approach that gave the temperance cause respectability. Willard harnessed the religious impulse to an immediate need and produced an organization that grew rapidly. The WCTU drew American women from the north and south together after the War Between the States. Then the movement spread around the world and fulfilled the same basic need in many nations. As they banded together (shielded by a mantle of piety) in what they perceived as a just cause, women like Mary Clement Leavitt could dedicate their lives to temperance in a socially acceptable framework. Once they became members, they broadened their social awareness and range of activities under Willard's "Do Everything" policy.

Leavitt was able to develop the World WCTU because alcohol abuse established a common bond across cultures and languages. Her eight-year odyssey to form WCTUs around the world is remarkable. She overcame obstacles of inadequate funding, difficult travel, and limited communication options. Through the bond of religion, missionaries, and other colonial women rendered substantial assistance, even as they protected one another from acknowledging the actual circumstances of indigenous women's lives. The element of class snobbery in the way missionaries assumed the superiority of their own religion and culture, a feminine twist on the "white man's burden" to uplift the "little brown brothers" now seems offensive. However, the system at least allowed native women to achieve new levels of awareness as missionaries attempted to outlaw what they regarded as offensive practices such as slavery, polygamy, and maintaining concubines and prostitutes.

While the imposition of colonial values is now held in ill repute, missionaries in their various world outposts laid a foundation of education and English language communication on which other women's rights leaders were able to capitalize. Missionaries primarily wanted to Christianize the local people, but they more often achieved their secondary goal to educate them. International bonds were also formed by student exchanges among countries. For example, Cornelia Sorabji was educated in England and practiced law in India before English women had that right. Similarly, Ume Tsuda spent eleven years in the United States and then founded Tsuda College in Japan. Missionaries began the first women's college in Korea and many others as well. Although their efforts to convert the natives to Christianity often failed, they bridged language and cultural gaps to create modern expectations and pave the way for international organizations.

While the WWCTU evolved through common needs and interests among women in a wide variety of circumstances, better education and aspirations for professional status motivated the formation of other organizations. The ICW was formed to campaign for the ballot, and then the IWSA splintered off when the ICW became immersed in other women's rights issues. Ultimately, both organizations extended the battle for equality and drew on one another for mutual support. Their hierarchical structures brought leaders of national organizations together (such as in National Councils of Women) and so helped to coordinate their efforts as well. Among their goals were the right of married women to retain their nationality and the obligation to assist refugees in wartime.

Woman suffrage was not always as much of a priority as it has often appeared in later accounts. Over the decades, between the early calls for woman suffrage and the not always directly associated right to run for political office, women initially won the right to stand for election to local school boards and in municipalities. Denied access to political office directly or representation through suffrage in state and national governments, bright and increasingly well-educated women continued to be excluded from suitable employment. Women's organizations provided them with opportunities to exercise their leadership skills and offered a forum in which to debate women's appropriate place in society and how to achieve it. Women delineated their priorities and devised campaigns to achieve them.

The debate over peace or war aroused a wider ethical debate among both men and women. Like slavery, it was a socially accepted issue to address publicly. However, antiwar activities were not generally acceptable to the male hierarchy. Fawcett and her militant competitors, the Pankhursts, maintained some popularity as they supported British colonial incursions and other male-initiated wars. How much the tradeoff in support for various war efforts won them cooperation in the suffrage movement is difficult to assess. Fawcett dismally concluded that if women had not gotten the vote with soldiers in World War I, they might never have done so.

Certainly Jane Addams' leadership of the women's peace initiative in 1915 demonstrated how tenuous prominence could be when all forms of public recognition were dominated by male values. As the press turned against her, she was publicly castigated by women as well as men. Carrie Chapman Catt's sympathies were also with the peace movement, but she recognized that popular support for woman suffrage (her priority) hinged on retaining male cooperation. Like Fawcett, Catt, and Anna Howard Shaw, ultimately Jane Addams supported the war effort in World War I to continue momentum toward woman suffrage. After the war when suffrage had also been won, Catt's belated open support for the peace movement diminished her public appeal. Addams also stayed on course and became president of the new WILPF. Both of them returned to favor as peace became a popular cause in the lull between world wars.

As external events such as wars challenged women's social awareness and leadership skills, their efforts coalesced in pressure to initiate the principle not only of equal rights for women, but also international cooperation for peace and human betterment overall. In 1893, May Wright Sewall foresaw an international governing body that would bring nations together for mutual support and assistance. Male leaders implemented this concept when the League of Nations was founded in 1920. It was a major landmark for women, too. At the end of World War I, after European women's groups drew representatives together to offer their unsolicited input to the peace conference at Versailles, a liaison committee of international organizations was formed to lobby for an equal rights charter at the League of Nations and an equal employment rights policy in the ILO. With consultative status extended to NGOs, they were able to pressure committees on which some of the women also had official standing, such as Margery Corbett Ashby's Disarmament Committee.

While equal rights feminists united in the peace movement and gradually renewed their standing, controversial issues like prostitution, venereal disease, and birth control were left to women who generally walked a tenuous line between acclaim and ostracism. As Catt and Fawcett concluded the women's suffrage campaigns in the United States and England, Marie Stopes and Margaret Sanger were fighting the battles over intimacy in print, in clinics, and in bedrooms. Margaret Sanger opened the first birth control clinic in America in 1916, and Marie Stopes published *Married Love,* the first how-to sex manual, in England in 1918. Sanger's campaign led to legalization of information about birth control in the United States, and she generated funding for the research that led to the discovery of the birth control pill. Although birth control has now become widely available, military and other suppressive governments can still limit women's access and ability to control reproduction.

Aletta Jacobs had opened the first birth control clinic in Holland in the late nineteenth century. A licensed physician, she was one of the few women who played a leadership role in the birth control movement while she was also active in the battle for woman suffrage. Certainly the women who played their politics carefully to maintain favor with the male patriarchy were more widely respected than those closer to the fringe of respectability, but the parallel movements contributed to progress in women's rights. Sanger and Stopes made birth control an international cause that Shidzue Kato also promoted in Japan. Later, Kato's acquaintance with Mary Ritter Beard also contributed to her effort to collect and preserve documents important to women's history. While this lacked the immediacy of the birth control movement, it was important in the long term.

The battle over the double standard of sexual behavior continues, although women are no longer persuaded that men require sexual intercourse to remain healthy. Recently, some scholarship has dealt with the more controversial issues, but activism remains the purview of missionaries and women directly affected. For example, the sex tours in Asia continue to be as popular as ever, although the advent of AIDs had made health a bigger issue than fidelity.[1] Consequently, Japanese women's groups like the JWCTU have taken the initiative to promote public awareness. In the west, AIDS has also become more of a mainstream issue. However, many middle-class women still manage not to see how drug use, prostitution, and other methods of transmission can have a direct bearing on their own health and well-being.

The rise of militarism in World War II demonstrated how fragile women's rights had been, as they were once again summarily put aside to support war machines. International women's meetings were restricted, and lobbying efforts at the League of Nations were put on hold. However, a new source of strength had arisen in Latin America. Whereas conservative North American organizations like the LWV tried to protect women from arduous working conditions, Alice Paul's National Woman's Party cooperated with European and Latin American women to fight protective legislation. Out of this association came a new force for women's equality.

Particularly in the absence of women at the Dumbarton Oaks planning session for the postwar era, the Inter-American Conference on Problems of War and Peace in Mexico City paved the way for an equal rights doctrine in the United Nations Charter. Consultantship rights for nongovernmental organizations had been validated in the decades before the United Nations continued the precedent in 1945 and adopted a policy of total equality between the genders. Then the Commission on the Status of Women was established in 1946. This body collects information and sponsors international meetings that publicize the extension of women's rights and highlights ongoing deficiencies. By 1948, when the Declaration of Human Rights was promulgated, both official and consultant NGOs were collecting information on women's status and pressuring national governments for change.

International women's organizations continue, and they deserve recognition for pioneering efforts to establish a network that lobbied for equal rights within nations, at the League of Nations, and then through the United Nations. Women's clubs have often been recognized largely for their social aspects, but organizations like the WWCTU, ICW, IAW, and WILPF accomplished much more. They struggled to improve women's status during a period when females lacked formal channels of authority. Now, although the United Nations is still a distinct patriarchy, women's organizations maintain their input and visibility, particularly in the Commission on the Status of Women. Also, more women—but still a small minority—occupy positions as delegates and officials. One, Vijaya Lakshmi Pandit, went from being an outsider at the UNO in 1945 to being its first woman president in the early 1950s.

Although the United Nations cannot impose its recommendations on member nations, this forum draws attention to their efforts and neglect as well. As more nations join the UN and more data on women are collected and compared, this pressure can intensify. John Stuart Mill's assertion is still applicable that the level of a civilization can be determined by the standing of its women. As the barbarism of war and the social stigma of prostitution as well as economic inequities continue to undermine women's advances, much remains to be accomplished before equal rights are achieved and their continuation assured.

While the focus of attention has shifted to the United Nations, women's organizations still contribute significantly, and their efforts demonstrate mutual support and an understanding of what can be accomplished through international cooperation. As in the past, women develop greater understanding of their common restrictions as they compare their familiar circumstances with those in other cultures. Then parallels emerge from what initially seem to be differences. Whether women live veiled and secluded in polygynous relationships or unveiled and monogamous, their circumstances remain widely controlled by men. Together, however, women have the opportunity to expand their understanding of and respect for themselves and others, to recognize similarities in their circumstances, and to broaden their visions of what they deserve and what they can accomplish.

Getting to this point was the major accomplishment of women's organizations in the last half of the nineteenth and first half of the twentieth century. With the recognition of their individual and collective worth and objectives, strategies for implementation followed inevitably. However, the fact that women now are being inducted into mainstream occupations has disadvantaged women's organizations in some respects. Many more women now apply their education and talents in industry, government, social services, and education. Nonetheless, mutual support enables them to maintain political coalitions to pressure dominant male power groups, while women's organizations continue to offer a basis for international as well as national organization and cooperation.

NOTES

Chapter 1

1. Arnold Whittick, *Woman into Citizen* (Santa Barbara, CA ABC-Clio, 1979), 24.

2. Christine Bolt, *The Women's Movements in the United States and Britain from the 1790s to the 1920s* (New York: Harvester Wheatsheaf, 1993), 296.

3. Ross Evans Paulson, *Women's Suffrage and Prohibition: A Comparative Study of Equality and Social Control* (Glenview, IL: Scott, Foresman and Company, n.d.), 45.

4. Madelyn Gutworth, "Madame de Staël, Rousseau and the Woman Question," *PMLA*, 86 (1971), 107.

5. Rosemary Cullen Owens, *Smashing Times; A History of the Irish Women's Suffrage Movement 1889-1922* (Dublin: Attic Press, 1984), 10.

6. Josephine Kamm, *Rapiers and Battle Axes* (London: George Allen and Unwin Limited, 1966), 22.

7. Paulson, 20.

8. Kamm, 29.

9. Paulson, 29.

10. *A Brief Review of the Women's Suffrage Movement Since Its Beginning in 1832: History of the Women's Suffrage Movement in Parliament* (Manchester: Manchester Central Library), Women's Suffrage Collection.

11. Owens, 11.

12. Ray Strachey, *The Cause: A Short History of the Women's Movement in Great Britain* (London: Virago Limited, 1978), 39.

13. Bolt, 99.

14. Whittick, 23-24.

15. Harriet Martineau, *Harriet Martineau's Autobiography with Memorials by Maria Weston Chapman* (London: Smith Elder and Company, 1877), 181, 182.

16. Letter of Grimke to Weld, August 12, 1837, in Paulson, 14.

17. Miriam Schneir, "Lucretia Mott: Not Christianity, but Priestcraft," in *Feminism: The Essential Historical Writings,* ed. Miriam Schneir (New York: Vintage Books, 1972), 99.

18. Paulson, 16.

19. Theodore Stanton and Harriot Stanton Blatch, eds., *Elizabeth Cady Stanton,* 2 (New York: Arno Press, 1969), 18 n.3.

20. Stanton and Blatch, eds., 2:40.

21. Paulson, 30.

22. Kamm, 29.

23. Paulson, 37.

24. "Married Women's Property Act, New York, 1848," in Schneir, 73.

25. *Women in a Changing World: The Dynamic Story of the International Council of Women Since 1888* (London: Routledge & Kegan Paul, 1966), 7.

26. Paulson, 52.

27. ICW Dynamic, 9.

28. Paulson, 32.

29. Alice Stone Blackwell, *Lucy Stone* (New York: Kraus Reprint Co., 1971), 98.

30. Blackwell, 99.

31. Ida Husted Harper, *Life and Work of Susan B. Anthony*, 1 (Salem, NH: Ayer Company, Publishers, Inc., 1983, reprint of 1898-1908 edition), 59.

32. Harper, 1, 61.

33. Blackwell, 101.

34. Harper, 1, 65.

35. Harper, 1, 72.

36. Bolt, 96-97.

37. Elizabeth Cady Stanton, "Address to the New York State Legislature, 1854," in Schneir, 113.

38. Elizabeth Cady Stanton," Address to the New York State Legislature, 1860," in Schneir, 118.

39. "Married Women's Property Act, New York, 1860," in Schneir, 122.

40. Bolt, 51.

41. Bolt, 161.

42. Kamm, 47.

43. Whittick, 28.

44. Whittick, 28.

45. Cullen Owens, 31.

46. Page Smith, *Daughters of the Promised Land: Women in American History* (Boston: Little, Brown and Company, 1970), 181.

47. Raj Kumar, *Annie Besant's Rise to Power in Indian Politics 1914-1917* (New Delhi: Concept Publishing Company, 1981), 136.

48. Paulson, 181.

49. Paulson, 89.

50. Bolt, 119.

51. Bolt, 119.

52. Clifford, 178.

53. Paulson, 97.

54. "Woman's Suffrage Is 75 Years Old Today: Idea Started at a Tea Party in Wyoming," *New York Times*, 10 Dec. 1944: 48.

55. Shaw, 243-44.

56. Chrystal Macmillan chair, title page missing, book published by the International Woman Suffrage Alliance, Edinburgh Scotland, May 26, 1913,

Woman Suffrage Collection microfilm, Manchester Central Library, Manchester England, 33.

57. Macmillan, IWSA history, 32.

58. Macmillan, IWSA history, 86.

59. Paulson, 91.

Chapter 2

1. Millicent Garrett Fawcett, "England," in *The Woman Question in Europe: A Series of Original Essays,* ed. Theodore Stanton (New York: Putnam's, 1884), 4.

2. John Stuart Mill, *Autobiography and Literary Essays, I,* ed. John M. Robson and Jack Stillinger in *The Collected Works of John Stuart Mill,* 33 vol., ed. John M. Robson (London: Oxford UP, 1969), 63, 147.

3. Michael St. John Packe, *The Life of John Stuart Mill* (New York: MacMillan, 1954), 58.

4. Cullen Owens, 19.

5. Packe, 89.

6. Packe, 90.

7. John Stuart Mill to Harriet Taylor, letter after Oct. 29, 1850, No. 30, in *The Later Letters of John Stuart Mill 1849-1873* 15, eds. Francis E. Mineka and Dwight N. Lindley, in *The Collected Works of John Stuart Mill* (Toronto: U of Toronto P, 1972), 49.

8. Packe, 347.

9. John Stuart Mill to Augustus DeMorgan, letter of July 21, 1850, No. 29 in *The Later Letters of John Stuart Mill 1849-1873,* 15 in *The Collected Works of John Stuart Mill,* 48 n2.

10. Pugh, 435.

11. Packe, 347.

12. "XLVII.—The Enfranchisement of Women," *The English Women's Review,* 13.77 (1 July 1864): 289-96.

13. Packe, 315.

14. Ruth Borchard, *John Stuart Mill: The Man* (London: Watts, 1957), 99.

15. Borchard, 100.

16. Packe, 315.

17. Borchard, 117.

18. Gertrude Himmelfarb, *On Liberty and Liberalism: The Case of John Stuart Mill* (New York: Knopf, 1974), 181.

19. Borchard, 117.

20. B. R. P. [Bessie Raynor Parkes], "The Opinions of John Stuart Mill," *The English Woman's Journal,* Part 1, 6.31 (Sept. 1860): 1.

21. *Ibid.,* 3.

22. *Ibid.,* 3, 4.

23. *Ibid.,* 6.

24. *Ibid.,* 11

25. Evelyn L. Pugh, "John Stuart Mill and the Women's Question in Parliament," *The Historian*, 42.3 (May 1980): 406.

26. "IV.—Some Probable Consequences of Extending the Franchise to Female Householders," *The Englishwoman's Review*, 1 (Oct. 1866): 26-34.

27. "I.—The Debate on the Enfranchisement of Women," *The Englishwoman's Review*, 1.4 (July 1867): 199-208.

28. Strachey, 42.

29. *A Brief Review of the Women's Suffrage Movement Since Its Beginning in 1832*, Women's Suffrage Collection (Manchester: Manchester Central Library), 9.

30. Fawcett in Stanton, 8.

31. Borchard, 140.

32. Cullen Owens, 30.

33. Helen Blackburn, *Women's Suffrage*, Women's Suffrage Collection (Manchester: Manchester Central Library), 8.

34. *A Brief Review of the Women's Suffrage Movement Since Its Beginnings in 1832*, 10.

35. Fawcett in Stanton, 12.

36. Millicent Garrett Fawcett, *Women's Suffrage: A Short History of a Great Movement* (London: T. C. and E. C. Jack, n.d.), 9.

37. David Tyler, "Introduction," Lydia Becker Papers, Women's Suffrage Collection (Manchester: Manchester Central Library), 8.

38. Strachey, 43.

39. Cullen Owens, 22.

40. Packe, 419.

41. Ray Strachey, *Millicent Garrett Fawcett* (London: John Murray, 1931), 16.

42. Packe, 418.

43. Fawcett in Stanton, 10.

44. Pugh (1973), 431.

45. Pugh (1973), 428.

46. Pugh (1973), 429.

47. Pugh (1973), 435.

48. Packe, 479.

49. Fawcett in Stanton, 4.

50. Tyler, 8.

51. Borchard, 97.

Chapter 3

1. Millicent Garrett Fawcett and E. M. Turner, *Josephine Butler: Her Work and Principles, and Their Meaning for the Twentieth Century* (London: The Association for Moral and Social Hygiene, 1927), 39.

2. Annie Besant, *Annie Besant: An Autobiography* (London: Unwin, n.d.), 71.

3. Susan Kingsley Kent, *Sex and Suffrage in Britain, 1860-1914* (Princeton: Princeton UP, 1987), 133.

4. Erna Olason Hellerstein, Leslie Parker Hume, and Karen M. Offen, eds., *Victorian Women: A Documentary Account of Women's Lives in Nineteenth-Century England, France, and the United States* (Stanford, CA: Stanford UP, 1981), 411.

5. Hellerstein et al., 415.

6. E. Moberly Bell, *Josephine Butler: Flame of Fire* (London: Constable, 1912), 71.

7. Fawcett and Turner, 57.

8. Fawcett and Turner, 42.

9. Fawcett and Turner, 26.

10. Kent, 19.

11. Kent, 55.

12. Fawcett and Turner, 10.

13. Paulson, 92.

14. Bolt, 145.

15. Cullen Owens, 23.

16. Cullen Owens, 24.

17. Petrie, 20.

18. Fawcett, 47.

19. Fawcett, 23.

20. Fawcett, 22.

21. George W. and Lucy A. Johnson, eds., *Josephine Butler: An Autobiographical Memoir* (Bristol: Arrowsmith, 1911), 32.

22. Fawcet, 58.

23. Fawcett, 58.

24. Kent, 79.

25. Fawcett, 3.

26. Fawcett, 5.

27. Harriet Martineau, *Harriet Martineau's Autobiography with Memorials by Maria Weston Chapman* 3 (London: Smith Elder and Company, 1877), 434.

28. Fawcett, 64.

29. Fawcett, 58.

30. Kent, 106.

31. Kent, 111.

32. Kent, 134.

33. Josephine E. Butler, *Personal Reminiscences of a Great Crusade* (Chatham: Mackay, 1896), 64.

34. Johnsons, 127.

35. Butler, 109-10.

36. Bell, 127.

37. Fawcett, 116.

38. Johnsons, 218.

39. Bell, 224.
40. Paulson, 117.
41. Paulson, 102.
42. Fawcett, 114.
43. Butler, 115.
44. Bell, 132.
45. Butler, 107.
46. Butler, 111.
47. Fawcett, 97.
48. Fawcett, 102.
49. Johnsons, 306.
50. Fawcett, 127.
51. Fawcett, 130.
52. Johnsons, 211.
53. Bell, 232.
54. Cullen Owens, 122.
55. Cullen Owens, 123.
56. Fawcett, 131.
57. Kent, 195.
58. Kent, 159.
59. Kent, 163.
60. Kent, 160.
61. Kent, 178.
62. Kent, 160.
63. Kent, 227

Part II

1. R. Pierce Beaver, *American Protestant Women in World Mission: A History of the First Feminist Movement in North America* (Grand Rapids, MI: William B. Eerdmans Publishing Company, 1980), 14.

2. Beaver, 13.

3. Kenneth E. Wells, *History of Protestant Work in Thailand 1828-1958* (Bangkok, Thailand: 1958), 195, 22.

4. Wells, 19.

5. Sophia Blackmore, *Sophia Blackmore in Singapore: Educational and Missionary Pioneer 1887-1927*, ed. Theodore R. Doraisarny (Singapore: General Conference Women's Society of Christian Service, the Methodist Church in Singapore, 1987), 56.

6. Paulson, 70.

7. Ida Husted Harper, *The Life and Work of Susan B. Anthony,* 1 (Indianapolis: Hollenbeck Press, 1898), 67.

8. *Ibid.*

9. Harper, 1, 71.

10. Paulson, 114.

11. Paulson, 115.

12. Paulson, 58.

13. Paulson, 60.

14. John Stuart Mill, *Utilitarianism, Liberty, and Representative Government,* reprint edition (New York: E. P. Dutton & Co., 1951), 206.

15. Paulson, 83.

Chapter 4

1. Paulson, 113.

2. Elizabeth Putnam Gordon, *Women Torch-bearers: The Story of the Woman's Christian Temperance Union* (Evanston: National Woman's Christian Temperance Union, 1924), 2.

3. Gordon, 11.

4. Gordon, 3.

5. Gordon, 7.

6. Paulson, 113.

7. Gordon, 16.

8. Gordon, 19.

9. Paulson, 113.

10. Mary I. Wood, *The History of the General Federation of Women's Clubs for the First Twenty-two Years of Its Organization* (Norwood, MA: Norwood Press, 1912), 27.

11. Earhart, 135.

12. Wood, 31.

13. Anna Garlin Spencer, *The Council Idea: A Chronicle of Its Prophets and a Tribute to May Wright Sewall, Architect of Its Form and Builder of Its Method of Work* (New Brunswick, NJ: J. Heidingsfeld Co., 1930), 4.

14. Spencer, 5.

15. Deborah Pickman Clifford, *Mine Eyes Have Seen the Glory: A Biography of Julia Ward Howe* (Boston: Little, Brown, 1979), 201.

16. Mary Earhart, *Frances Willard: From Prayers to Politics* (Chicago: U of Chicago P, 1944), 129.

17. Earhart, 130.

18. Gordon, 193.

19. Earhart, 152.

20. Gordon, 4.

21. Gordon, 265.

22. Gordon, 194.

23. Gordon, 195.

24. Gordon, 196.

25. Gordon, 197-98.

26. Gordon, 198.

27. Gordon, 200.

28. Paulson, 113.

29. Paulson, 115.
30. Earhart, 245.
31. Gordon, 102.
32. Earhart, 261.
33. Gordon, 234.
34. Earhart, 185.
35. Gordon, 132.

Chapter 5

1. Gordon, 270.
2. E. K. Stanley, *Ten Decades of White Ribbon Service* (Cincinnati: Revivalist P, 1983), 10.
3. Gordon, 78.
4. Stanley, 11.
5. Gordon, 70.
6. Gordon, 71.
7. Earhart, 271.
8. Mark Edward Lender, ed., "Leavitt, Mary Greenleaf Clement," *Dictionary of American Temperance Biography from Temperance Reform to Alcohol Research: The 1600s to the 1980s* (Westport: Greenwood P, 1984), 290.
9. Earhart, 270.
10. Paul S. Boyer and Janet Wilson James, "Leavitt, Mary Greenleaf Clement," *Notable American Women 1607-1950, A Biographical Dictionary* 2, G-O (Boston: Belknap P of Harvard UP, 1971), 384.
11. "Mary Clement Leavitt," *The Union Signal,* 14 Nov. 1891.
12. "Leavitt, Mary Greenleaf Clement," *Dictionary of American Temperance Biography from Temperance Reform to Alcohol Research: The 1600s to the 1980s,* ed. Mark Edward Lender (Westport: Greenwood P, 1984), 290.
13. Boyer and James, 384.
14. "Our National Organizers," *Union Signal,* 13 Nov. 1884.
15. Note, *Union Signal,* 4 Dec. 1841.
16. Frances Willard, "Miss Willard's Plea for Mrs. Leavitt," *Union Signal,* 8 Jan. 1885.
17. Mary Clement Leavitt, "Correspondence: The W.C.T.U. in the Sandwich Islands," *Union Signal,* 22 Jan. 1885.
18. *First Annual Report of the Woman's Christian Temperance Union, 1885,* Hawaiian Historical Society, 7.
19. Mary Clement Leavitt, "Correspondence: Our Round-the World Missionary," *Union Signal,* 27 Aug. 1885.
20. Mary Clement Leavitt, "The New Zealand W.C.T.U.," *Union Signal,* 9 Apr. 1885.
21. Mary Clement Leavitt, "The Ends of the Earth Come to Us: Our Round the World Correspondence," *Union Signal,* 11 June 1885.
22. *Ibid.*

23. Mary Clement Leavitt, "Correspondence: Our Round the World Missionary," *Union Signal,* 27 Aug. 1885.

24. Mary Clement Leavitt, "The Work in New Zealand," *Union Signal,* 22 Oct. 1885.

25. Mary Clement Leavitt," Our Round-the-World Missionary," *Union Signal,* 15 Apr. 1886.

26. Paulson, 125.

27. Jessie Ackerman, "South Australian Convention," *Union Signal,* 17 Dec. 1891.

28. Melanie Nolan and Caroline Daley, "International Feminist Perspectives on Suffrage: An Introduction," *Suffrage & Beyond: International Feminist Perspectives,* ed. Caroline Daley and Melanie Nolan (New York: New York UP, 1994), 1.

29. Paulson, 128.

30. Mary A. Livermore, "The W.C.T.U. Missionary," *Union Signal,* 16 July 1885.

31. Mary Clement Leavitt, "Our Round-the-World Missionary," *Union Signal,* 10 Dec. 1885.

32. Mary Clement Leavitt, "Our Round the World Missionary," *Union Signal,* 8 July 1886.

33. Mary Clement Leavitt, "Our Round the World Missionary: Tasmania," *Union Signal,* 6 May 1886.

34. Mary Clement Leavitt, "Our Round-the-World Missionary," *Union Signal,* 30 July 1891.

35. Catherine T. Wallace, "The New Federated W.C.T.U. of Australia," *Union Signal,* 30 July 1891.

36. Paulson, 128.

37. Paulson, 123.

38. Paulson, 124.

39. Mary Clement Leavitt, "Correspondence: Our Round-the-World Missionary, *Union Signal,* 5 Aug. 1886.

40. "World's W.C.T.U.," *Union Signal,* 1 Dec. 1887.

41. "A Japanese Girl's Letter," *Union Signal,* 14 Apr. 1892.

42. Masako Sato, Japanese WCTU historian, personal communication, Aug. 20, 1995.

43. Lizzie Nelson Fryer, "Temperance Progress in China," *Union Signal,* 18 Aug. 1887.

44. Mary Clement Leavitt, "Our Round the World Missionary," *Union Signal,* 2 June 1887.

45. Note, *Union Signal,* 28 Apr. 1887.

46. Mary Clement Leavitt, "Our Round the World Missionary," *Union Signal,* 9 June 1884.

47. "The Ends of the Earth," *Union Signal,* 12 May 1887.

48. Mary Clement Leavitt, "Our Round the World Missionary," *Union*

Signal, 23 June 1887.

49. Mary Clement Leavitt, "Our Round the World Missionary," *Union Signal,* 21 July 1887.

50. Mary Clement Leavitt, "Our Round the World Missionary," *Union Signal,* 28 July 1887.

51. Mary Clement Leavitt, "Extract from a Letter from Mrs. Mary Clement Leavitt to Pundita Ramabai," *Union Signal,* 21 Nov. 1887.

52. Mary Clement Leavitt, "Our Round the World Missionary, *Union Signal,* 8 Oct. 1891.

53. Mary Clement Leavitt, "Our Round the World Missionary," *Union Signal,* 20 Aug. 1891.

54. Mary Clement Leavitt, "Our Round the World Missionary," *Union Signal,* 17 Sept. 1891.

55. Mary Clement Leavitt, "Our Round the World Missionary," *Union Signal,* 24 Sept. 1891.

56. Mary Clement Leavitt, "Our Round the World Missionary in the Dark Continent," *Union Signal,* 12 June 1890.

57. Paulson, 118.

58. Mary Clement Leavitt, "Our Round the World Missionary," *Union Signal,* 16 July 1891.

59. Mary Clement Leavitt, "Our Round the World Missionary," *Union Signal,* 2 Sept. 1886.

60. Mary Clement Leavitt, "Work in Madagascar," *Union Signal,* 3 Jan. 1889.

61. Mary Clement Leavitt, "Work in Madagascar," *Union Signal,* 24 Jan. 1889.

62. Mary Clement Leavitt, "Our Round the World Missionary," *Union Signal,* 2 Sept. 1886.

63. Frances Willard, "President's Address," *Union Signal,* 2 Aug. 1888.

64. Stanley, 12.

65. Stanley, 16.

66. Esther Pugh, "The Genesis of the World's W.C.T.U.," *Union Signal,* 14 May 1891.

67. Stanley, 25.

68. Stanley, 25.

69. Stanley, 20.

70. Gordon, 72.

71. Gordon, 20.

72. Boyer and James, 384.

73. Frances Willard, "President's Address," *Union Signal,* 2 Aug. 1888.

74. "Relation of the W.C.T.U. to Missions," *Union Signal,* 14 May 1891.

75. "Missions and Temperance," *Union Signal,* 4 Mar. 1886.

76. "Mrs. Mary Clement Leavitt," *Union Signal,* 14 Nov. 1891.

77. "Welcome Home," *Union Signal,* 2 July 1891.

78. Mary Clement Leavitt, "Mrs. Leavitt's Experiences in South America," *Union Signal,* 29 Sept. 1892.

79. Mary Clement Leavitt, "Mrs. Leavitt in South America," *Union Signal,* 16 June 1892.

80. Mary Clement Leavitt, "Mrs. Leavitt in South America," *Union Signal,* 6 Oct. 1892.

81. Mary Clement Leavitt, "Mrs. Leavitt in South America," *Union Signal,* 16 June 1892.

82. "Mrs. Mary Clement Leavitt," *Union Signal,* 14 Nov. 1892.

83. "Welcome Home," *Union Signal,* 2 July 1891.

Chapter 6

1. Stanley, 18.
2. Stanley, 25.
3. Stanley, 29.
4. Stanley, 30.
5. Stanley, 37.
6. Stanley, 14.
7. Gordon, 108.
8. Gordon, 111.
9. Gordon, 112.
10. Gordon, 109.
11. Stanley, 51.
12. Paulson, 159.
13. Stanley, 37.
14. Stanley, 52.
15. Gordon, 123, 124.
16. Gordon, 134.
17. Stanley, 46-47.
18. Gordon, 135.
19. Gordon, 201-02.
20. Gordon, 150.
21. Gordon, 142.
22. Gordon, 220-21.
23. Gordon, 223-25.
24. Paulson, 161.
25. Gordon, 192.
26. Gordon, 187-88.
27. Gordon, 204.
28. Stanley, 109.
29. Ian Tyrrell, *Woman's World: Woman's Empire, The Woman's Christian Temperance Union in International Perspective, 1880-1930* (Chapel Hill: U of North Carolina P, 1991), 257.
30. Stanley, 56.

31. Gordon, 215-16.

32. Gordon, 216.

33. Gordon, 35.

34. Stanley, 57.

35. Stanley, 80.

Chapter 7

1. Paulson, 33.

2. May Wright Sewall, *Genesis of the International Council of Women and the Story of Its Growth, 1888-1893* (Indianapolis: n.p., 1914), 1.

3. Rosemary T. Van Arsdel, *Florence Fenwick Miller,* unpublished manuscript, Fawcett Library, London, 1991, 211.

4. Sewall, 2.

5. Sewall, 3.

6. Sewall, 6.

7. Sewall, 7.

8. Sewall, 10.

9. Spencer, 11.

10. Harper, 2, 636.

11. Elizabeth Cady Stanton, opening remarks, NWSA *Report,* 35.

12. *Ibid.,* 33.

13. Clifford, 250.

14. Ida Husted Harper, *Life and Work of Susan B. Anthony Including Public Addresses, Her Own Letters and Many from Her Contemporaries during Fifty Years* 2 (Indianapolis: Hollenbeck P, 1898), 627.

15. Elizabeth Cady Stanton, remarks, *NWSA Report,* 322-23.

16. Frederick Douglass, remarks, *NWSA Report,* 329.

17. *Women in a Changing World: The Dynamic Story of the International Council of Women Since 1888* (London: Routledge & Kegan Paul, 1966), 14.

18. Paulson, 118.

19. Harper, 2, 639.

20. Spencer, 52.

21. National Woman Suffrage Association, *Report of the International Council of Women* condensed from the Stenographic Report made by Mary F. Seymour and Assistants (Washington, D.C.: Darby, 1888), 110, 222, 286, 319, 422.

22. NWSA *Report,* 449.

23. Marjorie Pentland, *In the Nineties* (London: Caxton P, 1947), 7.

24. Sewall, 29-30.

25. Sewall, 36.

26. Mary I. Wood, *The History of the General Federation of Women's Clubs for the First Twenty-two Years of Its Organization* (Norwood, MA: Norwood P, 1912), 32-33.

27. Sewall, 53.

28 Anna Garlin Spencer, *The Council Idea: A Chronicle of Its Prophets and a Tribute to May Wright Sewall, Architect of Its Form and Builder of Its Methods of Work* (New Brunswick, NJ: Heidingsfeld, 1930), v.

29. Sewall, 43.

Chapter 8

1. Harper, 2, 744.

2. Jeanne Madeline Weimann, *The Fair Women* (Chicago: Academy, 1981), 28.

3. Weimann, 32.

4. Weimann, 38.

5. Weimann, 43.

6. Weimann, 49.

7. Weimann, 48.

8. Ishbel Ross, *Silhouette in Diamonds: The Life of Mrs. Potter Palmer* (New York: Harper & Brothers, 1960), 71.

9. Ross, 72.

10. Sewall, 51.

11. Weimann, 524.

12. Sewall, 57.

13. Weimann, 525.

14. Weimann, 526.

15. Weimann, 529.

16. Sewall, 63.

17. Weimann, 526.

18. Weimann, 530.

19. Letter of Mrs. Potter Palmer to May Wright Sewall, Chicago Historical Society.

20. Harper, 2, 742.

21. Mary Gray Peck, *Carrie Chapman Catt: A Biography* (New York: Wilson, 1944), 72.

22. Pentland, *In the Nineties,* 8.

23. Weimann, 533.

24. Jacqueline Van Voris, *Carrie Chapman Catt: A Public Life* (New York: Feminist P, 1987), 31-37.

25. Bordin, 201.

26. Harper, 2, 751.

27. Blackwell, 276.

28. Van Voris, 37.

29. Harper, 2, 748.

30. Harper, 2, 746.

31. Harper, 2, 749-51.

32. Harper, 2, 750.

33. Marjorie Pentland, *A Bonnie Fechter: The Life of Ishbel Marjoribanks*

Marchioness of Aberdeen & Temair, G.B.E., L.L.D., J.P. 1857 to 1939 (London: Batsford, 1952), 98.

34. David Rubinstein, *Before the Suffragettes: Women's Emancipation in the 1890s* (Brighton, Sussex: Harvester P, 1986), 151.

35. *Women in a Changing World: The Dynamic Story of the International Council of Women Since 1888*, 18.

36. Sewall, 70.

37. Sewall, 66.

Chapter 9

1. *Women in a Changing World: The Dynamic Story of the International Council of Women Since 1888*, 18.

2. Rubinstein, 152.

3. *Women in a Changing World*, 21.

4. Marjorie Pentland, *In the Nineties: Ishbel Aberdeen and the I.C.W* (London, Caxton P, 1947), 18.

5. *Ibid.*

6. Pentland, *In the Nineties*, 17.

7. Jill Liddington, *The Long Road to Greenham: Feminists and Anti-Militarism in Britain Since 1920* (London: Virago P, 1989), 37.

8. *Women in a Changing World*, 22.

9. Cliona Murphy, *The Women's Suffrage Movement and Irish Society in the Early Twentieth Century* (New York: Wheatsheaf P, 1989), 15.

10. *Women in a Changing World*, 23.

11. *Women in a Changing World*, 27-28.

12. Pentland, *In the Nineties*, 29.

13. *Women in a Changing World*, 24.

14. *Women in a Changing World*, 32.

15. *Women in a Changing World*, 36.

16. Gordon, 149-50.

17. *Women in a Changing World*, 46.

18. Pentland, *A Bonnie Fechter*, 141.

19. *Women in a Changing World*, 56.

20. *Women in a Changing World*, 62.

21. *Women in a Changing World*, 66.

22. *Women in a Changing World*, 72.

23. Pentland, 147.

24. *Women in a Changing World*, 83.

Chapter 10

1. *Women in a Changing World*, 22.

2. Liddington, 37.

3. Anna Howard Shaw with Elizabeth Jordan, *The Story of a Pioneer* (New York: Harper & Brothers, 1915), 189.

4. Van Voris, 12.

5. Van Voris, 19.

6. Van Voris, 31.

7. *Ibid.*

8. Van Voris, 57.

9. Adele Schreiber and Margaret Mathieson, *Journey Towards Freedom: Written for the Golden Jubilee of the International Alliance of Women* (Copenhagen, Denmark: International Alliance of Women, 1955), 2.

10. *Women in the World,* 26.

11. Whittick, 33.

12. Whittick, 34.

13. *Women in the World,* 27.

14. Schreiber and Mathieson, 4.

15. Van Voris, 68.

16. Schreiber and Mathieson, 4-5.

17. Arnold Whittick, *Woman into Citizen* (Santa Barbara, CA: ABC-Clio P, 1979), 32.

18. Schreiber and Mathieson, 5.

19. Schreiber and Mathieson, 6.

20. Schreiber and Mathieson, 6.

21. Whittick, 38.

22. Schreiber and Mathieson, 8.

23. Zeneide Mirovitch, "Russia," *History of the International Woman Suffrage Alliance,* Women's Suffrage Collection (Manchester: Manchester Central Library), 116.

24. Schreiber and Mathieson, 8.

25. Identified as Briet Asmundsson in IWSA literature, the Deputy Chief of Mission of the Icelandic Embassy, Peter Thorsteinsson gave Briet Bjarnhedinsdottir as the correct name. Personal communication, Jan. 2, 1997.

26. Whittick, 38.

27. Cullen Owens, 39.

28. Cullen Owens, 40.

29. Whittick, 18.

30. Cullen Owens, 42.

31. Murphy, 63.

32. Schreiber and Mathieson, 11.

33. Schreiber and Mathieson, 9.

34. No title, identified as "Tribute written by the late Mrs CCC at the age of 85 in honour of her "adopted daughter," Rosa Manus materials, file 38, International Information Centre and Archives for the Women's Movement, Amsterdam, The Netherlands.

35. Whittick, 47.

36. Schreiber and Mathieson, 9.

37. Schreiber and Mathieson, 12.

38. Whittick, 48.

39. Whittick, 51.

40. Schreiber and Mathieson, 14.

41. Schreiber and Mathieson, 15.

42. Schreiber and Mathieson, 17.

43. Schreiber and Mathieson, 18.

Chapter 11

1. Carrie Chapman Catt, "Introduction," Unpublished Journal Manuscript in Library of Congress.

2. See correspondence of Carrie Chapman Catt with Aletta Jacobs, International Information Centre and Archives for the Women's Movement, Amsterdam, The Netherlands.

3. Catt, "South Africa," Journal Manuscript, 21.

4. Van Voris, 88.

5. Catt, "South Africa," Journal Manuscript, 86.

6. Catt, "South Africa," Journal Manuscript, 159.

7. Vera Brettain, *Envoy Extraordinary: A Study of Vijaya Lakshmi Pandit and Her Contribution to Modern India* (London: Allen & Unwin, 1965), 77.

8. Paulson, 154.

9. Catt, "South Africa," Journal Manuscript, 180.

10. Catt, "The Holy Land," Journal Manuscript, 47.

11. Van Voris, 91.

12. Catt, "The Holy Land," Journal Manuscript, 21.

13. Catt, "The Holy Land," Journal Manuscript, 26.

14. Peck, 190.

15. Catt, "India," Journal Manuscript, 8.

16. Van Voris, 93.

17. Cullen Owens, 46.

18. Peck, 191.

19. Schreiber and Mathieson, 19.

20. Ray Strachey, *Millicent Garrett Fawcett* (London: Murray, 1931), 336.

21. Peck, 191.

22. Peck, 193.

23. Peck, 194.

24. Catt, "Java," Journal Manuscript, 2.

25. Catt, "Java," Journal Manuscript, 56.

26. Catt, "Philippines," Journal Manuscript, 6.

27. Catt, "Philippines," Journal Manuscript, 5.

28. Catt, "Philippines," Journal Manuscript, 36.

29. Catt, "Macao," Journal Manuscript, 3.

30. Catt, "Canton," Journal Manuscript, 5-6.

31. Catt, "Canton," Journal Manuscript, 7.

32. Van Voris, 96.

33. Peck, 199.
34. Van Voris, 100.
35. Peck, 200.
36. Van Voris, 99.
37. Catt, "Shanghai," Journal Manuscript, 29.
38. Peck, 201.
39. Catt,"China," Journal Manuscript, 44.
40. Peck, 200.
41. Dorothy Robins-Mowry, *Hidden Sun: Women of Modern Japan* (Boulder: Westview P, 1983), 47.
42. Van Voris, 104.
43. Catt, "Japan," Journal Manuscript, 34.
44. Catt, "Hawaii," Journal Manuscript, 42.
45. Catt, "End of Trip," Journal Manuscript, 44.

Chapter 12

1. Van Voris, 106.
2. Van Voris, 108.
3. Van Voris, 110.
4. Schreiber and Mathieson, 20.
5. Van Voris, 110-11.
6. Schreiber and Mathieson, 22.
7. Whittick, 58.
8. Schreiber and Mathieson, 21.
9. Millicent Garrett Fawcett and E. M. Turner, *Josephine Butler: Her Work and Principles and Their Meaning for the Twentieth Century* (London: Association for Moral and Social Hygiene, 1927).
10. Whittick, 60.
11. Liddington, 74.
12. Whittick, 60.
13. Van Voris, 156.
14. Peck, 350.
15. Van Voris, 170.
16. Schreiber and Mathieson, 29.
17. Schreiber and Mathieson, 28.
18. Schreiber and Mathieson, 27.
19. Van Voris, 171.
20. Schreiber and Mathieson, 28.
21. Whittick, 77.
22. Schreiber and Mathieson, 29.
23. Whittick, 74.
24. Whittick, 76.
25. Schreiber and Mathieson, 30.
26. Van Voris, 172.

27. Van Voris, 162.

28. Van Voris, 164.

29. Whittick, 79.

30. Schreiber and Matheison, 30.

31. J. Stanley Lemons, *The Woman Citizen: Social Feminism in the 1920s* (Urbana: U of Illinois P, 1973), 212.

32. Van Voris, 173.

33. *Women of the World,* 49.

34. Van Voris, 176.

35. Peck, 374.

36. Catt, "South America," Journal Manuscript, 32.

37. Peck, 376.

38. Van Voris, 177.

39. Catt, "South America," Journal Manuscript, 53.

40. Catt, "South America," Journal Manuscript, 62.

41. Catt, "South America," Journal Manuscript, 63.

42. Catt, "South America," Journal Manuscript, 68.

43. Catt, "South America," Journal Manuscript, 78.

44. Peck, 382.

45. Peck, 387.

46. Peck, 388.

47. Peck, 386.

48. Catt, "South America," Journal Manuscript, 92.

49. Catt, "South America," Journal Manuscript, 8-9.

50. Catt, "South America," Journal Manuscript, 10.

51. Peck, 389.

52. Van Voris, 180.

53. Schreiber and Mathieson, 32.

54. Whittick, 85.

55. Whittick, 86.

56. Whittick, 82.

57. Van Voris, 179.

58. Schreiber and Mathieson, 31.

59. Schreiber and Mathieson, 34.

Chapter 13

1. Whittick, 91.

2. Whittick, 89.

3. Whittick, 92.

4. Schreiber and Mathieson, 35.

5. Schreiber and Mathieson, 37.

6. Whittick, 94.

7. Schreiber and Mathieson, 36.

8. Schreiber and Mathieson, 37.

9. Whittick, 96.
10. Whittick, 93.
11. Schreiber and Mathieson, 35.
12. Schreiber and Mathieson, 39.
13. Whittick, 92.
14. Schreiber and Mathieson, 38.
15. Schreiber and Mathieson, 39.
16. Schreiber and Mathieson, 40.
17. Whittick, 102.
18. Schreiber and Mathieson, 43.
19. Whittick, 119.
20. Whittick, 120.
21. Schreiber and Mathieson, 44.
22. Schreiber and Mathieson, 45.
23. Schreiber and Mathieson, 48.
24. Schreiber and Mathieson, 48.
25. Whittick, 121.
26. Schreiber and Mathieson, 47.
27. Whittick, 121.
28. Schreiber and Mathieso, 49.
29. Whittick, 127.
30. Schreiber and Mathieson, 51.
31. Schreiber and Mathieson, 50.
32. Margery Corbett Ashby, unpublished Mt. Holyoke Speech Notes, "U.S. Trip 1937," Margery Corbett Ashby Papers, Box 484, Fawcett Library, 1.
33. Corbett Ashby, Mt. Holyoke Speech Notes, 4.
34. Whittick, 136.
35. Schreiber and Mathieson, 51.
36. Whittick, 139.
37. Schreiber and Mathieson, 52.
38. Schreiber and Mathieson, 54.
39. Whittick, 145.
40. Egon Stern, letter to Millicent Garrett Fawcett, Amsterdam, 1946, Millicent Garret Fawcett Papers, Box 484, "International Letters on Conditions of Refugee Friends at End of WW II 1944-45," Fawcett Library, London.
41. Schreiber and Mathieson, 56.
42. Whittick, 149.
43. Whittick, 154.
44. Schreiber and Mathieson, 57.
45. Whittick, 154.
46. Whittick, 158.
47. Schreiber and Mathieson, 117.

Chapter 14

1. Jill Liddington, *The Long Road to Greenham: Feminism & Anti-Militarism in Britain Since 1820* (London: Virago P, 1989), 15.

2. Liddington, 17.

3. Sewall, *Genesis,* 36.

4. Liddington, 21.

5. Deborah Pickman Clifford, *Mine Eyes Have Seen the Glory: A Biography of Julia Ward Howe* (Boston: Little, Brown, 1979), 187.

6. Liddington, 24.

7. Liddington, 28.

8. Earhart, 265.

9. Earhart, 262.

10. Stanley, 43.

11. Pentland, *In the Nineties,* 26.

12. Pentland, *A Bonnie Fechter,* 136.

13. Liddington, 36.

14. Liddington, 41.

15. Spencer, 38.

16. Helena M. Swanwick, *I Have Been Young* (London: Gollancz, 1935), 259.

17. David Tyler, Introduction to Millicent Garret Fawcett Papers, the Woman Suffrage Collection, microfilm (Manchester: Manchester Central Library), 516.

18. Cullen Owens, 28.

19. Murphy, 54.

20. Murphy, 19.

21. Murphy, 74.

22. Liddington, 58.

23. Liddington, 59.

24. Liddington, 31.

25. Allen F. Davis, *American Heroine: The Life and Legend of Jane Addams* (New York: Oxford UP, 1973), 36.

26. Davis, 55.

27. Jeffrey Furst, *The Return of Frances Willard: Her Case for Reincarnation* (New York: Coward, McCann & Geoghegan, 1971), 87.

28. Davis, 277.

29. James Weber Linn, *Jane Addams* (New York: Appleton-Century, 1935), 359.

30. Linn, 288.

31. Linn, 295.

32. Spencer, 38.

33. Linn, 152.

34. Linn, 267.

35. Davis, 187.

36. Davis, 176.

37. Linn, 296.

38. Davis, 197.

39. Liddington, 74.

40. Schreiber and Mathieson, 24.

41. Liddington, 75.

42. Whittick, 25.

Chapter 15

1. Liddington, 79.

2. Liddington, 90.

3. Chrystal Macmillan, "The History of the Congress," *International Congress of Women The Hague—Holland. April 28th, 29th, 30th, 1915,* ed. Chrystal Macmillan (n.p., n.p., Manchester: Manchester Central Library, Women's Suffrage Collection Microfilm), xiii.

4. Schreiber and Mathieson, 26.

5. Liddington, 96.

6. Cullen Owens, 120.

7. Macmillan, xiv.

8. Ray Strachey, *Millicent Garrett Fawcett* (London: Murray, 1931), 289.

9. Liddington, 97.

10. Swanwick, 259.

11. See the correspondence of Kathleen Courtney and Millicent Garrett Fawcett in Fawcett's papers, Fawcett Library, London.

12. Macmillan, xv.

13. *Ibid.*

14. Van Voris, 123.

15. Liddington, 80.

16. John C. Farrell, *Beloved Lady: A History of Jane Addams' Ideas on Reform and Peace* (Baltimore: Johns Hopkins P, 1967), 148.

17. Farrell, 150.

18. Van Voris, 126.

19. Farrell, 153.

20. Linn, 298.

21. Liddington, 97.

22. Liddington, 65.

23. Liddington, 100.

24. Liddington, 71.

25. Liddington, 94.

26. Liddington, 98.

27. Liddington, 102.

28. Murphy, 24.

29. Cullen Owens, 99.

30. Jane Addams, *Peace and Bread in Time of War* (New York: Macmillan,

1922), 13.

31. Macmillan, xxii.

32. Linn, 303.

33. Catherine Foster, *Women for All Seasons: The Story of the Women's International League for Peace and Freedom* (Athens: U of Georgia P, 1989), 12.

34. Macmillan, xxiii.

35. Davis, 226.

36. Papers of Aletta Jacobs, Box 156, International Information Centre and Archives for the Women's Movement, Amsterdam, The Netherlands.

37. Davis, 240.

38. Davis, 243.

39. Van Voris, 138.

40. Davis, 247.

41. Bosch, 173.

42. Davis, 254.

43. Linn, 340.

44. Linn, 344.

45. Liddington, 106.

46. Liddington, 119.

47. Liddington, 107.

48. Liddington, 136.

49. Davis, 275.

50. Davis, 269.

51. Carrie A. Foster, *The Women and the Warriors: The U.S. Section of the Women's International League for Peace and Freedom, 1915-1946* (Syracuse: Syracuse UP, 1995), 116.

52. Van Voris, 192.

53. Davis, 276.

54. Davis, 271.

55. Linn, 357.

56. Jane Addams' letter to Aletta Jacobs of Oct. 3, 1923, Aletta Jacobs Box Number 1, International Information Centre and Archives for the Women's Movement, Amsterdam, The Netherlands.

57. Linn, 356.

58. Davis, 273.

59. Margaret Solberg, "What Is PPSEAWA?" in *Women of the Pacific and Southeast Asia: Proceedings of the Sixteenth International Conference of the Pan Pacific and Southeast Asia Women's Association,* Tokyo, Japan, National Women's Education Centre, Aug. 20-27, 1984: 6.

60. Liddington, 147.

61. Linn, 351.

62. Linn, 389.

63. Van Voris, 213.

Chapter 16

1. Carrie Chapman Catt, letter to Millicent Garrett Fawcett of Oct. 24, 1918 (Manchester: Manchester Central Library), Women's Suffrage Collection, microfilm.

2. Carrie Chapman Catt, letter to Millicent Garrett Fawcett of Nov. 22, 1918 (Manchester: Manchester Central Library), Women's Suffrage Collection, microfilm.

3. Van Voris, 152.

4. Mineke Bosch with Annemarie Kloosterman, eds., *Politics and Friendship: Letters from the International Woman Suffrage Alliance, 1902-1942* (Columbus, OH: Ohio State UP, 1990), 173.

5. Whittick, 70.

6. Whittick, 71.

7. Spencer, 51.

8. Pentland, *A Bonnie Fechter,* 138.

9. Pentland, *A Bonnie Fechter,* 144.

10. Liddington, 141.

11. Whittick, 72.

12. Gordon, 150.

13. Stanley, 49.

14. Gordon, 99.

15. Stanley, 50.

16. Whittick, 79-80.

17. Schreiber and Mathieson, 31.

18. Whittick, 84.

19. Gertrude Bussey and Margaret Tims, *Pioneers for Peace: Women's International League for Peace and Freedom 1915-1965* (Oxford: Alden P, 1980), 74.

20. *Ibid.*

21. Liddington, 141.

22. Whittick, 121.

23. Bosch, 181.

24. Whittick, 97.

25. Schreiber and Mathieson, 39.

26. Whittick, 97.

27. Schreiber and Mathieson, 39.

28. Whittick, 101.

29. Van Voris, 206.

30. Van Voris, 211.

31. Schreiber and Mathieson, 43.

32. Whittick, 107.

33. Whittick, 109.

34. Whittick, 110.

35. Stanley, 71.

36. Liddington, 149.
37. Liddington, 152.
38. Liddington, 162.
39. Liddington, 151.
40. Van Voris, 215.
41. Whittick, 130.
42. Schreiber and Mathieson, 51.
43. Whittick, 131.
44. Whittick, 132.
45. Whittick, 133.
46. Liddington, 171.

Chapter 17

1. J. Stanley Lemons, *The Woman Citizen: Social Feminism in the 1920s* (Urbana: U of Illinois P, 1973), 212.

2. Lemons, 192.

3. Inez Hayes Irwin, *The Story of Alice Paul and the National Woman's Suffrage Party* (Fairfax, VA: Denlinger's, 1977), 159.

4. Carrie Chapman Catt, letter to Millicent Garrett Fawcett of Oct. 3, 1916 (Manchester: Manchester Central Library, Women's Suffrage Collection, Microfilm).

5. Mildred Adams, *The Right to Be People* (Philadelphia: Lippincott, 1967), 171.

6. Susan D. Becker, *The Origins of the Equal Rights Amendment: American Feminism Between the Wars* (Westport: Greenwood P, 1981), 32.

7. Mary Anderson, *Woman at Work: The Autobiography of Mary Anderson As Told to Mary N. Winslow* (Minneapolis: U of Minnesota P, 1951), 33.

8. Becker, 215.

9. Becker, 17.

10. Becker, 122.

11. Jason Berger, *A New Deal for the World: Eleanor Roosevelt and American Foreign Policy* (New York: Columbia UP, 1981), 2.

12. William H. Chafe, "Biographical Sketch," *Without Precedent: The Life and Career of Eleanor Roosevelt*, ed. Joan Hoff-Wilson and Marjorie Lightman (Bloomington: Indiana UP, 1984), xi.

13. Lois Scharf, "Eleanor Roosevelt and Feminism," *Without Precedent: The Life and Career of Eleanor Roosevelt*, 251.

14. Chafe, xii.

15. Becker, 150.

16. Becker, 167.

17. Becker, 168.

18. Becker, 23.

19. Becker, 82.

20. Becker, 163.

21. IWSA Minutes of Headquarters Meeting, Jan. 23, 1917 (Manchester: Manchester Central Library, Women's Suffrage Collection).
22. IWSA Minutes of Headquarters Committee, Oct. 22, 1918 (Manchester: Manchester Central Library, Women's Suffrage Collection).
23. Becker, 172.
24. Becker, 163.
25. Lemons, 196.
26. Lemons, 197.
27. Becker, 172.
28. Becker, 93.
29. Becker, 96.
30. Becker, 169-70.
31. Lemons, 237.
32. Becker, 103.
33. Becker, 174.
34. Lemons, 198.
35. Becker, 175.
36. Becker, 223.
37. Becker, 176.
38. Becker, 165.
39. Becker, 25.
40. Becker, 215.
41. Becker, 92.
42. Becker, 176-77.
43. Scharf, 241.
44. Becker, 68.
45. Becker, 164.
46. Scharf, 241.
47. Samuel Guy Inman, *Inter-American Conferences 1826-1954: History and Problems* (Washington, D.C.: UP of Washington, D.C., 1965), 189.
48. Scharf, 241.
49. Becker, 46.
47. Samuel Guy Inman, *Inter-American Conferences 1826-1954: History and Problems* (Washington, D.C.: UP of Washington, D.C., 1965), 189.
48. Scharp, 241.
49. Becker, 46.

Chapter 18
1. Ann J. Lane, *Mary Ritter Beard: A Source Book* (New York: Schocken Books, 1977), 1.
2. Lane, 7.
3. Lane, 24.
4. Lane, 19.
5. Lane, 22.

6. Lane, 240.

7. Dorothy Hamilton Dick Brush to Margaret Grierson, June 21, 1960, Sophia Smith Collection, Northampton, Smith College.

8. Lane, 70.

9. Lane, 25.

10. Lane, 29.

11. Shidzue Ishimoto (now Kato), *Facing Two Ways* (New York: Farrar and Rinehart, 1935).

12. Ishimoto, 175.

13. Ishimoto, 177.

14. Kato, personal communication, Sept. 9, 1987.

15. Margaret Sanger, *Margaret Sanger: An Autobiography* (Elmsford: Maxwell Reprint Company, 1970), 321.

16. Sanger, 316.

17. Mary Ritter Beard, "The New Japanese Women," *The Woman Citizen,* 12 Jan. 1922: 10, 28-29.

18. Kathleen Susan Molony, *One Woman Who Dared: Ichikawa Fusae and the Japanese Women's Suffrage Movement* (Ann Arbor, MI: Unpublished Dissertation, University of Michigan, 1980), 184.

19. Beard, "The New Japanese Women," *The Woman Citizen,* 12 Jan. 1924: 29.

20. Mary Ritter Beard to Ethyl B. Weed, Dec. 24, 1946, Sophia Smith Collection, Northampton, Smith College.

21. Ishimoto, 369.

22. Mary Ritter Beard, *The Force of Women in Japanese History* (Washington, D.C.: Public Affairs Press, 1953), 172.

23. Lane, 43-44.

24. Lane, 34.

25. Lane, 58.

26. Mary Ritter Beard to Margaret Grierson, Apr. 6, 1944, Sophia Smith Collection, Northampton, Smith College.

27. Mary Ritter Beard to Margaret Grierson, Oct. 28, 1945, Sophia Smith Collection, Northampton, Smith College.

28. Mary Ritter Beard to Margaret Grierson, Dec. 27, 1945, Sophia Smith Collection, Northampton, Smith College.

29. Mary Ritter Beard to Margaret Grierson, June 6, 1946, Sophia Smith Collection, Northampton, Smith College.

30. Shidzue Kato to Mary Ritter Beard, June 17, 1946, Sophia Smith Collection, Northampton, Smith College.

31. Dorothy Hamilton Dick to Ethyl B. Weed, Aug. 8, 1946, Sophia Smith Collection, Northampton, Smith College.

32. Dorothy Hamilton Dick Brush to Margaret Grierson, June 21, 1960, Sophia Smith Collection, Northampton, Smith College.

33. Mary Ritter Beard to Ethyl B. Weed, Nov. 5, 1947, Sophia Smith Col-

lection, Northampton, Smith College.

34. Mary Ritter Beard, *The Force of Women in Japanese History,* 175.

35. Dorothy Hamilton Dick Brush to Margaret Grierson, June 21, 1960, Sophia Smith Collection, Northampton, Smith College.

36. Mary Ritter Beard, *The Force of Women in Japanese History,* Preface.

Chapter 19

1. Beard, *The Force of Women in Japanese History,* 122.

2. Dorothy Robins-Mowry, *Hidden Sun: Women of Modern Japan* (Boulder: Westview P, 1983), 50.

3. Beard, *The Force of Women in Japanese History,* 125-26.

4. Beard, *The Force of Women in Japanese History,* 60, 61.

5. Robins-Mowry, 47.

6. Beard, *The Force of Women in Japanese History,* 142.

7. Karen L. Sievers, *Flowers in Salt: The Beginnings of Feminist Consciousness in Modern Japan* (Stanford, CA: Stanford UP, 1983), 13.

8. Ishimoto, 360.

9. Molony, 30.

10. Ishimoto, 360.

11. Robins-Mowry, 47.

12. Taki Fujita, personal communication, Aug. 12, 1980.

13. Beard, *The Force of Women in Japanese History,* 162.

14. Beard, *The Force of Women in Japanese History,* 163.

15. Frances E. Willard, *Glimpses of Fifty Years: The Autobiography of an American Woman* (Evanston, IL: National Woman's Christian Temperance Union, 1904), 431.

16. Masako Sato, personal communication, July 18, 1987.

17. Molony, 27.

18. Nancy Boyd, *Emissaries: The Overseas Work of the American YWCA 1895-1970* (New York: Woman's P, 1986), 132.

19. Molony, 101-02.

20. Kato, 365.

21. Beard, *The Force of Women in Japanese History,* 148.

22. Molony, 53.

23. "Woman Suffrage in Japan: Movement Tentative Here though in Full Swing in China and Elsewhere," *Nippon Times,* 20 Oct. 1912: 1.

24. Masako Sato, personal communication, July 18, 1986.

25. Fusae Ichikawa, ed., "50th Anniversary of S.F.K.," *Japanese Women* 28 Feb. 1970: 1.

26. Akiko Tokuza, "Oku Mumeo and the Movements to Alter the Status of Women in Japan from the Taisho Period to the Present." Ph.D. diss., U of Michigan, 1988, 289.

27. Molony, 126.

28. Molony, 119.

29. Molony, 130.

30. Masako Sato, personal communication, July 24, 1987.

31. Molony, 180.

32. Molony, 149.

33. Molony, 148.

34. Molony, 179.

35. Masako Sato, personal communication, July 18, 1987.

36. Taki Fujita, personal communication, Sept. 14, 1987.

37. Molony, 168.

38. Bernice Guttmann, personal communication, Oct. 22, 1987.

39. Bernice Guttmann, personal communication, Evanston, IL, Oct. 23, 1987.

40. Molony, 143.

41. Molony, 184.

42. Molony, 209.

43. Molony, 225.

44. Molony, 227.

45. Fusae Ichikawa, personal communication, Aug. 4, 1980.

46. Molony, 246.

47. Molony, 252.

48. Molony, 280.

49. Molony, 337.

50. Molony, 344.

51. "MacArthur to Institute Woman Suffrage Here," *Nippon Times* 25 Sept. 1945: 1.

52. "Stern U.S. Policy Is Reaffirmed as Order to MacArthur Is Bared," *New York Times,* 23 Sept. 1945: 2.

53. "Hirohito's Sister-in-Law Hopes That Women Will Take Democratic Role in Japanese Life," *New York Times,* 10 Oct. 1945: 22.

54. George E. Jones, "Democratic Rule Ordered in Japan: MacArthur Directs Shidehara to Give Women Vote and Encourage Labor Unions," *New York Times,* 12 Oct. 1945: 1.

55. Robins-Mowry, 337.

56. "Woman to Run for Diet: Baroness Would Promote Birth Control for Japanese," *New York Times,* 15 Nov. 1945: 2.

57. "Imperial Prince Gives Up in Japan: Relative of Emperor Enters Prison as Peers Discuss Status of Hirohito: Homma Sent to Manila: Trials of Prison Guards Will Begin in Special Courts Next Monday," *New York Times,* 12 Dec. 1945: 19.

58. Lindesay Parrott, "Japan's War Diet to Dissolve Today: Election, Labor, Land Laws Have Been Approved—New Session in February," *New York Times,* 18 Dec. 1945: 3.

59. "Tokyo Women Organize: New Special Political Party to Take Part in Coming Elections," *New York Times,* 29 Dec. 1945: 5.

60. "Message from Japanese Women," *New York Times,* 9 Apr. 1946: 24.
61. Taki Fujita, personal communication, Aug. 12, 1980.
62. Taki Fujita, personal communication, Sept. 14, 1987.
63. "Moderates Ahead in Japanese Vote," *New York Times,* 12 Apr. 1946: 15.
64. Barbara Malony, "Afterword" in *Facing Two Ways: The Story of My Life* by Baroness Shidzue Ishmoto (Stanford: Stanford UP, 1984), xxiv.
65. Lindesey Parrott, "Japan's Moderates Win Diet Control: Coalition of Leading Parties Looms—Communists Get Only 5 of 466 Seats: 38 Women Are Elected: MacArthur Headquarters Calls Result 'Satisfactory'—Fate of Shidehara in Balance," *New York Times,* 13 Apr. 1946: 12.
66. Lindesay Parrott, "Japanese Election Sets New Course: People Voting Freely Choose to Keep Emperor and Set up Conservative Parliament," *New York Times,* 14 Apr. 1946: E5.
67. "Japanese Women Scolded," *New York Times,* 9 Aug. 1946: 28.
68. "Most Tokyo Papers Laud Constitution," *New York Times,* 6 May 1947: 18.

Chapter 20

1. Van Voris, 217.
2. "Women in Tribute to Mrs. Catt at 85: Mrs. Roosevelt Hails Suffrage Pioneer, Urges Peace Plans Be Put above Politics," *New York Times,* 11 Jan. 1944: 16.
3. "Peace Preservation Urged by Mrs. Catt," *New York Times,* 27 Aug. 1945: 16.
4. "Women Can 'Compel Cessation of War,' Mrs. Catt Tells Alliance She Founded," *New York Times,* 9 Aug. 1946: 28.
5. "Nicaragua Liberals Act: Convention Favors Presidential Re-election and Woman Suffrage," *New York Times,* 11 Jan. 1944: 5.
6. "Women Again Demanding Egyptian and Iraqi Vote," *New York Times,* 16 Jan. 1944: 11.
7. "Arab Women Hold a Historic Meeting: Their First Conference in Cairo Starts Fund to Prevent Palestine Land Sale," *New York Times,* 20 Jan. 1945: 8.
8. "Soviet Union Pays Homage to Women: Their Vital Role in Red Army, in Factories and on Farms Earns Nation's Plaudits," *New York Times,* 9 Mar. 1955: 3.
9. "Confidence Voiced by Mrs. Churchill: Women's Parley Is Told That Oppressed Will Get Relief from Nazis within Year," *New York Times,* 6 Mar. 1944: 12.
10. Mrs. Florence L. C. Kitchelt, "Progress Toward Equal Rights: To the Editors of *The New York Times,*" *New York Times,* 1 Apr. 1944: 12.
11. "Poll in France Discloses Trend for 2-Party Politics," *New York Times,* 9 Feb. 1945: 4.
12. A. C. Sedgwick, "Women May Vote in Italian Regime: Universal Suffrage Proposed by Badoglio Government in Return to Democracy: May Day to

Be Observed," *New York Times,* 28 Apr. 1944: 7.

13. "Vote Promised Women: Togliatti Says Communists Will Push for Suffrage in Italy," *New York Times,* 29 Aug. 1944: 6.

14. "Italy's 6-Party Rule Held Near Collapse; Socialist Chief Calls Equality a Fiction," *New York Times,* 5 Sept.1944: 3.

15. Note, *New York Times,* 16 Dec. 1944: 9.

16. "Mrs. Luce Tells of Italy's Plight: Says Thousands Die of Cold and Starvation—Poletti Called Symbol of Broken Pledges," *New York Times,* 4 Jan. 1945: 4.

17. "Italian Women Get Vote; Age Requirement Is 21," *New York Times,* 31 Jan. 1945: 10.

18. "Women Voters 53% in Italy," *New York Times,* 10 July 1945: 9.

19. "Woman Sets Precedent: Talks in Italy's Chamber," *New York Times,* 2 Oct. 1945: 5.

20. "Italians Vote Today: 436 Towns and Villages Will Choose Local Officials," *New York Times,* 10 Mar. 1946: 17.

21 Sam Pope Brewer, "First Free Ballot in Italy in 26 Years: High Proportion of Women at Polls in Local Elections Amazes Authorities," *New York Times,* 11 Mar. 1946: 7.

22. Arnaldo Cortesi, "Italy Goes to Polls Quietly; Women Glory in First Vote," *New York Times,* 3 June 1946: 1.

23. *Ibid.,* 5.

24. "Women Obtain Equal Rights," *New York Times,* 23 Dec. 1947: 5.

25. "Belgian Women Get Vote in 1947," *New York Times,* 25 Oct. 1945: 4.

26. David Anderson, "Belgian Parliament Is Dissolved; General Election Set for Feb. 18," *New York Times,* 10 Jan. 1946: 13.

27. "Quiet Voting Seen in Belgium Today: Informed Observers Declare King's Return Will Not Be Vital Issue in Balloting," *New York Times,* 17 Feb. 1946: 26.

28. David Anderson, "Women Will Vote in Belgium Today: Communal Elections Are Likely to Result in Overthrow of Cabinet Before Christmas," *New York Times,* 24 Nov. 1946: 21.

29. "Belgian Women Nearer to Vote," *New York Times,* 28 Apr. 1949: 6.

30. "Yugoslav General Election Set," *New York Times,* 17 June 1945: 7.

31. "Fights for Women in House of Lords: Lady Astor to Continue Her Campaign—Denies Calling Churchill a Blunderer," *New York Times,* 20 June 1946: 15.

32. "Equality Plank Sought by Women," *New York Times,* 1 June 1944: 12.

33. "Hails Women's Vote Day: President Proclaims Enfranchisement Anniversary Today," *New York Times,* 2 Nov. 1945: 16.

34. "Elizabeth Cady Stanton Day Set," *New York Times,* 3 Nov. 1945: 17.

35. *Ibid.*

36. "Begin World Peace Drive: Women Voters Start Campaign with Backing of Stettinius," *New York Times,* 15 Jan. 1945: 12.

Chapter 21

1. Scharf, 243.

2. Robert C. Hilderbrand, *Dumbarton Oaks: The Origins of the United Nations and the Search for Postwar Security* (Chapel Hill: U of North Carolina P, 1990), 81.

3. Hilderbrand, 93.

4. Inman, 213.

5. Inman, 221.

6. Dorothy B. Robins, *Experiment in Democracy: The Story of U.S. Citizen Organizations in Forging the Charter of the United Nations* (New York: Parkside P, 1971), 291.

7. Robins, 122.

8. Virginia Crocheron Gildersleeve, *Many a Good Crusade: Memoirs of Virginia Crocheron Gildersleeve* (New York: Macmillan, 1955), 351.

9. Bertha Lutz, "Reminiscences of the San Francisco Conference That Founded United Nations," unpublished paper, Margery Corbett Ashby papers, Fawcett Library, London.

10. Elisabeth Israels Perry, "Training for Public Life: Eleanor Roosevelt and Women's Political Networks in the 1920s," *Without Precedent: The Life and Career of Eleanor Roosevelt,* eds. Joan Hoff-Wilson and Marjorie Lightman, 32.

11. Ingrid Winther Scobie, "Helen Gahagan Douglas and the Roosevelt Connection," *Without Precedent: The Life and Career of Eleanor Roosevelt,* eds. Joan Hoff-Wilson and Marjorie Lightman, 169.

12. Gildersleeve, 254.

13. Gildersleeve, 351.

14. Lutz, Notes on UNO, Margery Corbett Ashby papers, Fawcett Library, London.

15. Vijaya Lakshmi Pandit, *The Scope of Happiness: A Personal Memoir* (New York: Crown, 1979), 216.

16. Lutz, Notes on UNO, Margery Corbett Ashby papers, Fawcett Library, London.

17. Robins, 135.

18. Scharf, 243.

19. "Women Hail Principles of Equal Rights in Charter," *New York Times,* 27 June 1945: 11.

20. Gildersleeve, 351.

21. Robins, 130.

22. Gildersleeve, 350.

23. Gildersleeve, 351.

24. "Hails Women's Vote Day: President Proclaims Enfranchisement Anniversary Today," *New York Times,* 2 Nov. 1945: 16.

25. "Women Seek Inclusion in United Nations' Councils," *New York Times* Feb. 1945: 4.

26. Scharf, 244.

27. "U.N. Urged to Act on Women's Vote," *New York Times,* 14 Nov. 1946: 11.

28. "War Scored in U.N. by Warsaw Woman: Bombing Survivor Pleads for Equal Rights—Chilean Takes Issue with Mrs. Roosevelt," *New York Times,* 16 Nov. 1946: 4.

29. "Carrie C. Catt Dies of Heart Attack: Woman's Suffrage Pioneer, Long an Advocate of World Peace, Succumbs at 88: Urged Support of U.N.: Leader in Tolerance Drives Organized Fight for Vote Along Political Lines," *New York Times,* 10 Mar. 1947: 21.

30. Joseph P. Lash, *Eleanor: The Years Alone* (New York: Norton, 1972), 70.

31. Lash, 79.

32. Whittick, 164.

33. Schreiber and Mathieson, 62.

34. Whittick, 166.

Chapter 22

1. Chikako Uemura, Senior Researcher, National Women's Education Centre, Ranzan-Machi, Hiki-Gun, Saitama, Japan, personal communication, Aug. 4, 1994.

LIMITED BIBLIOGRAPHY

Periodicals

"I.—The Debate on the Enfranchisement of Women." *The Englishwoman's Review* 4 (1 July 1867): 199-208.

"IV.—Some Probable Consequences of Extending the Franchise to Female Householders." *The Englishwoman's Review* 1 (Oct. 1866): 26-35.

"XLVII.—The Enfranchisement of Women." *The Englishwoman's Review* 77 (July 1864): 289-97.

"50th Anniversary of S. F. K." *Japanese Women* 28 (Feb. 1970): 1.

Beard, Mary R. "The New Japanese Women." *The Woman Citizen* 10 (12 Jan. 1922): 28-29.

Blom, Ida. "A Centenary of Organized Feminism in Norway." *Women's Studies International Forum* 5.6 (1982): 569-74.

Boxer, Marilyn J. "'First Wave' Feminism in Nineteenth-Century France: Class, Family and Religion." *Women's Studies International Forum* 5.6 (1982): 551-59.

Caine, Barbara. "John Stuart Mill and the English Women's Movement." *Historical Studies* 18.70 (Apr. 1978): 52-67.

Costin, Lela B. "Feminism, Pacifism, Internationalism and the 1915 International Congress of Women." *Women's Studies International Forum* 5.34 (1982): 301-15.

Duelli-Klein, Renate. "Accounts of 'First Wave' Feminism in Germany by German Feminists." *Women's Studies International Forum* 5.6 (1982): 691-96.

Gerhard, Ute. "A Hidden and Complex Heritage: Reflections on the History of Germany's Women's Movements." *Women's Studies International Forum* 5.6 (1982): 561-67.

Gutwirth, Madelyn. "Madame de Staël, Rousseau and the Woman Question." *PMLA* 86 (Jan. 1971): 100-09.

Jeffreys, Sheila. "Free from All Uninvited Touch of Man: Women's Campaigns around Sexuality, 1880-1914." *Women's Studies International Forum* 5.6 (1982): 629-45.

Kaplan, Marion. "Prostitution, Morality Crusades and Feminism: German-Jewish Feminists and the Campaign Against White Slavery." *Women's Studies International Forum* 5.6 (1982): 619-27.

Mann, Glenn K. S. "John Stuart Mill and Harriet Taylor." *Antigonish Review* 14 (Summer 1973): 43-50.

Molony, Kathleen." Feminist Ideology in Prewar Japan." *Proceedings of the Tokyo Symposium on Women. Tokyo: International Group for the Study of Women* 1979: 13-24.

"The Opinions of John Stuart Mill." *The English Woman's Journal* Part I 31 (Sept. 1860): 1-11; Part II 4.31 (Nov. 1860): 1-11.

Pfeffer, Paula F. "'A Whisper in the Assembly of Nations: United States' Participation in the International Movement for Women's Rights from the League of Nations to the United Nations." *Women's Studies International Forum* 8.5: 459-71.

Pugh, Evelyn L. "John Stuart Mill, Harriet Taylor, and Women's Rights in America, 1850-1873." *Canadian Journal of History* 13.1 (Mar. 1973): 423-42.

——. "John Stuart Mill and the Women's Question in Parliament." *The Historian* 42.3 (May 1980): 399-418.

Rasmussen, Janet E. "Sisters Across the Sea: Early Norwegian Feminists and Their American Connections." *Women's Studies International Forum* 5.6 (1982): 647-54.

Register, Cheri. "Motherhood at Center: Ellen Key's Social Vision." *Women's Studies International Forum* 5.6 (1982): 599-610.

Sherrick, Rebecca L. "Toward Universal Sisterhood." *Women's Studies International Forum* 5.6 (1982): 655-61.

Taylor, Harriet. "Enfranchisement of Women." *Westminster Review* 55 (July 1851): 289-311.

Walker, Cherryl. "The Women's Suffrage Movement in South Africa." *Communications No. 2.* Cape Town: Centre for African Studies, U of Cape Town, 1979. 1-109.

Newspapers

New York Times 11 Jan. 1944
16 Jan. 1944
20 Jan. 1944
9 Mar. 1944
6 Mar. 1944
1 Apr. 1944
28 Apr. 1944
1 June 1944
19 Aug. 1944
5 Sept. 1944
10 Dec. 1944
16 Dec. 1944
4 Jan. 1945
15 Jan. 1945
31 Jan. 1945
9 Feb. 1945
17 June 1945
27 June 1945
10 July 1945

27 Aug. 1945
2 Oct. 1945
12 Oct. 1945
25 Oct. 1945
2 Nov. 1945
3 Nov. 1945
15 Nov. 1945
12 Dec. 1945
10 Jan. 1946
1 Feb. 1946
17 Feb. 1946
10 Mar. 1946
11 Mar. 1946
9 Apr. 1946
12 Apr. 1946
13 Apr. 1946
14 Apr. 1946
2 June 1946
9 Aug. 1946
14 Nov. 1946
16 Nov. 1946
24 Nov. 1946
10 Mar. 1947
6 May 1947
23 Dec. 1947
27 Dec. 1947
20 Feb. 1948
28 Apr. 1949

Union Signal
9 June 1884
13 Nov. 1884
8 Jan. 1885
22 Jan. 1885
9 Apr. 1885
11 June 1885
27 Aug. 1885
22 Oct. 1885
10 Dec. 1885
4 Mar. 1886
15 Apr. 1886
6 May 1886
8 July 1886
5 Aug. 1886
2 Sept. 1886

12 May 1887
2 June 1887
23 June 1887
21 July 1887
28 July 1887
18 Aug. 1887
21 Nov. 1887
1 Dec. 1887
2 Aug. 1888
3 Jan. 1889
24 Jan. 1889
12 June 1890
14 May 1891
2 July 1891
16 July 1891
30 July 1891
20 Aug. 1891
17 Sept. 1891
24 Sept. 1891
8 Oct. 1891
14 Nov. 1891
17 Dec. 1891
14 Apr. 1892
16 June 1892
29 Sept. 1892
6 Oct. 1892
14 Nov. 1892

Letters

Beard, Mary R. to Margaret Grierson Apr. 6, 1944; Oct. 28, 1945; Dec. 27, 1945; June 6, 1946; to Ethyl Weed, Nov. 5, 1947. Sophia Smith Collection. Northampton: Smith College.

Brush, Dorothy Hamilton Dick to Margaret Grierson, June 21, 1960; to Ethel Weed, Aug. 8, 1946. Sophia Smith Collection. Northampton: Smith College.

Ishimoto (Kato), Shidzue to Mary R. Beard. June 17, 1946. Sophia Smith Collection. Northampton: Smith College.

Dissertations

Molony, Kathleen Susan. "One Woman Who Dared: Ichikawa Fusae and the Japanese Women's Suffrage Movement." Diss. University of Michigan, 1980.

Tokuza, Akiko. "Oku Mumeo and the Movements to Alter the Status of Women in Japan from the Taisho Period to the Present." Diss. University of Michigan, 1988.

Books

Adams, Mildred. *The Right to Be People*. Philadelphia: Lippincott, 1967.

Addams, Jane. *Peace and Bread in Time of War*. New York: Macmillan, 1922.

Anderson, Mary. *Woman at Work: The Autobiography of Mary Anderson as Told to Mary N. Winslow*. Minneapolis: U of Minnesota P, 1951.

Barrett, John. *The Pan American Union: Peace Friendship Commerce*. Washington, D.C.: Pan American Union, 1911.

Beard, Mary R. *The Force of Women in Japanese History*. Washington, D.C.: Public Affairs P, 1953.

——. *The Making of Charles A. Beard*. New York: Exposition P, 1955.

——. *Woman as Force in History: A Study in Traditions and Realities*. New York: Macmillan, 1946.

Beaver, R. Pierce. *American Protestant Women in World Mission: A History of the First Feminist Movement in North America*. Grand Rapids: Eerdmans, 1980.

Becker, Susan D. *The Origins of the Equal Rights Amendment: American Feminism Between the Wars*. Westport: Greenwood, 1981.

Bell, E. Moberly. *Josephine Butler: Flame of Fire*. London: Constable, 1912.

Berger, Jason. *A New Deal for the World: Eleanor Roosevelt and American Foreign Policy*. New York: Columbia UP, 1981.

Besant, Annie. *Annie Besant: An Autobiography*. London: Unwin, n.d.

Bidelman, Patrick Kay. *Pariahs Stand Up! The Founding of the Liberal Feminist Movement in France, 1858-1889*. Westport: Greenwood, 1982.

Birn, Donald S. *The League of Nations Union 1918-1945*. Oxford: Clarendon P, 1981.

Blackmore, Sophia. *Sophia Blackmore in Singapore: Educational and Missionary Pioneer 1887-1927*. Ed. Theodore R. Doraisarny. Singapore: General Conference Women's Society of Christian Service, 1987.

Blackwell, Alice Stone. *Lucy Stone*. New York: Kraus Reprint, 1971.

Blatch, Harriot Stanton, and Alma Lutz. *Challenging Years: The Memoirs of Harriet Stanton Blatch*. New York: Putnam's, 1940.

Borchard, Ruth. *John Stuart Mill: The Man*. London: Watts, 1957.

Bordin, Ruth. *Frances Willard: A Biography*. Chapel Hill: U of North Carolina P, 1986.

Bosch, Mineke, with Annemarie Kloosterman, eds. *Politics and Friendship: Letters from the International Woman Suffrage Alliance, 1902-1942*. Columbus: Ohio State UP, 1990.

Boyd, Nancy. *Emissaries: The Overseas Work of the American YWCA 1895-1970*. New York: Woman's P, 1988.

Bussey, Gertrude, and Margaret Tims. *Pioneers for Peace: Women's International League for Peace and Freedom 1915-1965*. Oxford: Alden P, 1980.

Butler, Josephine E. *Personal Reminiscences of a Great Crusade*. Chatam: Mackay, 1896.

Catt, Carrie Chapman. Unpublished Journals. Carrie Chapman Catt Papers. Washington, D.C.: Library of Congress microfilm, n.d.

Ceadel, Martin. *Pacifism in Britain 1914-1935: The Defining of a Faith.* Oxford: Clarendon P, 1980.

Clifford, Deborah Pickman. *Mine Eyes Have Seen the Glory: A Biography of Julia Ward Howe.* Boston: Little Brown, 1979.

Committee for the Compilation of The History of Korean Women. *Women of Korea: A History from Ancient Times to 1945.* Ed. Yung-Chung Kim. Seoul, Korea: Ewha Woman's UP, 1976.

Cullen Owens, Rosemary. *Smashing Times: A History of the Irish Women's Suffrage Movement 1889-1922.* Dublin: Attic P, 1984.

Davis, Allen F. *American Heroine: The Life and Legend of Jane Addams.* New York: Oxford UP, 1973.

Davis, Paulina W. *A History of the National Woman's Rights Movement for Twenty Years, with the Proceedings of the Decade Meeting Held at Apollo Hall, October 20, 1870, from 1850 to 1870, with an Appendix Containing the History of the Movement during the Winter of 1871, in the National Capitol.* New York: Journeymen Printers' Co-operative Association, 1871; Kraus Reprint, 1971.

Deckard, Barbara Sinclair. *The Women's Movement: Political, Socioeconomic, and Psychological Issues.* 2nd ed. New York: Harper & Row, 1979.

Director General, Governing Board of the Pan American Union. *Inter-American Conference on Problems of War and Peace Mexico City, February 21-March 8, 1945.* Washington, D.C.: Pan American Union, 1945.

Earhart, Mary. *Frances Willard: From Prayers to Politics.* Chicago: U of Chicago P, 1944.

Establishment and Composition of the Commission on the Status of Women, Economic and Social Council Resolutions 2/11 and 2/12 both of 21 June 1946, documents E/84/Rev. 1 and E/90.

Evans, Richard J. *The Feminist Movement in Germany 1894-1933.* London: Sage, 1976.

——. *The Feminists: Women's Emancipation Movements in Europe, America and Australasia 1840-1920.* New York: Barnes & Noble, 1977.

Fawcett, Millicent G., and E. M. Turner. *Josephine Butler: Her Work and Principles, and Their Meaning for the Twentieth Century.* London: Association for Moral and Social Hygiene, 1927.

First Annual Report of the Woman's Christian Temperance Union. Honolulu: Hawaiian Historical Society, 1885. n.p.

Foster, Carrie A. *The Women and the Warriors: The U.S. Section of the Women's International League for Peace and Freedom, 1915-1946.* Syracuse: Syracuse UP, 1995.

Foster, Catherine. *Women for All Seasons: The Story of the Women's International League for Peace and Freedom.* Athens, GA: U of Georgia P, 1989.

Furst, Jeffrey. *The Return of Frances Willard: Her Case for Reincarnation*. New York: Coward, McCann & Geoghegan, 1971.

Gage, Matilda Joslyn, and Susan B. Anthony. *History of Woman Suffrage*. 1881. 6 vol. Salem: Ayer, 1985.

Gildersleeve, Virginia Crocheron. *Many a Good Crusade: Memoirs of Virginia Crocheron Gildersleeve*. New York: Macmillan, 1955.

Gordon, Elizabeth Putnam. *Women Torch-bearers: The Story of the Woman's Christian Temperance Union*. Evanston: National Woman's Christian Temperance Union, 1924.

Grimshaw, Patricia. *Women's Suffrage in New Zealand*. Auckland: Auckland UP, 1972.

Harper, Ida Husted. *The Life and Work of Susan B. Anthony*. 2 vol. Indianapolis: Hollenbeck P, 1898. Also 3 volumes reprinted from 1898-1908. Salem: Ayer, 1983.

Haouse, Steven C., with Anne R. Kenney. *Hubertine Auclert: The French Suffragette*. New Haven: Yale UP, 1987.

——. *Women's Suffrage and Social Politics in the French Third Republic*. Princeton: Princeton UP, 1984.

Hay-Cooper, L. *Josephine Butler and Her Work for Social Purity*. London: Society for Promoting Christian Knowledge, 1922.

Hayek, F. A. *John Stuart Mill and Harriet Taylor: Their Correspondence and Subsequent Marriage*. Chicago: U of Chicago P, 1951.

Hellerstein, Erna Olason, Leslie Parker Hume, and Karen M. Offen, eds. *Victorian Women: A Documentary Account of Women's Lives in Nineteenth-Century England, France, and the United States*. Stanford: Stanford UP, 1981.

Hilderbrand, Robert C. *Dumbarton Oaks: The Origins of the United Nations and the Search for Postwar Security*. Chapel Hill: U of North Carolina P, 1990.

Himmelfarb, Gertrude. *On Liberty and Liberalism: The Case of John Stuart Mill*. New York: Knopf, 1974.

Hoff-Wilson, Joan, and Marjorie Lightman, eds. *Without Precedent: The Life and Career of Eleanor Roosevelt*. Bloomington: Indiana UP, 1984.

Inman, Samuel Guy. *Inter-American Conferences 1826-1954: History and Problems*. Washington, D.C.: UP of Washington, D.C., 1965.

Inter-American Institute of International Legal Studies. *The Inter-American System: Its Development and Strengthening*. Dobbs Ferry: Oceana, 1966.

Irwin, Inez Haynes. *The Story of Alice Paul and the National Woman's Party*. Fairfax: Denlinger's, 1977.

——. *The Story of the Woman's Party*. New York: Harcourt, Brace, 1921.

Ishimoto (Kato), Shidzue. *Facing Two Ways; the Story of My Life*. New York: Farrar and Rinehart, 1935.

Johnson, George W., and Lucy A., eds. *Josephine Butler: An Autobiographical Memoir*. Bristol: Arrowsmith, 1911.

Kamm, Josephine. *Rapiers and Battle Axes*. London: Allen and Unwin, 1966.

Kearney, James R. *Anna Eleanor Roosevelt*. Boston: Houghton Mifflin, 1968.

Kent, Susan Kingsley. *Sex and Suffrage in Britain, 1860-1914*. Princeton: Princeton UP, 1987.

Kumar, Raj. *Annie Besant's Rise to Power in Indian Politics 1914-1917*. New Delhi: Concept, 1981.

Lacey, Candida Ann, ed. *Barbara Leigh Smith Bodichon and the Langham Place Group*. New York: Routledge & Paul, 1987.

Lane, Ann J. *Mary Ritter Beard: A Sourcebook*. New York: Schocken, 1977.

Lash, Joseph P. *Eleanor: The Years Alone*. New York: Norton, 1972.

Lemons, J. Stanley. *The Woman Citizen: Social Feminism in the 1920s*. Urbana: U of Illinois P, 1973.

Liddington, Jill, and Jill Harris. *The Long Road to Greenham: Feminism & Anti-Militarism in Britain Since 1820*. London: Virago P, 1989.

——. *One Hand Tied Behind Us: The Rise of the Women's Suffrage Movement*. London: Virago P, 1978.

Linkugel, Wilmer A. *The Speeches of Anna Howard Shaw*. 2 vol. Doctoral diss. U of Wisconsin, 1960.

Linn, James Weber. *Jane Addams*. New York: D. Appleton-Century, 1935.

Lutz, Bertha. Unpublished Account of the formation of the United Nations at San Francisco, 1945, Margery Corbett Ashby Papers, the Fawcett Library, London.

MacMinn, Ney, J. R. Hainds, and James McNab McCrimmon, eds. *Bibliography of the Published Writings of John Stuart Mill*. Evanston: Northwestern UP, 1945.

Martineau, Harriet. *Harriet Martineau's Autobiography with Memorials by Maria Weston Chapman*. London: Smith Elder, 1877.

Mill, John Stuart. *Autobiography*. Ed. Jack Stillinger. London: Oxford UP, 1969.

——. *The Later Letters of John Stuart Mill 1849-1873*. Vol. 14-17. *The Collected Works of John Stuart Mill*. Ed. Francis E. Mineka and Dwight N. Lindley. Toronto: U of Toronto P, 1972.

——. *Unitarianism, Liberty, and Representative Government*, reprinted. New York: Dutton, 1951.

Murphy, Cliona. *The Women's Suffrage Movement and Irish Society in the Early Twentieth Century*. New York: Harvester Wheatsheaf, 1989.

National Woman Suffrage Association, eds. *Report of the International Council of Women*. Washington, D.C.: Darby, 1888.

Okin, Susan Moller. *Women in Western Political Thought*. Princeton: Princeton UP, 1979.

Packe, Michael St. John. *The Life of John Stuart Mill*. London: Secker and Warburg, 1954.

Palmer, Bertha Potter. *Correspondence, Chicago Historical Society*. London: Unwin, 1900.

Pandit, Vijaya Lakshmi. *The Scope of Happiness: A Personal Memoir.* New York: Crown, 1979.

Pankhurst, E. Sylvia. *The Suffragette Movement: An Intimate Account of Persons and Ideals.* London: Longmans, Green, 1932.

Paulson, Ross Evans. *Women's Suffrage and Prohibition: A Comparative Study of Equality and Social Control.* Glenview, IL: Scott, Foresman, 1973.

Peck, Mary Gray. *Carrie Chapman Catt: A Biography.* New York: Wilson, 1944.

Pentland, Marjorie. *A Bonnie Fechter: the life of Ishbel Marjoribanks, Marchioness of Aberdeen and Temair, G.B.E., LL.D., JP., 1857 to 1939* London: Batsford, 1952.

——. *In the Nineties: Ishbel Aberdeen and the I.C.W.* London: Caxton P, 1947.

Petrie, Glen. *A Singular Inquiry: The Campaigns of Josephine Butler.* New York: Viking P, 1971.

Pivar, David J. *Purity Crusade: Sexual Morality and Social Control, 1868-1900.* Westport, CT: Greenwood, 1973.

Randall, Vicky. *Women and Politics.* New York: St. Martin's, 1982.

Rice, Anna V. *A History of the World's Young Women's Christian Association.* New York: Woman's P, 1947.

Robins, Dorothy B. *Experiment in Democracy: The Story of U.S. Citizen Organizations in Forging the Character of the United Nations.* New York: Parkside P, 1971.

Robins Mowry, Dorothy. *Hidden Sun: Women of Modern Japan.* Boulder: Westview P, 1983.

Roe, Clifford G. *The Great War on White Slavery or Fighting for the Protection of Our Girls.* n.p., 1911.

Roosevelt, Eleanor. *The Autobiography of Eleanor Roosevelt.* New York: Harper & Brothers, 1961.

——. *It's Up to the Women.* New York: Stokes, 1933.

Ross, Ishbel. *Silhouette in Diamonds: The Life of Mrs. Potter Palmer.* New York: Harper & Brothers, 1960.

Rubinsein, David. *Before the Suffragettes: Women's Emancipation in the 1890s.* Brighton: Harvester P, 1986.

Russell, Ruth B. *A History of the United Nations Charter: The Role of the United States 1940-1945.* Washington, D.C.: Brookings, 1958.

Sanger, Margaret. *Margaret Sanger; An Autobiography.* New York: Norton, 1938.

Schreiber, Adele, and Margaret Mathieson. *Journey Towards Freedom Written for the Golden Jubilee of the International Alliance of Women.* Copenhagen, Denmark: International Alliance of Women, 1955.

Scott, Benjamin. *A State Iniquity: Its Rise: Extension and Overthrow.* London: Paul, Trench, Trubner, 1890.

Sewall, May Wright, ed. *Genesis of the International Council of Women and the Story of Its Growth: 1888-1893.* Indianapolis: n.p., 1914.

——. *The World's Congress of Representative Women.* Chicago: Rand, McNally, 1894.

Shaw, Anna Howard, with Elizabeth Jordan. *The Story of a Pioneer.* New York: Harper, 1915.

Sievers, Sharon L. *Flowers in Salt: The Beginnings of Feminist Consciousness in Modern Japan.* Stanford, CA: Stanford UP, 1983.

Smith, Page. *Daughters of the Promised Land: Women in American History.* Boston: Little, Brown, 1970.

Spencer, Anna Garlin. *The Council Idea: A Chronicle of Its Prophets and a Tribute to May Wright Sewall Architect of Its Form and Builder of Its Method of Work.* New Brunswick, NJ: Heidingsfeld, 1930.

Stanley, E. K. *Ten Decades of White Ribbon Service.* Cincinnati: Revivalist P, 1983.

Stanton, Elizabeth Cady. *Eighty Years and More (1815-1897) Reminiscences of Elizabeth Cady Stanton.* New York: European, 1898.

Stanton, Theodore, ed. *The Woman Question in Europe: A Series of Original Essays.* New York: Putnam's, 1884.

Stanton, Theodore, and Harriot Stanton Blatch, eds. *Elizabeth Cady Stanton.* 2 vol. New York: Arno P, 1969.

Stenton, Doris Mary. *The English Woman in History.* London: Allen & Unwin, 1957.

Strachey, Ray. *The Cause: A Short History of the Women's Movement in Great Britain.* London: Bell, 1928. Reprinted by Virago P, 1978.

——. *Frances Willard: Her Life and Work.* London: Unwin, 1912.

——. *Millicent Garrett Fawcett.* London: Murray, 1931.

Swanwick, Helena M. *I Have Been Young.* London: Gollancz, 1935.

Thomas, Ann Van Wynen, and A. J. Thomas, Jr. *The Organization of American States.* Dallas: Southern Methodist UP, 1963.

Thönnessen, Werner. *The Emancipation of Women: The Rise and Decline of the Women's Movement in German Social Democracy 1863-1933.* Trans. Joris de Bres. London: Pluto P, 1973.

Tims, Margaret. *Mary Wollstonecraft: A Social Pioneer.* London: Millington, 1976.

Tiwari, S. C. *Genesis of the United Nations.* n.c., India: Lokbharti, 1968.

Tulloch, Gail. *Mill and Sexual Equality.* Boulder: Rienner, 1989.

Tyrell, Ian. *Woman's World, Woman's Empire: The Woman's Christian Temperance Union in International Perspective, 1880-1930.* Chapel Hill: U of North Carolina P, 1991.

Van Arsdel, Rosemary T. *Florence Fenwick Miller.* Unpublished manuscript. Fawcett Library, London, 1991.

Van Voris, Jacqueline. *Carrie Chapman Catt: A Public Life.* New York: Feminist P, 1987.

Walters, F. P. *History of the League of Nations.* 2 vols. London: Oxford UP, 1952.

Ware, Susan. *Beyond Suffrage: Women in the New Deal.* Cambridge: Harvard UP, 1981.

——. *Holding Their Own: American Women in the 1930s.* Boston: Twayne, 1982.

Weimann, Jeanne Madeline. *The Fair Women.* Chicago: Academy P, 1991.

Wells, Kenneth E. *History of Protestant Work in Thailand 1828-1958.* Bangkok: Church of Christ in Thailand, 1958.

Whittick, Arnold. *Woman into Citizen.* Santa Barbara: ABC-Clio, 1979.

Willard, Frances E. *Glimpses of Fifty Years.* Evanston, IL: National Woman's Christian Temperance Union, 1904.

Women in a Changing World: The Dynamic Story of the International Council of Women Since 1888. London: Routledge & Paul, 1966.

Wood, Mary I. *The History of the General Federation of Women's Clubs for the First Twenty-two Years of Its Organization.* Norwood, MA: Norwood P, 1912.

Zimmern, Alice. *Women's Suffrage in Many Lands.* London: Francis, 1909.

Chapters in Books

Boyer, Paul S., and Janet Wilson James. "Leavitt, Mary Greenleaf Clement." *Notable American Women 1607-1950, A Biographical Dictionary.* 3 vols. G-O. Boston: Belknap P of Harvard UP, 1971.

Cooper, Sandi E. "Women's Participation in European Peace Movements: The Struggle to Prevent World War I." *Women and Peace: Theoretical, Historical and Practical Perspectives.* Ed. Ruth Roach Pierson. London: Croom Helm, 1987. 51-75.

Fawcett, Millicent Garrett. "England." *The Woman Question in Europe: A Series of Original Essays.* Ed. Theodore Stanton. New York: Putnam's, 1884. 1-138.

Lender, Mark Edward. "Leavitt, Mary Greenleaf Clement." *The Dictionary of American Temperance Biography from Temperance Reform to Alcohol Research the 1600s to the 1980s.* Westport: Greenwood, 1984.

Macmillan, Chrystal. "The History of the Congress." *International Congress of Women The Hague—Holland, April 28th, 29th, 30, 1915.* Ed. Chrystal Macmillan. n.p., n.d.

Nolan, Melanie, and Caroline Daley. "International Feminist Perspectives on Suffrage: An Introduction." *Suffrage and Beyond: International Feminist Perspectives.* Ed. Caroline Daley and Melanie Nolan. New York: New York UP, 1993. 1-22.

INDEX

Aberdeen, Ishbel, 70, 85-86
  ICW president, 83, 87
  peace movement, 126
  Post World War I, 87,142-43
  World's Congress of Representa -
    tive Women, 75
Addams, Jane, 82, 85, 105, 201
  anti-prostitution, 129
  Chicago Emergency Federation of
    Peace Forces, 133
  Hague Peace Conference, The
    124, 134-35
  Hull House, 127, 137, 177
  Ichikawa, Fusae, 177-78
  International Committee of Women
    for Permanent Peace, 137
  IWSA, 129
  Japan, 139
  labor, 46
  National Peace Federation, 133
  NAWSA, 128-29, 162
  Negative publicity, 136-38
  Newer Ideals of Peace, 128
  Nobel peace prize, 139
  Peace movement, 126-28, 133
    Henry Ford's peace ship, 136
  PPWA, 139, 147
  Roosevelt, Theodore, 129
  suffrage, 127
  Why Wars Must Cease, 148
  see WILPF
  Woman's Peace Party, 137
  world tour, 138
Alcohol abuse, 2, 4, 34, 38, 41, 44, 51
Alcoholics Anonymous (AA), 41
  Mothers Against Drunk Drivers
    (MADD), 41
  WCTU link to suffrage, 44

Alliance for Participation of Women
  in Government (Japan), 176-77
American Association of University
  Women, 187
American Woman Suffrage Associa-
  tion, 16, 40 150
  see Stone, Lucy
Anderson, Mary, 156, 158
  Equal Rights Treaty, 157
  ILO, 157
  social reformers, 157
  Women's Bureau of the U.S.
    Department of Labor, 156
Anthony, Susan B., 2, 8, 11-12, 15-18,
  25, 38, 46, 65, 75, 91-92, 109, 113,
  169, 198
  amendment, U.S. Constitution, 109
  American Equal Rights Associa-
    tion, 15
  Chicago World's Columbian
    Exposition, 76-77, 81-82
  History of Woman Suffrage, 2
  ICW, 69, 71, 85
  IWSA, 93-94
  NAWSA, 72
  NCW, 73
  NWSA, 16
  see Stanton, Elizabeth Cady
  teachers' convention, 13
  temperance, 13, 38
  Woman's State Temperance Soci-
    ety, 38
  women's rights, 12, 15, 38
Anti-Corn Law agitation, 9
antislavery, 11
  French colonies, 12
  Quakers, 11
  Stanton, Elizabeth Cady, 11

India, 102
  Besant, Annie, 15, 27, 102, 107
    Indian National Congress, 27,
    102
  Contagious Diseases Acts, 34
  Cousins, Margaret, 95, 102
  education, 15
  Gandhi, Mahandas K., 15, 100
  law, 15
  Metha, Hansa, 195
  Mudaliar, Ramaswami, 193, 194
  Naidu, Sarojini, 15
  Pandit, Vijaya Lakshimi, 192-93,
    203
  prostitution, 34
  Ramabai, Pandita, 61
  Sorabji, Cornelia, 102, 200
Inter-Allied Suffrage Congress, 142-
  43
Inter-American Commission of
  Women, 156, 158, 189
  Breckinridge, Sophonisba, 156
  equal civil and political rights, 156
  Equal Nationality Treaty, 156
  reorganization, 158
  Stevens, Doris, 155, 158
  Winslow, Mary, 158
Inter-American Conference on Prob-
  lems of War and Peace, 189, 202
  recommendations, 189
  resolutions, 189
  No. XXXI, Cooperation of
    Women in International Con-
    ferences, 189
  NGOs, 191
  Vandenburg, Arthur H. 190
Inter-American Congress of Women,
  154-55
  Stevens, Doris, 155
International Alliance of Women for
  Suffrage and Equal Citizenship
  (IAW), 114, 119, 150, 200, 203
  Alliance Peace Committee meeting,
    145
  see Ashby, Margery Corbett

  see Catt, Carrie Chapman
  child bearing rights, 158
  committees, 115, 120-21, 145
  congresses, 115-17, 119-22, 146
  deMadariaga, Sig–or, 146
  equal rights, 156-57
  IAW name change, 121
  ICW, 116
  ILO, 118
  International Bibliographical
    Bureau, 116
  international cooperation, 105-106
  see IWSA (became International
    Alliance of Women, Equal
    Rights, Equal Responsibilities,
    121)
  Kluyver, Clasina Albertina, 146
  Latin America, 154
  League of Nations, 116
  Liaison Committee, 147
  see Manus, Rosa
  Members, 116-17
  Morgan, Ruth, 145-46
  national accomplishments, 118-22
  Nationality Report, 115, 120
  NWP, 153, 158
  peace, 118
  protective legislation, 155
  public sessions, 116
  Rydh, Hanna, 196
  Study Conference, 147
  suffrage, 116
  World Peace Congress, 148
International Committee of Women
  for Permanent Peace, 137
International Council of Women
  (ICW), 39-40, 42, 69, 90, 110, 142,
  150, 154, 200, 203
  Cadbury, Elizabeth, 130
  committees, 86
  conventions, 126
  formation, 71-72, 83
  IAW, 116
  IWSA, 93
  Liaison Committee, 147

Universal Peace Union, 125
Uruguay, 110, 193
  deVidal, Isabel R., 110, 191
  Luisi, Paulina, 115, 144
  WCTU, 110
  YWCA, 110
Utilitarianism, 9

venereal disease, 27-28, 32, 41, 115,
  198, 201
  Ireland, 34
VonSuttner, Bertha, 126
  Boer War, 127
  Lay Down Your Arms, 126
  Nobel Peace Prize, 126
Victoria, Queen of England, 86

Wald, Lilian, 133, 162
  Henry Street Settlement, 133
Weed, Ethyl B., 166-68
Wheeler, Anna, 19
Willard, Frances, 39-43, 45, 48, 50,
  57-58, 127, 147, 199
  Association for the Advancement
    of Women, 44
  ICW forerunner, 44
  AWSA, 44
  Catt's, Carrie Chapman, tribute, 65
  Do Everything Policy, 39, 43, 58,
    63, 199
  Home Protection, 45-46
    petition, 45
    policy, 46
  ICW, 39-40, 72
  labor reform, 43
  Livermore, Mary, 43-44
  memorialized, 66-67
  NCW, 73
  peace movement, 43, 125, 128
  prior to WCTU, 43-44
  social purity, 43
  Sorosis, 43-44
  support of Leavitt, Mary Clement,
    53
  see WCTU

woman suffrage, 43-45
women's rights, 43
world vision, 48
World's Congress of Representative
  Women, 82-83
Wilson, Woodrow, 133, 136-37, 142,
  150
Wollstonecraft, Mary, 1, 7-8, 11
  *A Vindication of the Rights of
  Women*, 7
woman suffrage, 94, 200
  after World War I, 107, 113, 116
  Australia, 52
  Belgium, 182, 187
  Chile, 111
  Colorado, 90
  England, 138
  Finland, 94
  France, 185
  India, 55
  Isle of Man, 93
  Italy, 113, 182, 186
  Myanmar, 138
  New Zealand, 52
  reverses, 184
  United States, 39, 65, 151, 177,
    187
  Wyoming, 17, 93
  Yugoslavia, 182, 187
woman suffrage campaigns, 9, 15, 24,
  27, 86, 115, 118, 178, 198, 201-02
  Addams, Jane, 127
  see Anthony, Susan B.
  Chicago World's Columbian Expo-
    sition, 83
  Church of England, 97
  Contagious Diseases Acts, 35
  defeats, 33, 63
  German campaign, 94
  international efforts, 71, 92-93,
    196
  Ireland, 126
  Latin America, 87
  Middle East, 185
  militancy, 35, 105